MODERN HUMANITIES RESEARCH ASSOCIATION
TEXTS AND DISSERTATIONS
VOLUME 97

INSTITUTE OF GERMANIC AND ROMANCE STUDIES
(UNIVERSITY OF LONDON)
BITHELL SERIES OF DISSERTATIONS
VOLUME 41

PHANTOM IMAGES
THE FIGURE OF THE GHOST IN THE
WORK OF CHRISTA WOLF AND IRINA LIEBMANN

INSTITUTE OF GERMANIC AND ROMANCE STUDIES
BITHELL SERIES OF DISSERTATIONS

Launched in 1978, this series publishes outstanding recent doctoral theses, accepted by universities in the United Kingdom and Ireland, across all fields of Germanic studies. Since 1989 the series has been published in collaboration with the Modern Humanities Research Association.

Recommendations for theses which might be considered for possible inclusion in the series should be made by the supervisor and/or examiner(s), and sent to Professor Ritchie Robertson, Convenor of the Bithell Editorial Board, St John's College, Oxford OX1 3JP. Proposals must be accompanied by a copy of the Examiners' Report and Abstract.

Editorial Board
Dr Judith Beniston, University College London
Professor Sarah Colvin, University of Birmingham
Professor Pól O Dochartaigh, University of Ulster
Professor Ritchie Robertson (*Convenor*), St John's College, Oxford
Professor Bill Marshall,
Institute of Germanic and Romance Studies, University of London
Dr John Walker, Birkbeck College London
Dr Godela Weiss-Sussex,
Institute of Germanic and Romance Studies, University of London
Professor David Wells, Birkbeck College London

MODERN HUMANITIES RESEARCH ASSOCIATION
TEXTS AND DISSERTATIONS

Established in 1970, the series promotes important work by younger scholars by making the most accomplished doctoral research available to a wider readership. Titles are selected and edited by a Board of distinguished experts from across the modern Humanities.

Editorial Board
English: Professor Catherine Maxwell, Queen Mary, University of London
French: Professor William Brooks, University of Bath
Germanic: Professor Ritchie Robertson, University of Oxford
Hispanic: Professor Derek Flitter, University of Exeter
Italian: Professor Brian Richardson, University of Leeds
Portuguese: Professor Thomas Earle, University of Oxford
Slavonic: Professor David Gillespie, University of Bath

Managing Editor: Dr Graham Nelson

PHANTOM IMAGES

THE FIGURE OF THE GHOST IN THE WORK OF CHRISTA WOLF AND IRINA LIEBMANN

by
CATHERINE SMALE

Modern Humanities Research Association
2013

Published by

The Modern Humanities Research Association
1 Carlton House Terrace
London SW1Y 5AF
United Kingdom

© Modern Humanities Research Association and the
Institute of Germanic and Romance Studies, University of London, 2013

Catherine Smale has asserted her right under the Copyright, Designs and Patents Act 1988 to be identified as the author of this work. Parts of this work may be reproduced as permitted under legal provisions for fair dealing (or fair use) for the purposes of research, private study, criticism, or review, or when a relevant collective licensing agreement is in place. All other reproduction requires the written permission of the copyright holder who may be contacted at rights@mhra.org.uk.

Copy-Editor: Nigel Hope

First published 2013

ISBN 978-1-78188-026-5 (hardback)
ISBN 978-1-78188-027-2 (paperback)
ISSN (Bithell Series of Dissertations) 0266-7932
ISSN (MHRA Texts and Dissertations) 0957-0322

CONTENTS

Acknowledgements	vii
Abbreviations	ix
List of Illustrations	x

Introduction   1

    The Afterlife of the GDR   3
    Figures of the Uncanny   6
    Intergenerational Phantoms   9
    Derrida and Hauntology   11
    Media and Mediation   14
    Conditions of Haunting   16
    Ghosts of Romanticism   20
    Outline   23

1   Phantom Images: Christa Wolf's *Was bleibt*   34

    Unwahrscheinliche Geschichten   37
    Dystopian Prospects   40
    Ghosts of Surveillance   43
    Self-Scrutiny   47
    Visitations   49

2   'Abschied von Phantomen'? Christa Wolf's *Leibhaftig*   56

    'Ein fremder Mensch tritt mir gegenüber'   59
    The Spirit Medium   63
    Tricks of the Light   66
    Gothic Bodies   69
    Ghosts in the Machine   73

3   Spectral Images: Irina Liebmann's *Stille Mitte von Berlin*   82

    'Allgemeiner Stillstand'   84
    'Dialektik im Stillstand'   90
    The Scene of the Crime   96
    'Living Dead'   102

4   'Lebendige Bilder': Irina Liebmann's *In Berlin*   112

    Ekphrastic Images   115
    'Lauter angehaltene Bilder'   120
    'Glasige Augen'   125

	'Tote Hände'	129
	'Im Spiegel'	134
5	A Haunting Legacy: Irina Liebmann's *Die freien Frauen*	143
	Familial Haunting	146
	'Eine Verwechslung im Grunde'	149
	Uchronian Narratives	153
	Other Spaces	157
	'Eine unsterbliche Geschichte'	161
	Conclusion	169
	Bibliography	173
	Index	186

ACKNOWLEDGEMENTS

This book originated as an AHRC-funded doctoral thesis at Trinity Hall, Cambridge, and was completed at the Freie Universität Berlin on a Hanseatic Scholarship funded by the Alfred Toepfer Foundation. Above all, my thanks must go to my supervisor, Professor Andrew Webber, for his insightful guidance and patient support throughout the course of my doctoral research. I would also like to thank my examiners, Dr Peter Hutchinson and Professor Karen Leeder, for their constructive advice and enthusiasm for the project. I am grateful to Professor Pól Ó Dochartaigh and Professor Ritchie Robertson for their detailed comments on the manuscript of this book, and to Nigel Hope and Dr Graham Nelson for their help with the editing process.

Many others have played a significant role in ensuring that this project was realized. Irina Liebmann kindly allowed me to interview her, and was more than generous with her time and hospitality on that occasion. The development of the monograph has benefited considerably from discussions with Dr Brigitte Heymann, Professor Stefan Keppler-Tasaki, Dr Karolin Machtans, Dr Lyn Marven, Dr Georgina Paul, and Dr Charlotte Woodford. I am grateful to researchers at the Friedrich Schlegel Schule für literaturwissenschaftliche Studien and at the Institute for Cultural Inquiry in Berlin for their engagement with the project, and to Siobhán Carew at the University of Cambridge for her support during my doctoral studies. The process of editing the thesis for publication has taken place at King's College London, and I am indebted to my colleagues here, in particular Professor Erica Carter and Dr Ben Schofield, for creating such a supportive environment in which to work.

Parts of Chapters 2 and 4 of this monograph appeared in a different form in *Die Halbschlafbilder in der Literatur, den Künsten und den Wissenschaften*, ed. by Roger Paulin and Helmut Pfotenhauer (Würzburg: Königshausen & Neumann, 2011), and in *Popular Revenants: The German Gothic and its International Reception*, ed. by Andrew Cusack and Barry Murnane (Rochester, NY: Camden House, 2012). Parts of Chapters 3 and 4 appeared in a different form in *Twenty Years On: Competing Memories of the GDR in Postunification German Culture*, ed. by Renate Rechtien and Dennis Tate (Rochester, NY: Camden House, 2011), and in *Phantasmata: Techniken des Unheimlichen*, ed. by Martin Doll, Rupert Gaderer, Fabio Camiletti, and Jan Niklas Howe (Vienna: Turia & Kant, 2011). I am grateful to the editors of these volumes for their advice in producing my contributions.

Finally, I owe especial thanks to my family and friends. Without their unconditional support and encouragement, my work on this project would not have been possible.

I dedicate this book to Matthew.

c. s., August 2013

ABBREVIATIONS

~

The following abbreviations have been used for key texts:

Walter Benjamin

WB   Walter Benjamin, *Gesammelte Schriften*, ed. by Rolf Tiedemann and Hermann Schweppenhäuser, 7 vols (Frankfurt a. M.: Suhrkamp, 1991)

Sigmund Freud

SF   Sigmund Freud, *Studienausgabe*, ed. by Alexander Mitscherlich, Angela Richards, and James Strachey, 11 vols (Frankfurt a. M.: Fischer, 1969–75)

E. T. A. Hoffmann

H   E. T. A. Hoffmann, *Sämtliche Werke*, ed. by Wulf Segebrecht and Hartmut Steinecke, 6 vols (Frankfurt a. M.: Deutscher Klassiker, 1985–2004)

Irina Liebmann

DfF   Irina Liebmann, *Die freien Frauen: Roman* (Berlin: Berlin, 2004)
IB   Irina Liebmann, *In Berlin: Roman* (Cologne: Kiepenheuer & Witsch, 1994)
SM   Irina Liebmann, *Stille Mitte von Berlin: Eine fotografische Spurensuche rund um den Hackeschen Markt* (Berlin: Berlin, 2009). This volume is a largely unaltered reprint of *Stille Mitte von Berlin: Eine Recherche rund um den Hackeschen Markt* (Berlin: Nicolai, 2002). This book refers to the 2009 edition, rather than the original 2002 version, because the latter had a limited print-run and is consequently difficult to obtain.

Christa Wolf

L   Christa Wolf, *Leibhaftig: Erzählung* (Munich: Luchterhand, 2002)
CW   Christa Wolf, *Werke*, ed. by Sonja Hilzinger, 12 vols (Munich: Luchterhand, 1999–2001)

LIST OF ILLUSTRATIONS

~

Cover. Detail Eckhaus Oranienburger Straße, Tucholskystraße (c. 1984)
  © Berlin Verlag/Irina Liebmann
Fig. 3.1. Postfuhramt an der Oranienburger Straße, Ecke Tucholskystraße (1984)
  © bpk — Bildagentur für Kunst, Kultur und Geschichte/Irina Liebmann
Fig. 3.2. Abriss des Kolonistenhauses in der Sophienstraße (1984)
  © bpk — Bildagentur für Kunst, Kultur und Geschichte/Irina Liebmann
Fig. 3.3. Große Hamburger Straße mit Pfütze (1984)
  © bpk — Bildagentur für Kunst, Kultur und Geschichte/Irina Liebmann
Fig. 3.4. Große Hamburger Straße (c. 1984)
  © Berlin Verlag/Irina Liebmann
Fig. 3.5. Hofsynagoge in der Brunnenstraße (c. 1984)
  © Berlin Verlag/Irina Liebmann
Fig. 3.6. Rosenthaler Straße, Blick zum Hackeschen Markt (c. 1984)
  © Berlin Verlag/Irina Liebmann
Fig. 3.7. Detail Eckhaus Oranienburger Straße, Tucholskystraße (c. 1984)
  © Berlin Verlag/Irina Liebmann
Fig. 3.8. Rosenthaler Straße (c. 1984)
  © Berlin Verlag/Irina Liebmann
Fig. 3.9. Große Hamburger Straße. Gedenkstein für das jüdische Altersheim, ehemals Sammelstelle zur Deportation Berliner Juden (c. 1984)
  © Berlin Verlag/Irina Liebmann
Fig. 3.10. Friedhof der Sophiengemeinde (c. 1984)
  © Berlin Verlag/Irina Liebmann
Fig. 3.11. Große Hamburger Straße, Ecke Krausnickstraße (1984)
  © bpk — Bildagentur für Kunst, Kultur und Geschichte/Irina Liebmann
Fig. 3.12. Auguststraße (c. 1984)
  © Berlin Verlag/Irina Liebmann

INTRODUCTION

∽

This book examines the role of ghosts in the work of two East German writers: Christa Wolf and Irina Liebmann. Through close analysis of five texts published between 1990 and 2005 — Wolf's *Was bleibt* and *Leibhaftig*, and Liebmann's *Stille Mitte von Berlin*, *In Berlin*, and *Die freien Frauen* — it aims to show how these writers adopt the notion of haunting in their engagement with the double legacy of the Third Reich and the GDR. The imagery of ghostliness in these works is understood as a vehicle for uncovering memories which have been excluded from individual and collective historical narratives. As the purveyor of an unmastered past, the ghost raises ethical questions about the nature of society's engagement with the dead in a post-Holocaust age and highlights the need to cultivate a responsible attitude towards the other. At the same time, it will be argued that the ghost assumes a particular significance in the context of the *Wende* and the renegotiation of identity which has occurred in its wake: as a threshold figure, it serves to mediate between past and present, East and West, enabling a renegotiation of boundaries and challenging the apparent fixity of established limits.

In his study, *Die deutsche Gespenstergeschichte* (1994), Gero von Wilpert laments the demise of the ghost in the literature of the post-war period, suggesting that texts written after 1945 have been characterized by the 'allmähliche[s] Aussterben der Gespenster'.[1] While his proclamation of the gradual 'death' of the phenomenon leads him to predict a bleak future for those interested in literary depictions of ghosts, his curious turn of phrase serves to undermine the authority of his assertion: as figures of the undead, ghosts resist death, often resurfacing precisely when they appear to have been banished. Von Wilpert's obituary can be regarded as premature, an early dismissal of the ghost which fails to acknowledge the figure's predilection for unexpected acts of return and *revenance*. Indeed, had von Wilpert published his study a couple of years later, he would have had the opportunity to draw on the remarkable proliferation of references to the ghostly which have emerged in the literature of the post-*Wende* period. Authors such as Heiner Müller (*Germania 3: Gespenster am toten Mann*, 1996), Judith Hermann (*Nichts als Gespenster*, 2003), Marcel Beyer (*Spione*, 2000), and Stephan Wackwitz (*Ein unsichtbares Land: Familienroman*, 2003; *Neue Menschen: Bildungsroman*, 2005) have used images of spectrality and haunting in their literary engagement with the legacy of the recent German past. To date, critical examination of this literary phenomenon has tended to regard the references to the ghostly in texts written after 1990 as symptomatic of a 'kollektive Erblast über längere Perioden und Generationen' relating to the traumatic inheritance of the Holocaust and the Third Reich.[2] In particular, the prevalence of spectral themes is often considered to be related to the 'Aussterben der Zeitzeugen-Generation'[3] and the epochal transition from first-hand memory of the Third Reich to a reliance on what Marianne Hirsch terms 'postmemory',[4] the second-hand knowledge of historical events shaped by imaginative investment and creation rather than direct experience. Arising from the gaps and silences in inherited family narratives, the ghost tends to be regarded as a figure of 'Vergegenwärtigung — Re-Präsentation — des Vergangenen',[5] which appears in these texts as part of the authors' self-conscious reflection on the fluctuating boundary between reality and fantasy.[6]

While this critical focus on the relationship between the ghost and post-memorial narratives is illuminating for a certain number of texts written in recent years, it cannot fully explain why the imagery of ghostliness has become so popular in the context of the *Wende*. This book focuses on the writing of Christa Wolf and Irina Liebmann for two main reasons. First, the texts analysed here reveal the ghostly to be bound up not only with the legacy of the Third Reich and the Holocaust, but also with the more recent experience of the GDR and its demise.[7] Haunted by the retrospective spectre of Communism, these works grapple with the loss of hopes, illusions, and utopias which these writers experienced following the *Wende*,[8] and raise questions about the ambivalent legacy of the GDR in the period after 1990. The figure of the ghost can be viewed in this context as forming part of the writers' attempts to examine their relation to the lost State and reinvent their role as public figures in the new Federal Republic. Second, the different positions of Wolf and Liebmann within the GDR offer contrasting perspectives on its haunting legacy. While Wolf embraced the Socialist ideal, despite her criticism of its implementation in practice, and played a key role in the cultural sphere of the GDR, Liebmann's writing remained relatively unknown until the *Wende* and reveals a profound ambivalence towards the State and its ideology.[9] Although Liebmann's dissatisfaction led her to move to the West in 1988, becoming one of a stream of writers who left the GDR in the last decade of its existence,[10] she was never able to find fulfilment in the Federal Republic, and her resulting sense of homelessness, I suggest, is revealed in her texts through the imagery of haunting.[11] The generational difference between Wolf and Liebmann, born in 1929 and 1943 respectively, also complicates the suggestion that the current preoccupation with ghosts occurs primarily in family narratives written by the children and grandchildren of those involved in the Third Reich, since it reveals the imagery of haunting to be present in works which do not fit into this narrow category. Both writers are shown here to use this imagery as a means of exploring the relationship between individual and collective memory and the way it is passed on from one generation to the next.

Both Wolf and Liebmann have recently found themselves at the centre of critical attention, albeit for different reasons.[12] While Wolf was highly regarded as a writer in the GDR, she fell out of favour with scholars in the wake of the *Literaturstreit* of the early 1990s, facing accusations of hypocrisy and dishonesty. More recently, as Dennis Tate notes, she has had 'her status as a major author of post-1945 German literature' restored, and substantial new material has been released about her life and works which has contributed to this critical reassessment of her role.[13] Liebmann, by contrast, has only recently begun to attract scholarly interest,[14] and this is steadily increasing following her acceptance of the Preis der Leipziger Buchmesse in 2008. While surprisingly little mention has been made of the references to haunting in the work of either author,[15] this study draws on certain key trends in recent scholarship on Wolf and Liebmann. Following Michelle Mattson's investigation of notions of moral responsibility in the work of Christa Wolf, and in particular her suggestion that 'her efforts to historicize [...] seek to bring the past closer to the present, to examine the motives of those living at the time and to specify their level of responsibility',[16] I argue that the repertoire of ghostliness serves an ethical purpose in her writing, raising questions about the necessity and possibility of engaging with the experiences of others. Although Michelle Mattson adopts a feminist perspective in her argument, a viewpoint which could equally well be applied to the writing of Liebmann, with its focus on female subjectivity, this study does not consider the haunting in these texts to be a specifically female condition. Rather, it regards femininity as one constituent element among others in the depictions of self–other relations offered by these writers. Their portrayal of hauntedness does touch on questions of feminine identity, yet these are always shown to form part of a broader reflection on the nature of human interactions and their historical significance.

The Afterlife of the GDR

The book focuses primarily on texts by Wolf and Liebmann which were published in the post-*Wende* period between 1990 and 2005. The prefix 'post' highlights the retrospective condition of these texts, which 'come after' the demise of the GDR while also remaining bound to this bygone State. The recent literature of Wolf and Liebmann, it is argued, is influenced by the cultural climate of the GDR even as these writers seek to distance themselves from it. While two of the texts analysed here — *Was bleibt* and *In Berlin* — were published in the immediate aftermath of the events of 1989/90, the others appeared after the foundation of the Berlin Republic in 1998/99, in what has been described as a 'period of relative cultural calm'.[17] Despite the altered vantage point which this political stabilization appeared to bring, however, these later texts also remain marked by the tumultuous after-effects of the events of 1989 and by their continuing attachment to the lost GDR State. Although such texts seem to signal an attempt to let go of the past and turn towards the future, a move which is reflected above all in the verb 'loslassen' which recurs as a linguistic leitmotif throughout these works, the possibility of achieving any sense of closure is repeatedly undermined. The legacy of the GDR and its literature is shown to return whenever it appears to have been overcome; it haunts the writers' examination of their role in the wake of the *Wende* and shadows their efforts to reassert their influence in the new Federal Republic.

In this regard, the book contributes to the continuing discussion surrounding the future of GDR literature in post-*Wende* Germany. Such discussion has arisen from the various assertions made in 1989/90 that the end of the GDR would also lead to the demise of GDR literature.[18] In an article published in *The German Quarterly* in 1990, for example, the author Jurek Becker argued that 'DDR-Literatur in ihrer bisherigen Form aufhören wird zu existieren'.[19] GDR literature, he suggests, is conditioned by the political and social circumstances in which it was created, and so it follows that the alteration of these conditions would result in the end of this particular category of literature. More specifically, he argues that the removal of political restrictions and censorship would transform the subject matter and literary styles available to East German writers, and that this would result in what he terms a 'Wiedervereinigung der deutschen Literatur'.[20] Particularly striking here is the way in which Becker couches his proclamation of the end of GDR literature in the vocabulary of death and decay, using verbs such as 'untergehen' and 'erlöschen' to highlight the possibility that such literature might 'cease to exist'.[21] Becker is, in fact, not alone in adopting such imagery in discussions of the possible end of GDR literature: numerous critics have described their vision of the 'Tod der DDR Literatur' and regarded certain works by former GDR writers as examples of 'Grabsteine' which signal this death.[22] Their preoccupation with this apparent demise underlines their desire to lay the literature of the GDR to rest, to consign it to the past and thereby keep it in its historical place.

Becker's suggestion that GDR literature *in its hitherto existing form* might cease to exist is nevertheless ambiguous; although apparently emphasizing the death of such literature, his phrasing leaves open the possibility of it living on in an altered, spectral form. Through his suggestion that this literature will not *completely* expire,[23] he seems to imply that it will return in the post-*Wende* period as a kind of *revenant*, a transformed version of what it once was. In this respect, Becker apparently anticipates the phenomenon which Karen Leeder has termed 'the afterlife of the GDR': the notion that the GDR and its literature have persisted in ghostly forms in post-*Wende* works by writers of the former East German State.[24] Focusing specifically on the work of Volker Braun, Leeder argues that the prevalence of uncanny figures such as 'ghosts, spectres, vampires and zombies'[25] in literature from the former GDR is bound up with writers' attempts to renegotiate their role in the new Federal Republic. The act of 'remembering, re-imagining and re-presenting the past in ghostly forms',[26] she suggests, can be read as both an 'obituary [...] of the individual writer's commitment to the lost state and its ideals',[27] and as a reflection on the way in which these ideals exist in a kind of 'afterlife', living on in the present despite the disappearance of the State to which they are attached. This fascination with death and afterlife can be regarded as 'an exploration of literature as "postscript"',[28] a consideration of the way in which texts can reanimate and renovate past hopes in order to make them relevant to the present; as such, Leeder argues, the spectral imagery in post-*Wende* texts 'is perversely [...] a vital sign of life'.[29] Through their consideration of what remains of the GDR and its literature, such texts 'ironically exhume the disappearing dead in an effort to resuscitate the future'.[30]

While Leeder concludes that the afterlife of the GDR is a surprisingly positive, forward-looking phenomenon, which offers writers a means of overcoming their attachment to the past, the texts analysed in this study also reveal a darker side to this literary manifestation. Through various forms of intertextual recall, Wolf and Liebmann invoke aspects of their earlier work, reanimating their past convictions and breathing life into the remnants of their utopian thinking. On one level, this voluntary recollection of their previous writing signals an attempt to forge a continuing existence for their lost ideals, despite the disappearance of the social context with which they were associated. For Wolf in particular, it highlights a desire to reaffirm her commitment to the project of 'subjektive Authentizität' and the task of achieving a form of 'Selbstverwirklichung', even though her literature now operates in a very different ideological climate. At the same time, however, this technique of self-quotation is also shadowed by the involuntary return of failed projects and more questionable beliefs from the past, which the authors have sought to overcome. These unwanted *revenants* prove to be highly seductive, exerting a beguiling power over the writers and causing them to become fatally attached to their past selves. They assume an autonomy within the texts which works to undermine the positive renegotiation of past ideals and present reality and signals a bleak refusal or inability to turn towards the future. The afterlife of the GDR and its literature is thus shown to be characterized by ambivalence; while the post-*Wende* projects of Wolf and Liebmann are at times open to transformation and renewal, they are also shadowed by a mortal attachment to the lost State.

Figures of the Uncanny

As Freud observes in his essay of 1919, 'Das Unheimliche', ghosts and *revenants* are particularly uncanny figures (SF IV, 264). Assigning the term 'unheimlich' to everything, 'was mit dem Tod, mit Leichen und mit der Wiederkehr der Toten, mit Geistern und Gespenstern, zusammenhängt' (SF IV, 264), he attributes the uncanniness of these phenomena to the resurfacing of a repressed primitive fear of the dead, whose reappearance destabilizes society's fragile belief that this fear has been overcome. However, Freud seems strangely reluctant to elaborate on this claim, suggesting that his investigation into the return of the dead is limited both by the emotive nature of the topic and by the 'Unsicherheit unserer wissenschaftlichen Erkenntnis' (SF IV, 264). His hesitance is telling; despite his assertion to the contrary (SF IV, 244), he appears to have succumbed to the very sense of anxiety which his essay seeks to resolve. Because of his relative silence on the subject, the ghost becomes a kind of blind spot in Freud's work; through its unspoken presence, it haunts his attempts to rationalize the uncanny, repeatedly affirming the intellectual uncertainty which he seeks to overcome and undermining his efforts to shed light on the repressed aspects of the human psyche. The ghost signals the ineffable core of Freud's inquiry into the uncanny, the troubling lack of certainty which results in his 'notorious' failure 'to arrive at a satisfactory definition' of the phenomenon.[31] Above all, it reveals a darker side to his project of enlightenment, becoming 'a kind of toxic side-effect' which shadows his intellectual disenchantment with supernatural phenomena.[32]

What Freud fails to acknowledge in his essay is the way in which most of his general statements about the nature of the uncanny can be applied to the figure of the ghost. As a manifestation of 'etwas, was im Verborgenen hätte bleiben sollen und hervorgetreten ist' (SF IV, 264), the apparition of the ghost becomes linked with the revelation of repressed memories and mental states. Its appearance signals the disclosure of secrets which ought to remain untold and highlights the uncovering of sights which ought not to be witnessed. At the same time, the ghost's propensity to return repeatedly recalls Freud's assertion that the uncanny is bound up with a form of repetition compulsion (SF IV, 261), with a 'beständige Wiederkehr des Gleichen' (SF IV, 257) which aims to invoke and reanimate past realities. Such acts of repetition call into question the established boundaries between past and present, the living and the dead; they disturb chronology by recalling previous experiences and re-enacting them in the present. Finally, as a figure of the undead, the ghost marks an uncanny slippage between the animate and the inanimate; as a dead figure which appears to have come to life, it challenges its own status as a living being, evoking 'Zweifel, an der Beseelung eines anscheinend lebendigen Wesens und umgekehrt darüber, ob ein lebloser Gegenstand nicht etwa beseelt sei' (SF IV,

250). The ambiguous ontological status of the ghost troubles the boundary between fantasy and reality (SF IV, 267), making it impossible for the individual to determine whether or not the figure's apparent vitality is simply the product of his/her imagination. Although the ghost appears to take on the semblance of life, its animation might prove to be fictitious, revealing it to be a fantastic creation brought to life by the animating gaze of the human subject.

In its analysis of the work of Wolf and Liebmann, this book aims to show how the repertoire of the uncanny is related to their efforts to reveal repressed memories and bring to light events which have been excluded from conventional historiographical narratives. The ghost appears here as a figure of 'what is elusive, cryptic, still to come (back)',[33] yet it also emerges as an involuntary product of this revelation, as a troubling remainder which comes into view after a particular light has been shed on the past. In their fascination with the process of revelation and enlightenment, the texts analysed here depict the uncanny as a predominantly visual phenomenon, which works in and through the optical apparatus. The ghostly apparitions emerge in these texts as slippages and fixations in the visual field which deflect the writer's gaze and interrupt her attempts to shed light on the past. The visionary capability of the eye, its capacity to perceive that which normally remains hidden, is coupled with an inherent vulnerability which threatens to undermine its power to see. While the writer seeks to gain a particular clarity of vision, probing the blind spots in society (CW VIII, 341) and striving, in Liebmann's words, 'zu sehen, was man sieht',[34] her effort is always shadowed by the propensity of the eye to be blinded by the sights which it uncovers. Through their emphasis on the visual apparatus, the texts recall the proliferation of references to the ocular in the writing of E. T. A. Hoffmann, the classic author of the uncanny, whose tales depict the eye as a point of transition between external reality and the inner world of the artist. More specifically, the numerous references to 'tote Augen', 'erstarrte Augen', 'blinde Augen', and 'glasige Augen' in the writing of Wolf and Liebmann resonate with Hoffmann's portrayal of the visual apparatus as a point of transition between the animate and the inanimate, the living and the dead. The animating gaze with which the writer seeks to breathe life into her literary creation is perpetually at risk of becoming fixated and deadened through its contact with the ghostly apparitions which (s)he invokes.

This preoccupation with blockages and distortions in the visual field, it is argued, signals a reflection on the relationship between art and life, or, more specifically, on the Hoffmannesque predicament of the artist who is so enchanted by the seeming reality of his/her creation that (s)he becomes dead to the real world. The protagonists of Wolf and Liebmann's works are constantly in danger of becoming fatally absorbed in the imaginary realm of their respective literary projects; they risk losing touch with themselves and with the reality in which they live. Yet the texts analysed here move beyond a straightforward reflection on the mimetic potential of literature and the role of art as an uncanny double of life. Wolf and Liebmann both attempt, through their writing, to recuperate aspects of the past which have been irretrievably lost. By adopting a hybrid genre which blends elements of fiction and historiography, they blur the boundary between fantasy and reality, using their art as a means of creating an imaginary life for the dead. Through their creative practice, they attempt to bridge the gaps in historical understanding which have been transmitted by official narratives, weaving fictionalized accounts wherever it is necessary to construct an alternative view of the past to the one which has been passed on to them. While the notion of imaginative creation allows Liebmann and Wolf to counter historical repression by cultivating a subjective connection to the past, it is also ethically problematic, since it 'no longer requires historically verifiable remembrance of what happened' in the past.[35] The ghostly characters which exist in these texts therefore risk usurping the position of the actual historical figures whose experiences remain unknown and unknowable. Their semblance of life proves to be misleading and potentially dangerous, since it works to conceal the historical absence at its core.

The book goes on to argue that the imagery of the uncanny in these texts assumes a further dimension in its particular connection to the historical circumstances of the *Wende*. Signalling an experience of 'disjunction, when fixed boundaries become fluid',[36] this imagery is used as a means of renegotiating the distinctions between past and present, East and West, public and private. The ghost, as a figure which inhabits both the temporal threshold of the *Wende* and the spatial border between the GDR and the FRG, calls into question the fixity of these limits, opening them up to the possibility of alteration and fluctuation. This preoccupation with shifting boundaries in turn signals a more profound concern with questions of 'Heimat' and homelessness: is it possible, these writers ask, to feel 'at home' in the new Federal Republic? Peter Thompson has recently argued that post-*Wende* German culture is characterized by expressions of longing for an 'unheimliche Heimat', a homeland that 'both is and isn't, was and wasn't the GDR'.[37] Troubled by a sense of 'continuing dislocation' and experiencing a persistent sense of homelessness, many former East Germans have developed a nostalgia for the GDR, which needs to be understood as an expression of 'mourning [for] the passing of a Heimat which never was'.[38] Although Thompson's analysis of this pervasive cultural *Heimweh* is convincing, he does not explore all the implications of the term 'unheimlich'. By drawing on the Freudian notion of the uncanny as being fundamentally rooted in the home, this book suggests that the condition of post-*Wende* unhomeliness has its origin in the unrealized homeland of the GDR, whose utopian promise was always already shadowed by the dystopian prospect of its failure.

Intergenerational Phantoms

The book draws on the psychoanalytic model of haunting outlined by Nicholas Abraham in his essay, 'Notes on the Phantom' (1975),[39] in order to show how the ghostly apparitions in these texts can be read as manifestations of inherited trauma. The haunting legacy of National Socialism and the GDR is made apparent through the way in which the unassimilated experiences of one generation are transmitted, albeit unintentionally, to the next. The ghostly logic of these texts is understood here to operate within a familial, genealogical framework, as the parent–child relationship is characterized by the involuntary inheritance of traumatic memories, which return repeatedly to disrupt the stability of the family home. Although the works analysed here are not normally regarded as part of the 'remarkable upsurge in family stories' that has occurred in German literature since the *Wende*,[40] they nevertheless tend to depict the structure of the family as the prime vehicle for the transmission of an unmastered past. The family unit becomes, in Sigrid Weigel's words, the 'Schauplatz einer geheimnisvollen oder ungeklärten Vergangenheit',[41] a site rendered uncanny by the intergenerational consequences of violent histories. The book suggests that the adoption of a private, familial model in these texts is bound up with the technique of 'subjektive Authentizität' and the intention of these writers to cultivate a personal connection to historical events. The examination of the German past through the lens of the family serves to project the concerns of history at large onto the individual, highlighting the personal, psychic effects of collectively experienced events.

Nicholas Abraham's theory of intergenerational haunting was developed as a response to his clinical work with the children of Holocaust survivors. Observing that such patients often displayed symptoms which could not be traced to events in their own psychic lives, he theorized the phantom as a means of illustrating how individuals could be affected by the psychic aftermath of events which they had not experienced directly. Departing from Freudian and post-Freudian theories of psychopathology, Abraham suggests that the individual's symptoms stem from an act of 'phantomatic haunting',[42] or, more precisely, from his/her experience of being governed by the disavowed traumas and losses of a parental figure. The phantom, he argues, is 'an invention of the living',[43] whose purpose is 'to objectify [...] the gap produced in us by the concealment of some part of a love object's life. [...] What haunts are not the dead but the gaps left in us by the secrets of others'.[44] The term 'secret' refers to a traumatic event or unwanted loss, whose existence is too painful to be processed or assimilated by the ego, and whose occurrence and emotional consequences are therefore silenced and buried — 'entombed' — within the subject. Through the genealogical inheritance of the unconscious, these entombed secrets are then passed on to the child, who unwittingly becomes the carrier of his/her parent's silenced history. As Esther Rashkin observes, the child becomes 'a living tomb or repository in which an unspeakable drama, experienced as traumatic by someone else, lies buried yet alive, exerting its disruptive influence in a potentially infinite number of ways on the existence of the child or on the child grown into adulthood'.[45] The phantom is unknowingly created by the offspring as a means of filling in the gaps which (s)he has inherited; it is invoked involuntarily whenever the child comes into contact with the empty space in his/her psyche produced by the blocked memories of a parental figure.

The familial model which Abraham adopts is situated at the core of a broader network of relationships between self and other, and it therefore offers a paradigm for considering the influence of historical experiences on the development of individual subjectivity. The phantom, which emerges when normal patterns of genealogical inheritance are interrupted, operates on and through language, disrupting narrative and creating blockages and repetitions in the speech of the subject. Those who live through traumatic events often experience what Nicholas Rand terms 'psychic aphasia',[46] a condition which disturbs the expressive or representational power of language and obfuscates meaning. In order to protect the psyche against the overwhelming pain triggered by the memory of the traumatic event, these individuals tend to suppress the emotional content of language, employing words which have been 'stripped of their libidinal grounding'.[47] When this speech is passed on to the child, it becomes a kind of 'haunted language',[48] an emotionless idiom characterized by gaps and ellipses, which highlights the existence of a silenced, unspeakable history. This phantomatic language 'wreak[s] havoc'[49] in the psyche of the offspring, functioning 'like a ventriloquist, like a stranger within the subject's own mental topography'.[50] It compels the subject to speak in words which are not his/her own, to employ language which is already tainted by the experiences of another. This book considers the way in which linguistic haunting manifests itself — both thematically and formally — in the writing of Wolf and Liebmann. As a figure of disorder, the phantom is shown to undermine the narrative logic of these texts, signalling the presence of gaps and silences which 'elude rationalisation' and resist analysis.[51]

At the same time, phantoms are always deceptive figures, seeking to divert attention away from the secrets which they conceal. Abraham suggests that, while ghosts conventionally return from the dead in order to reveal information to the living, the phantom 'returns to haunt with the intention of lying'.[52] Its task is to conceal the secret and therefore ensure that the traumatic experience remains hidden. The haunted language which the subject inherits is therefore misleading, containing 'would-be "revelations"' which are 'false by nature' and blocking any explicit references to the trauma itself.[53] Above all, the phantom plays an active role in ensuring the continuation of the traumatic inheritance by instilling in the individual a sense of 'horror at [the possibility of] violating a parent's or family's guarded secret'; although 'the secret's text and content are inscribed within the patient's own unconscious',[54] they remain inaccessible, resisting efforts to uncover them. The disingenuous nature of the phantom assumes a particular significance in the work of Wolf and Liebmann, since it poses a constant threat to the writers' attempts to uncover the 'truth' of historical experience. While both writers place great emphasis on 'Wahrheit' as 'der Gegenstand der Kunst',[55] their pursuit of this goal is challenged by the false narratives and screen memories which they unearth. The figure of the phantom, I argue, is used by these writers as a self-conscious means of reflecting on the relationship between literature and truth; yet it is also shown to exist as an unwilled presence in these texts, casting doubt on the writers' claims to authenticity and veracity.

Finally, the book engages with and challenges Abraham's suggestion that the phantom can and should be laid to rest. While he admits that the phantom 'remains beyond the tools of classical analysis', because it is 'radically heterogeneous' to the human subject,[56] Abraham goes on to claim that the phantom can nevertheless be made to 'vanish'.[57] By 'reducing the sin attached to someone else's secret and stating it in acceptable terms',[58] he argues, it is possible to counter the phantom's deception and lead to it being 'successfully exorcised'.[59] Abraham's emphasis on laying the phantom to rest resonates with what Colin Davis has termed 'the "unfinished business" model' of communication between the living and the dead, according to which the ghost returns 'in order to be sent away again'.[60] Its existence signals a form of disturbance which needs to be corrected by the living if they wish to regain control over their lives. The texts analysed here all adopt certain features of this model, engaging with phantoms in an attempt to banish them completely. Yet the desire to be rid of these ghostly figures also proves to be ethically problematic, since any attempt to exorcise them would result in a denial of the traumatic legacy to which they are connected. The texts are therefore shown to be highly ambivalent in their attitude towards the phantom; oscillating between a desire to reject the past and a need to embrace it, they come to signal the writers' search for an alternative, more ethical engagement with the legacy of German history.

Derrida and Hauntology

In their attempt to develop an ethical relation to the past, Wolf and Liebmann at times undermine the 'unfinished business' model of haunting, casting doubt on its promise of closure and highlighting the potential reductionism of its genealogical approach. Moving away from an emphasis on personal ghosts, their writing comes to depict a more general form of hauntedness which cannot be reduced to the individual. This manifestation of ghostliness emerges primarily through the writers' adoption of the vocabulary of haunting in the context of their protagonists' everyday lives. As well as hosting the apparition of specific phantoms, the texts project the spectral condition onto the inhabitants of the city at large. Through verbs such as 'heimsuchen', 'schweben', 'plagen', and 'geistern', they lend these figures a ghostly existence, rendering the landscape of Berlin 'unheimlich' and 'ungeheuer' and revealing time itself to be 'out of joint'. This generalized condition of hauntedness, I argue, resonates with the mode of existence denoted by Jacques Derrida's term 'hauntology';[61] it signals the transition of 'being' into the liminal realm between different times and spaces, and reveals a preoccupation with the haunted and haunting character of human existence *per se*. The spectral logic of the hauntological condition transcends familial structures and resists attempts to trace its origin back to a specific historical moment. Instead, it demands that the ghostly be recognized and preserved as an irrecuperable other, whose existence can and should not be reduced to fit into existing intellectual and conceptual frameworks.

Although Derrida played a crucial role in publicizing the works of Nicholas Abraham and Maria Torok and was, to some extent, influenced by their notion of the 'secret',[62] his own theory of hauntology clearly differs from the psychoanalytic concept of the phantom. In *Specters of Marx*, his most sustained engagement with the notion of haunting, Derrida depicts the ghost as a form of alterity, which exists outside the realm of conceptual knowledge and whose message cannot be articulated in words. It is 'something that one does not know', a 'non-object' which resists categorization and therefore 'no longer belongs to knowledge'.[63] Through its unknowability, the ghost is protected from the kind of 'exorcism' advocated by Abraham, since its secret can never be brought to light. Whereas Abraham regards the secret as something which should be revealed in order for the phantom to be eliminated, Derrida regards the spectre as an 'enigma',[64] whose existence must be acknowledged but not explained away. The Derridean spectre becomes a figure of resistance, countering any attempts to reduce it to the status of an object of knowledge and thereby foreclosing the possibility of its expulsion or eradication. Thus, while Derrida repeatedly emphasizes the obligation to relate to the ghost, to address it and 'let [it] speak',[65] his intention 'is not to reveal the ghost's secret', but rather 'to attend to its mystery'.[66] The spectre presents us with an injunction to engage with alterity, to acknowledge the existence of this irrecuperable, ghostly other without seeking to control or dominate it. This ethical turn, I argue, chimes with the concern of Wolf and Liebmann to develop a mode of writing which 'rehears[es] individual and collective responsibility' towards alterity.[67] It resonates with their desire to cultivate a moral connection to the experiences of the other without appropriating them as their own.

For Derrida, the nature of our ethical engagement with the other is closely bound up with questions of legacy and debt. Calling for 'the principle of some *responsibility*, beyond all living present, [...] before the ghosts of those who are not yet born or who are already dead',[68] he disrupts the chronology inherent in the psychoanalytic understanding of phantomatic inheritance. The spectre, he suggests, is both a *revenant* and an *arrivant*, signalling our responsibility to face up to the past but also highlighting our obligation towards the future, towards what is still to come. In a series of puns based on the economic connotations of the terms 'revenance' and 'revenue', Derrida argues that the ghostly legacy which we inherit is contradictory: it signals what the past gives to us, but it also indicates the debt which we owe to the future. For Derrida, the experience of heirdom is an existential condition, inscribed into the very possibility of being of the human subject:

> *To be*, this word [...] means [...] to inherit. All the questions on the subject of being or of what is to be (or not to be) are questions of inheritance. [...] That we *are* heirs does not mean that we *have* or that we *receive* this or that, [...] but that the *being* of what we are *is* first of all inheritance.[69]

Through the implicit reference to Hamlet's existential dilemma, this passage highlights the inescapability of one's responsibility towards the past and the future, which is shown to be bound up with existence itself. In this regard, I suggest, the ethical implication of Derrida's argument correlates with Wolf's belief in 'Verantwortung' as a foundational principle of human subjectivity.[70] The texts analysed here all resort to the vocabulary of haunting as a means of exploring where the boundaries of individual and collective responsibility lie, and as a way of examining the precise nature of their ethical obligation towards the future.

The book argues that the move towards a more generalized form of haunting in the writing of Wolf and Liebmann signals their concern with the relations between self and other, subject and object, the individual and the collective. For Derrida, the condition of hauntology supplants the ontological concern with being and presence with a focus on the spectre as that which is neither present nor absent. In doing so, he prioritizes hauntedness as a fundamental condition of the human subject. He explains:

> This Ego, this *living individual* would itself be inhabited and invaded by *its own* specter. It would be constituted by specters of which it becomes the host and which it assembles in the haunted community of a single body. Ego = ghost. Therefore 'I am' would mean 'I am haunted' [...]. Wherever there is Ego, *es spukt*, 'it spooks'.[71]

Particularly striking here is the way in which Derrida blurs the distinction between the haunted and the haunting. The human subject is 'inhabited and invaded' by a spectre, and its body comes to act as the site of this haunting, yet (s)he also *becomes* a ghost, since, as Derrida observes, 'the phenomenological *ego* [...] is a specter'.[72] Signalled above all by the unspecific form of the German phrase, 'es spukt', which conceals the subject of the haunting, the Derridean spectre is at once intrinsic to and external to the human subject. At the same time, his references to the ghost as both a singular and plural entity challenge the distinction between the individual and the collective, revealing the spectre of personal identity to be inseparable from 'a more general ghost that haunts collective life in history'.[73] The move from the personal to the collective, from the specific to the general, I argue, can be read as a counter-current in the writing of Wolf and Liebmann. Challenging the private focus of their narratives, it serves to deflect individual concerns back onto the level of the collective, highlighting the different ways in which their experiences are bound up with the lives of others.

Media and Mediation

The role of the ghost as the purveyor of a disavowed traumatic history relates to questions about memory and memorialization, highlighting in particular the writers' search for a form of expression suited to the task of exposing this past. In this context, the book understands the ghost to be a self-conscious device which is employed as a means of reflecting on the mediation and medialization of individual and collective memory. The figure is often invoked in these texts in conjunction with references to different modes of artistic production. Depictions of the scene of writing are shadowed by ghostly apparitions which signal the transmission of messages between past and present through the medium of text, while the technological media of photography and film also convey spectral phenomena to the observer. Because of its link with the process of representation, the ghost can be regarded as a 'Figur medialer Selbstreferenz und Selbstreflexion',[74] which serves to highlight the ways in which different media forms can shape people's experience and memory of historical events.[75] As a figure lacking in physical presence, the existence of the ghost comes to depend on the medium which transmits it, while its form is defined by the nature of the apparatus which it haunts. In this regard, it is argued here that the writing of Wolf and Liebmann is based on a paradox: while these authors strive to create the impression of 'immediacy', to enable a direct, unmediated encounter with the past, their self-conscious exploration of the role of the medium reveals their awareness of the impossibility of achieving this goal.

As early as 1968, Wolf highlighted the position of the author as an intermediary figure, situated at the intersection between reality and the reader, and responsible for mediating between the two. Fundamental to artistic practice, she suggests, is 'die Vermittlung des Künstlers, der mit seinem Lebensschicksal und seinem

Lebenskonflikt zwischen der "Realität" und der leeren Seite steht und keine andere Wahl hat, diese Seite zu füllen, als die Auseinandersetzung zwischen der Welt und sich selbst darauf zu projizieren' (CW IV, 263). This emphasis on the active part played by the author in transmitting and influencing our experience of the world is central to Wolf's technique of 'subjektive Authentizität'; through her depiction of the productive role of the writer, she highlights his/her power to alter reality by changing how it is perceived by the individual. In the texts analysed here, the mediating role of the author is explored further through the use of imagery which depicts the figure of the writer as a spirit medium, whose task is to facilitate an encounter between past and present. The protagonists of these texts often draw upon their imaginative powers in order to invoke ghostly figures: their bodies act as a conduit between the real world and the realm of the supernatural, while their minds serve to transmit information from one party to the next. The act of mediation is depicted here in an ambivalent light; while the medium opens up the possibility of communication and exchange between two distinct realms, she also risks becoming possessed by the spirits which she invokes. In this regard, the texts exploit the classic predicament of the spirit medium, who, as the apparatus of mediation, also assumes the characteristics of the ghostly figures which she projects.[76] The task of the writer to mediate between past and present, fantasy and reality, is thus shadowed by the danger that she will be possessed by the phantoms which she invokes; her productive capacity is coupled with the risk of losing her identity to the ghosts which inhabit her.[77]

Historically, spirit mediums have tended to use technological devices in order to facilitate communication between the dead and the living.[78] While the techniques of photography, film, and telegraphy were used by mediums as a means of documenting ghostly apparitions and conveying messages from the spirit world, these devices also appeared to *create* phantoms by lending the illusion of presence to absent, non-material phenomena. Such technology therefore assumes a duplicitous function, testifying to the existence of phantoms which it has itself helped to create. In its examination of ghosts as 'Reflexionsfiguren der Medialität',[79] this book focuses on two particular examples of technological media: photography and film. While Liebmann's documentary volume, *Stille Mitte von Berlin*, contains actual photographs, the other texts discussed here refer to photography and film through ekphrastic description or, on a narratological level, through the adoption of the terminology associated with these forms of visual media to create a style of 'photographic' or 'filmic narrative'. These references to photography and film, I suggest, highlight two distinct points of tension in Wolf and Liebmann's work. First, the allusions to photography signal an attempt to validate the historical reference of their fiction by drawing on the documentary power of the camera; yet such an attempt is repeatedly countered by the realization that this history is characterized by gaps and absences which cannot be filled. Although the references to photography appear to endow the lost object with a spectral presence, this presence proves to be illusory, a sign of irrecuperable loss. Second, these allusions introduce a tension between photographic stasis and filmic animation. The texts here seek to breathe life into the figures which they create through the dynamic principle of the narrative; yet, just as the animation of the film reel is shadowed by the potential to slip back into a series of photographic stills, so too is the ghostly life fashioned by the author shown to be fragile, capable of returning at any moment to a state of arrest.

The book also considers the way in which the texts depict these technological devices in their interaction with the human body. As Jeffrey Sconce notes, the use of technological media transforms spirit mediums into 'wholly realized cybernetic beings — electromagnetic devices bridging flesh and spirit, body and machine, material reality and electronic space'.[80] The human body becomes a kind of apparatus, an uncanny interface between the living and the dead, the animate and the inanimate. In these texts, too, the distinction between human and machine is blurred through the protagonists' engagement with technology. Such devices often assume a prosthetic function, working to enhance the capabilities of the human body while at times replacing or supplanting the individual's organic functions. The camera, for example, operates as an artificial eye, heightening the writer's perception of the world around her, yet also taking over the role of her own visual apparatus. Like the optical instruments in the writing of E. T. A. Hoffmann, which serve as mechanical doubles of the human eye, the camera heightens the power of the real eye while also threatening to supersede it.[81] Organic, physical processes are rendered increasingly mechanistic as the body takes on the quality of apparatus which it operates, and it becomes unclear where the limits of the individual lie in relation to the technology it employs. In this regard, the texts raise questions about the nature of human agency and the capacity of the subject to direct his/her own actions. As the boundary between human and machine is blurred, so too is the distinction between subject and object, agent and victim. It is no longer clear who is governing whom, and this uncertainty casts doubt over the ability of the individual to take responsibility for his/her own behaviour.

Conditions of Haunting

The book identifies two psychological conditions which are particularly conducive to the experience of haunting: paranoia and melancholia. Symptoms of these conditions are displayed at different times by Wolf and Liebmann's protagonists, and their manifestation can frequently be traced back to the ambiguous status of the individual within the society of the GDR. As Mary

Fulbrook has observed, the power structures in the East German State were characterized by 'a curious combination of paranoia and paternalism'.[82] On the one hand, the SED, which was in principle inspired by 'the desire to make things better for the mass of the people',[83] adopted the role of a 'totally authoritarian parent', offering its citizens psychological and material security while also shielding them from potentially dangerous external influences.[84] On the other hand, the regime was plagued by an 'extraordinary' degree of insecurity, which meant that 'paranoia lay at the root of many of the measures taken by the state'.[85] The persistent fear of attack from perceived opponents within the GDR led to the curtailment of individual freedoms and the intrusion of the State into the private lives of its subjects through the mechanism of the Stasi.[86] The double-edged conception of the citizen as someone to be both protected and feared is, I suggest, reflected in the unsettled identity of the protagonists in the texts analysed here. At times, these figures reveal a melancholic attachment to the ideals of security and homeliness promised by the lost State; at others, their sense of home is rendered 'unheimlich' by the after-effects of surveillance and self-observation, and by their internalization of the State's paranoid quest to hunt down any potential enemies in the system.

Melancholia

In his essay 'Trauer und Melancholie', Freud famously defines mourning as 'die Reaktion auf den Verlust einer geliebten Person oder einer an ihre Stelle gerückten Abstraktion wie Vaterland, Freiheit, ein Ideal usw' (SF III, 197). The loss of a person, place or concept to which one was previously attached triggers a process of renegotiation, in which the individual's libidinal investment in the love object is withdrawn and invested elsewhere. The bereaved undergoes a process of reality-testing in which 'jede einzelne der Erinnerungen und Erwartungen, in denen die Libido an das Objekt geknüpft war, wird eingestellt, überbesetzt und an ihr die Lösung der Libido vollzogen' (SF III, 199). Although the process is time-consuming and 'außerordentlich schmerzhaft' (SF III, 199), it comes to a spontaneous and decisive end when the attachments to the other have been severed and the mourner has accepted the reality of the loss. By contrast, Freud theorizes melancholia as a pathological state which emerges when the individual fails to sever his/her emotional attachment to the lost love object. His/her identification with the lost object seeks to sustain the love relation with the other, denying the certainty of its loss and attempting to keep it alive in the psyche of the individual. Resisting closure, his/her mind works to prolong the existence of the other, lending it a fantasized afterlife in the present and endowing it with a spectral condition which persists beyond its demise.[87] The melancholic individual becomes haunted by the ghost of the lost other, whose existence signals the subject's continual inability or refusal to mourn.

What is particularly striking about Freud's understanding of melancholia is the way in which he depicts the individual's ambivalent struggle between his/her wish to remain among the living and his/her desire to be at one with the dead. (S)he is torn between the necessity of living with the pain of the loss which (s)he has experienced, and the longing to numb this pain by existing in a death-like state, free from the demands of reality. In oscillating between the demands of life and the temptation of death, the melancholic comes to lead a liminal, ghostly existence which resembles that of his/her lost love object. This ambiguity has been developed further by Nicholas Abraham and Maria Torok in their engagement with Freudian psychoanalysis. For them, the psychic denial of loss and the preservation of the lost love object occurs through the process of 'incorporation', a fantasy in which this object is 'swallowed and preserved' inside the subject.[88] The individual's memories of the love object are entombed within the unconscious, 'buried alive in the crypt as a full-fledged person', and this living-dead figure at times resurfaces to plague the subject, taking on the role of a 'ghost [that] comes back to haunt the cemetery guard'.[89] The melancholic individual becomes a kind of medium, who 'lend[s] [his/her] own flesh to the phantom object of love'.[90] At the same time, through the preservation of the lost object inside his/her psyche, (s)he becomes a 'living corpse',[91] assuming the features of the ghosts which inhabit him/her and, in doing so, embodying the very loss which (s)he seeks to deny.

Departing from these explanations of melancholia, I argue that the protagonists in the writing of Wolf and Liebmann betray a persistent attachment to the ideals and security offered by the lost GDR. Their ambiguous position as figures that are both haunted and haunting, caught in a struggle between life and death, is characteristic of the melancholic condition, while their preoccupation with salvaging the traces and remainders of the Socialist State signals an attempt to resuscitate the lost regime and maintain their emotional connection to it. At times, this melancholic condition resonates with the negative pathology attributed to it by Freud, Abraham, and Torok; its destructive quality manifests itself in various physical symptoms which plague the protagonists, as well as in the psychological stasis which repeatedly threatens to overwhelm them. At other times, however, it assumes a more positive dimension, fuelling the protagonists' creative projects and enabling them to maintain an open, personal connection to the past. Their melancholic stance, I suggest, has an ethical function which recalls Derrida's emphasis on melancholia as a means of 'porter l'autre en [soi] pour lui être fidèle'.[92] Through their continuous engagement with the past, they seek to recuperate some of the lost possibilities and opportunities occasioned by the passage of time, opening themselves up to the alternative histories hinted at by these losses. In this regard, the melancholic condition of the protagonists can also be regarded as a reflection on the way in which the texts themselves relate to a past which is 'neither fixed nor complete'.⁹³ Unlike the elegiac works which Charity Scribner has analysed in her study, *Requiem for Communism*, these texts are less concerned with presenting a nostalgic vision of the past than with cultivating a productive commitment to it.⁹⁴ Rather than simply fixating on aspects of the past for their own sake, these texts draw the past into the present in order to reveal how it relates to the future.

Paranoia

Paranoia or 'delusional disorder', according to the most recent edition of the *Diagnostic and Statistical Manual* published by the American Psychiatric Association, is a condition characterized by the presence of one or more 'non-bizarre' delusions which persist for at least a month.⁹⁵ 'Non-bizarre' refers to the fact that the delusions are to some degree plausible, in that they relate to circumstances and events which could conceivably occur in everyday life, such as being observed or stalked, or being at the centre of a malicious conspiracy. Moreover, these delusions do not markedly impair the normal functioning of the individual, and his/her outward behaviour is not noticeably odd or bizarre. The manual then goes on to list various types of delusional thinking, ranging from erotomania to somatic delusions, based on the specific theme of the patient's paranoia. Particularly relevant for this book is the subtype known as persecutory mania, which revolves around the individual's conviction that (s)he is being observed, watched, or persecuted in some way. This type of delusional disorder manifests itself in a heightened sense of suspicion towards those surrounding the individual, together with a readiness to perceive threats where none actually exist.⁹⁶ In addition, it often involves a fear of 'loss of autonomy', a conviction that one is being 'controlled by forces outside oneself'.⁹⁷

The book suggests that the texts analysed here can be regarded as examples of what David Trotter has termed 'paranoid narrative', a form of writing which is conditioned by the psychological structures of paranoia.⁹⁸ Trotter's understanding of paranoid narrative is largely influenced by the writings of Freud, and in particular his notes on the case of Daniel Schreber. For Freud, paranoia always arises from a psychic conflict within the patient which he cannot tolerate. When the individual experiences a libidinal attachment to a love object which his conscious mind cannot accept, this attachment undergoes a process of repression, resulting in its complete disavowal. His love for the other is negated ('Ich liebe ihn ja nicht — ich hasse ihn' — SF VII, 187) and the hatred which ensues is in turn projected onto another, external figure ('Ich liebe ihn nicht — ich hasse ihn ja, weil er mich verfolgt' — SF VII, 187). The person who was once loved and honoured by the patient is now hated and regarded as a persecutor. The characteristics of paranoia emerge when the repressed emotional connection to the other returns in the form of a perceived attack on the self from an external threat. The repressed material haunts the patient in the form of an estranged other, who is considered by the subject to have malevolent intent. Crucially, Freud emphasizes the constructive function of the paranoid delusion: although apparently pathological, it actually signals an unconscious attempt on the part of the individual to reconstruct the integrity of the psyche by ridding it of unwanted emotions and desires.

Drawing on Freud's analysis, Trotter argues that paranoid narratives emerge as a defence against what might be regarded as the confusion and chaos of the modern world.[99] Paranoid fantasies of persecution, he suggests, are employed by writers whenever the boundary between subject and object, self and other, is called into question.[100] They signal an obstinate 'striving towards structure',[101] an attempt to reassert a kind of order when the logic of reality threatens to fall apart. While Trotter's argument focuses on the work of English modernist writers, this book identifies a similar logic of paranoia at work in the writing of Wolf and Liebmann. The mysterious stalker figure which pursues the protagonist of *Die freien Frauen* is understood in this context as a projection of the threat to herself created by her knowledge of the murky past which she uncovers. And the phantom image of the Stasi officers which haunts the protagonist of *Was bleibt* can be read as a paranoid fantasy created by the mind of an individual whose world is on the verge of collapse. Signalling a potential loss of autonomy and a slippage of identity between subject and object, the image is regarded by the protagonist as an external threat to her fragile sense of self; it plays on her fear of being watched, becoming a kind of ghost which is always observing her and from whose gaze she can never escape. Yet this 'Phantombild' can be regarded as a projective image, an externalization of a threat which actually originates inside the protagonist, in that part of her which understands and sympathizes with the aims of the Stasi agents. As a ghostly remainder of her disavowed complicity with the regime, the image refuses denial, returning repeatedly and threatening to destroy the very security which it was intended to preserve.

Ghosts of Romanticism

As well as considering the significance of haunting on a thematic level, the book also understands the ghost to be a figure of intertextual *revenance*, whose presence reveals the way in which these works are inhabited by traces and fragments of other literary texts. While, as Julian Wolfreys has observed, it is possible to view any work of literature as a kind of ghost story, '"haunted" by voices from the past',[102] this study focuses more specifically on the ghost as an after-image of the Romantic imagination. At times, Wolf's and Liebmann's texts include direct references to the work of particular Romantic writers such as E. T. A. Hoffmann and Adelbert von Chamisso, whose fiction displays a preoccupation with uncanny figures such as ghosts, phantoms, and doubles. At other times, their writing alludes more generally to the spirit of Romanticism: the colour blue, for example, which was prized by Romantic authors as a symbol of transcendence,[103] reappears in these texts in the form of a ghostly blue light that is at once revelatory and potentially destructive. Whereas the colour once signalled the capacity of the human imagination to move beyond the earthly realm, it now reveals this prospect of transcendence to be spectral in inclination, characterized by a ghostly remainder which returns to haunt any form of creative endeavour. Such allusions to the repertoire of Romanticism, the book suggests, highlight the way in which the Romantic spirit has returned as a kind of 'cultural revenant' following the original demise of the movement.[104] This return of the Romantic imagination is understood to be highly ambivalent, enhancing the literary projects of Wolf and Liebmann while also threatening to undermine them through its inherent attachment to death and mortality.

The fact that the Romantic impulse resurfaces in the literature of former East German writers in the wake of the *Wende* assumes a particular significance given the status attributed to Romanticism in the GDR. Until the mid-1970s, the literature of the Romantic movement was largely dismissed by politicians and academics, who, following Goethe's famous proclamation,[105] tended to regard Romanticism as the unhealthy antithesis of Classicism.[106] East German cultural policy in this period was heavily influenced by the work of Georg Lukács, who understood 'die Kritik der Romantik' to be 'eine höchst aktuelle Aufgabe der deutschen Literaturgeschichte' and stressed that this criticism 'kann niemals tiefschürfend und scharf genug sein'.[107] Lukács considered Romantic writing to be inherently reactionary and thus at odds with the revolutionary principles of Socialism. This, together with his consideration of the prominent role played by Romanticism in the ideology of National Socialism, led him to denounce the movement as a negative principle which ought to be excluded from the literary canon of the GDR.[108] While some Romantic writers, such as E. T. A. Hoffmann and Friedrich Hölderlin, appear to have been spared such harsh criticism, their reception in this period was nevertheless distorted by critics' attempts to 'redeem' them by overemphasizing the Classicist elements of their work.[109] This pronounced criticism of Romanticism also influenced the creative output of East German writers, who were compelled to follow the restrictive tenets of Socialist Realism in their work. These tenets condemned the use of Romantic subject matter such as dreams, fantasy, and the irrational, demanding instead that writers focus on prosaic scenarios rooted in everyday life; at the same time, any efforts to replicate the experimental techniques characteristic of Romantic writing were decried as being detrimental to the didactic function of Socialist Realist literature.

The Romantic movement thus became what Hans-Georg Werner terms 'eine verdrängte Tradition',[110] a literary mode which was marginalized by those in authority. The 1970s and 1980s, however, witnessed a revival of this repressed tradition, with the publication of new editions of works by Romantic writers and a sudden proliferation of critical commentaries aiming to rehabilitate these marginalized figures into the cultural landscape of the GDR.[111] Influenced by developments in West German literary criticism, which sought to emphasize the transformative or redemptive potential of Romantic writing, academics in the East began to explore the ways in which this tradition could shed light on certain aspects of GDR society.[112] In his essays on E. T. A. Hoffmann, for example, Franz Fühmann placed particular emphasis on the previously ignored irrational quality of his tales; this quality, Fühmann argued, challenges the reader to acknowledge the potential monstrosities in him/herself and in the world, and encourages him/her to be on his/her guard against them.[113] A similar exploration of the transformative potential of Romantic literature can be found in short stories by Anna Seghers (*Sonderbare Begegnungen*, 1973) and Christa Wolf (*Unter den Linden: Drei unwahrscheinliche Geschichten*, 1974), which explore the possibility of harnessing the fantastic style of Romantic writers to a utopian purpose. Romantic motifs and experimental techniques are used here as a means of exposing the roots of society's problems and opening them up to the possibility of change. In this regard, the irrational or uncanny quality can be seen to operate in a similar way to the Brechtian *Verfremdungseffekt*, rendering everyday reality strange in order to unsettle the reader into acknowledging the avoidability of seemingly inevitable events. It offers a means of developing an active, productive relation to the present, enabling writers to cultivate alternative models of reality and in doing so highlight the latent potential inherent in the actual situation of the GDR.

If the Romantic tradition was initially suppressed by the GDR authorities, its reappearance in the 1970s and 1980s can be understood as a return of the repressed, a potentially subversive act of literary *revenance* which worked to undermine the validity of Socialist Realism as the dominant model of literary expression. As Hans Kaufmann explains in his influential essay, 'Versuch über das Erbe' (1980), the return of Romanticism in this period posed a challenge to the GDR's understanding of literary heritage, which had previously been based on a conscious appropriation of aspects of the past which were deemed to be of positive value for the furtherance of Socialism.[114] Following the revival of Romantic literature, the notion of 'Erbe' had to be adapted to include material which was 'bisher etwas vergessen';[115] it had to acknowledge that the inheritance of past literature could not necessarily be controlled, and that the present could be subjected to the return of literary forms which were previously considered negative. This acknowledgment involved calling into question the official conception of literary history as a teleological progression towards a truly Socialist form of expression; instead, it demanded recognition of the repetitions and returns inherent in the course of such a history. Above all, this revival of Romantic writing signalled a transfer of agency from the cultural authorities of the GDR to the literary texts themselves; because of their 'Wiederbelebung' at the hands of writers and critics, these texts seemed to possess a life of their own, living on in a revised form despite the official attempts to silence them.

Viewed against this backdrop, the book considers the return of Romantic imagery in the literature of the post-*Wende* period as a further manifestation of this repressed tradition. Whereas the appearance of Romantic motifs in texts of the 1970s and 1980s largely served to further the writers' utopian intent, their role here is more ambiguous, often highlighting a dystopian prospect which shadows the writers' creative vision. The productive fantasy which previously accompanied the repertoire of Romanticism is now coupled with a destructive potential, which threatens to subvert the artistic practices of Wolf and Liebmann. Recalling the 'chronic dualism' of Romantic irony, which affirmed 'creative vitality' while at the same time undermining it with 'a darker view of irredeemable mortality',[116] these post-*Wende* texts are paradoxically animated by their peculiar attachment to their own demise. The fantastic visions which they present are founded on the very possibility that such visions are, in fact, deceptive phantoms with the power to mislead the reader while holding him/her in their thrall. And the fictional life which they create is shown to be an illusion, an uncanny reanimation of the ghosts and golems of the Romantic imagination, whose semblance of life is at once seductive and potentially harmful. The texts analysed here are thus shown to work against themselves, undermining the writers' productive intention and ultimately casting doubt on the positive resolution of the psychic conflicts which they depict. These subversive counter-currents, I suggest, challenge the generic coherence of Wolf and Liebmann's post-*Wende* texts, revealing them to be highly unstable sites of hybridity and fluctuation.

Outline

The book is divided into five chapters, each of which is devoted to the analysis of one particular work. In Wolf's case, I have chosen to focus on texts published after the *Wende* whose imagery bears a particular relation to the Romantic tradition which she first embraced in the 1970s. Although this criterion necessarily excludes certain key works in her oeuvre, it enables a more detailed consideration of the significance of the tradition in question for Wolf in the wake of the GDR's demise. The second half of the book turns to the work of Liebmann. While the primary focus here is her fictional writing, I also consider the photographic project published under the title *Stille Mitte von Berlin*, since the evacuated scenes of her photographs are recalled in her novels through forms of ekphrastic description as the setting for ghostly manifestations and uncanny revelations of a repressed past. The book addresses the works of each author in chronological order of their genesis: the intention of this grouping is not so much to indicate a sense of progression or teleology in the work of either writer, but rather to demonstrate how they draw on techniques of intertextual recall and self-quotation in their engagement with questions of legacy and haunting.[117]

The first chapter focuses on Wolf's controversial *Erzählung*, *Was bleibt* (1990), whose publication in 1990 quickly propelled the author to the centre of what later became known as the *Deutsch–deutsche Literaturstreit*. The initial accusations made against Wolf following critics' reading of the text — namely, that she depicted herself as a victim of the GDR regime while actually profiting from her privileged role as a 'Staatsdichterin' — were compounded by the revelation in 1993 that she had herself worked as an *inoffizielle Mitarbeiterin* for the Stasi between 1959 and 1962. While criticism of *Was bleibt* has been influenced by the *Literaturstreit* insofar as it tends to focus on questions surrounding the autobiographical authenticity of the text, this chapter offers a reading which highlights the range of Romantic imagery present in the tale. Examining the text through the lens of Wolf's earlier short story, 'Unter den Linden' (1974), it argues that the imagery of ghostliness in *Was bleibt* serves to highlight the pathological undertones which haunt Wolf's utopian vision. More specifically, the chapter traces the way in which the notion of the 'Phantombild' — the ghostly after-image of the Stasi agents which lingers in the mind's eye of protagonist — destabilizes the relationship between subject and object, observer and observed. Working to call into question the boundary between autonomy and complicity, the phantom image reveals the way in which Wolf's commitment to Socialist ideals is always shown to be shadowed by the possibility of their betrayal.

The second chapter examines the depiction of the elusive boundary between victimhood and culpability in Wolf's more recent *Erzählung*, *Leibhaftig* (2002). It begins by outlining the way in which she uses the imagery of phantoms and haunting in her recent theoretical work both as a means of engaging with the repressed aspects of the collective German past and, on a more personal level, as a way of alluding to her own complicity with the Stasi. While she calls on Germany to take leave of its phantoms, she also embarks on a more private quest to come to terms with the repressed ghosts of her own history. The chapter goes on to argue that the metaphor of the phantom is rendered literal in *Leibhaftig* through the image of the protagonist's body as a spirit medium which facilitates ghostly encounters between past and present. Developing the notion of the mediating role of the writer which she first outlined in *Kindheitsmuster* (1974), Wolf depicts her protagonist's body as a technological apparatus for conjuring up spirits. By drawing on an allusion to E. T. A. Hoffmann's portrayal of the human being as an electric circuit, I argue that Wolf's depiction of the body as an apparatus introduces a slippage between autonomy and possession, subjecthood and objectification, which calls into question the protagonist's ability to act of her own volition. Although the text does not directly allude to Wolf's relationship with the Stasi, the descriptions of her protagonist's condition at the boundary of agency and victimhood resonate with the vocabulary which she uses in her more direct references to her role. Viewed in this light, the chapter suggests that the legacy of Wolf's ambivalent relationship with the Stasi is revealed in *Leibhaftig* to be a ghost in the machine of her protagonist's body, a persistent reminder of her double agency which haunts her corporeal existence.

The two halves of the book are linked by the overriding premise that references to the ghostly are used in these texts to highlight an underlying ambivalence towards the writer's task of engaging with the past. While the experience of haunting is often shown to open up a productive dimension, shedding new light on the relations between past and present, it also possesses a more ominous quality, threatening to destabilize the position of the subject and calling into question her autonomy as an individual. Chapter 3 goes on to illustrate this ambivalence through an examination of Liebmann's documentary volume, *Stille Mitte von Berlin* (2002), which contains photographs of the district of Mitte taken by the author in the 1980s. Drawing on the references to the early twentieth-century genre of spirit photography in the canonical theories of Walter Benjamin and Roland Barthes, which consider the camera to be kind of a spirit medium and the photograph a ghostly emanation of its referent, the chapter suggests that the haunting quality of Liebmann's images lies in their ability to create an atmosphere of standstill, to freeze their referents and suspend them in a perpetual moment of death-in-life. On the one hand, their apparent ability to resist the passage of time recalls Benjamin's notion of 'Dialektik im Stillstand' (WB v.1, 578), the explosive but frozen collision of past and present which exposes the underlying dialectical relationship between the two and prompts a clearer understanding of the way in which they interact. Her images work to reveal aspects of the past which usually remain imperceptible to the human eye, thus invoking an uncanny return of repressed memories. On the other hand, I argue that the potential of the photographic medium to create what Barthes terms 'the stasis of an *arrest*' is used here to indicate a sense of lifelessness, a pervasive deadening of human life which threatens to spill out of the photograph, arresting the observer and suspending him/her in a state of living death.

The fourth chapter of the book focuses on Liebmann's novel, *In Berlin* (1994), whose central character leads an unsettled existence, haunted by the ghosts of her past while also becoming a haunting figure, compulsively visiting and revisiting certain locations in the city in search of a sense of belonging. While the previous chapter examined the way in which her photography exploits the potential of the camera to create a state of living death, it is argued here that Liebmann's fiction is founded on the Hoffmannesque notion of the 'lebendiges Bild'. Her text often makes reference to the frozen scenes of her photographs, yet it seeks to animate these through the dynamic principle of the narrative. The evacuated streets of Berlin are shown to host a series of ghostly encounters and uncanny events as aspects of the past come alive in the present, while the temporal logic of her photographs, their ability to mediate between past, present, and future, is transformed here into a living encounter with the city's history. However, the chapter suggests that the animating principle of Liebmann's narrative is always shadowed by the threat of seizure, by the potential for these living images to return to a state of arrest. Focusing in particular on the human eye and the hand as points of transition between the animate and the inanimate, the chapter highlights the way in which the writer's task of animating her subject matter is shadowed by the danger she faces of being paralysed by the force of her imaginative vision. Her capacity to breathe life into her artistic creation is shown to be founded on the possibility of her own mortification, as the logic of the ghostly is projected back onto the subject. The internal deadening felt by the protagonist, I suggest, serves in Liebmann's work to raise questions about the function of identification and empathy in literary attempts to engage with experiences which are not one's own. Though derived from the fantastic writing of E. T. A. Hoffmann, this spectral logic serves an ethical purpose in Liebmann's writing, highlighting the dangers associated with appropriating the historical experiences of others in literary texts.

Finally, the book examines Liebmann's most recent novel, *Die freien Frauen* (2004), which has been described as belonging to the 'Tradition der romantischen deutschen Erzählung, wie sie von E. T. A. Hoffmann bis Gustav Meyrink die Leser faszinierte'.[118] Continuing Liebmann's project of delving beneath official narratives and revealing hidden aspects of the past, the novel employs the form of the family narrative in its exploration of the way in which historical events influence the construction of individual subjectivity. The chapter draws on Nicholas Abraham's 'Notes on the Phantom' in order to reveal how the protagonist is haunted by the ghosts of her father's past, which have been passed on to her through silences and somatic symptoms. It suggests that her sense of psychic displacement can be related directly to her identification with the ghosts of those murdered in the Third Reich, whose existence has been denied by her family, yet whose continuing spectral presence signals a resistance against erasure and disavowal. The chapter goes on to address how the protagonist's engagement with these ghosts leads her to develop alternative, uchronian narratives which open up a realm beyond the chronology of historical time. Occupying a position between historiography and fiction, these narratives offer the protagonist a means of attending to the ghosts of her family's past by refiguring the events of their lives and thereby endowing them with a fictive presence in her imagination. This aesthetic, I argue, is characteristic of Liebmann's work as a whole; combining factual material and fictional techniques, she blurs the boundary between 'Geschichte' and 'Geschichten', using alternative narratives as a means of shedding new light on the past and recovering the unrealized opportunities and possibilities inherent in it. Through her imagination, she adopts a playful approach to historical subject matter, using it as the impetus for her own creative reflection and thereby cultivating a living connection to the ghostly figures which haunt her.

Notes to the Introduction

1. Gero von Wilpert, *Die deutsche Gespenstergeschichte: Motiv, Form, Entwicklung* (Stuttgart: Kröner, 1994), p. 439. See also Muriel Stiffler, *The German Ghost Story as Genre* (New York: Lang, 1993), p. 131.
2. Bart Philipsen, 'Literatur und Spektralität: Zur Einführung', in *Literatur im Krebsgang: Totenbeschwörung und memoria in der deutschsprachigen Literatur nach 1989*, ed. by Arne de Winde and Anke Gilleir, Amsterdamer Beiträge zur neueren Germanistik, 64 (Amsterdam: Rodopi, 2008), pp. 13–22 (p. 14). On the relationship between the ghost and the so-called 'paradox of witnessing', see the essays in *Figures and Figurations of the (Un-)Dead*, ed. by Robert Buch and Johannes Türk, Special Issue of *Germanic Review*, 82 (2007).
3. Philipsen, p. 15.
4. Marianne Hirsch, *Family Frames: Photography, Narrative and Postmemory* (Cambridge, MA: Harvard University Press, 1997).
5. Philipsen, p. 15.
6. See also Silke Horstkotte, 'Die Geister von Auschwitz: Fotografie und spektrale Erinnerung in Stephan Wackwitz' *Ein unsichtbares Land* und *Neue Menschen*', in *Literatur im Krebsgang*, ed. by de Winde and Gilleir, pp. 273–98.
7. As Peter Graves notes, the Holocaust and the *Wende* are 'two events [...] that mark out the ideological poles of Wolf's experience, and they continue to resonate throughout her work'. Peter Graves, 'Christa Wolf in the 1990s', in *Legacies and Identity: East and West German Literary Responses to Unification*, ed. by Martin Kane, British and Irish Studies in German Language and Literature, 31 (Oxford: Lang, 2002), pp. 167–80 (p. 179).
8. Jörg Magenau suggests that the post-*Wende* period for Wolf has been characterized by 'Abschiede von Hoffnungen, von Illusionen, von Utopien'. Jörg Magenau, *Christa Wolf: Eine Biographie* (Berlin: Kindler, 2002), p. 445.
9. Her ambivalence might be related to her childhood experience of forced resettlement following her father's expulsion from the Politburo in 1953, an event which shadows all of her literary work.
10. For a list of these writers, see Ricarda Schmidt, 'GDR Women Writers: Ways of Writing for, within and against Socialism', in *A History of Women's Writing in Germany, Austria*

and Switzerland, ed. by Jo Catling (Cambridge: Cambridge University Press, 2000), pp. 190–99 (p. 196). Wolf has also admitted to considering the possibility of leaving in an interview with Hanns-Bruno Kammertöns und Stephan Lebert, published under the title 'Bei mir dauert alles sehr lange', in *Die Zeit*, 29 September 2005, pp. 17–20.

11. Monika Hohbein-Deegen suggests that she led a kind of 'Transitexistenz', 'da sie sich weder im Westteil, noch im Ostteil der Stadt heimisch fühlt'. Monika Hohbein-Deegen, *Reisen zum Ich: Ostdeutsche Identitätssuche in Texten der neunziger Jahre*, East German Studies, 17 (Berne: Lang, 2010), p. 132.
12. This book was written before Wolf's death in 2011 and therefore refers to her in the present tense throughout.
13. In particular, we have witnessed the publication of Sonja Hilzinger's twelve-volume edition of Wolf's works, two new biographies of the author (Magenau, *Christa Wolf*; and Peter Börthig, *Christa Wolf: Eine Biografie in Bildern und Texten* (Munich: Luchterhand, 2004)) and the release of unseen diary material in *Ein Tag im Jahr* (Munich: Luchterhand, 2003).
14. The most significant analyses of Liebmann's work can be found in Astrid Köhler, *Brückenschläge: DDR-Autoren vor und nach der Wiedervereinigung* (Göttingen: Vandenhoek & Ruprecht, 2007), pp. 103–30; Katharina Gerstenberger, *Writing the New Berlin: The German Capital in Post-Wall Literature* (Rochester, NY: Camden House, 2008), pp. 98–101; Lyn Marven, '"Die Landschaft ihrer Gedanken": Autobiography and Intertextuality in Irina Liebmann's Berlin Texts', in *New German Literature: Life-Writing and Dialogue with the Arts*, ed. by Julian Preece, Frank Finlay, and Ruth J. Owen, Leeds-Swansea Colloquia on Contemporary German Literature, 1 (Oxford: Lang, 2007), pp. 267–82; and Lyn Marven, '"Souvenirs de Berlin-Est": History, Photos, and Form in Texts by Daniela Dahn, Irina Liebmann, and Sophie Calle', *Seminar*, 43 (2007), 220–33.
15. See Elizabeth Boa, 'Christa Wolf: Kindheitsmuster', in *Landmarks in the German Novel 2*, ed. by Peter Hutchinson and Michael Minden, British and Irish Studies in German Language and Literature, 47 (Oxford: Lang, 2010), pp. 77–92 (p. 87); Elke Brüns, '*Leibhaftig*: Christa Wolfs Gang ins Totenreich', in *Literatur im Krebsgang*, ed. by de Winde and Gilleir, pp. 145–58; and Susanne Ledanff, *Hauptstadtphantasien: Berliner Stadtlektüren in der Gegenwartsliteratur 1989–2008* (Bielefeld: Aisthesis, 2009), p. 199.
16. Michelle Mattson, *Mapping Morality in Postwar German Women's Fiction: Christa Wolf, Ingeborg Drewitz, and Grete Weil* (Rochester, NY: Camden House, 2010), p. 103.
17. Dennis Tate, *Shifting Perspectives: East German Autobiographical Narratives before and after the End of the GDR* (Rochester, NY: Camden House, 2007), p. 54. See also Paul Cooke, '"GDR Literature" in the Berlin Republic', in *Contemporary German Fiction: Writing in the Berlin Republic*, ed. by Stuart Taberner (Rochester, NY: Camden House, 2005), pp. 56–71 (pp. 56–58).
18. For two more detailed analyses of this discussion, see Stephen Brockmann, 'Literature and Convergence: The Early 1980s', in *Beyond 1989: Re-reading German Literary History since 1945*, ed. by Keith Bullivant, Modern German Studies, 3 (Providence: Berghahn, 1997), pp. 49–67 (pp. 49–50); and Ruth J. Owen, *The Poet's Role: Lyric Responses to German Unification by Poets from the GDR*, Amsterdamer Publikationen zur Sprache und Literatur, 147 (Amsterdam: Rodopi, 2001), pp. 278–80.
19. Jurek Becker, 'Die Wiedervereinigung der deutschen Literatur', *The German Quarterly*, 63 (1990), 359–66 (p. 363).
20. Ibid., p. 359.
21. Ibid., pp. 364, 366.
22. See, for example, Siegrun Wildner, *Experimentum mundi: Utopie als ästhetisches*

Prinzip: Zur Funktion utopischer Entwürfe in Irmtraud Morgners Romanwerk (St Ingbert: Röhrig, 2000), p. 17; Gustav Seibt, 'Wer mit dem Meißel schreibt, hat keine Handschrift: Ein neuer Anfang lyrischen Sprechens im Ausgang einer Epoche. Aus Anlaß eines Gedichts von Heiner Müller', *Frankfurter Allgemeine Zeitung*, 1 June 1993; and Richard Herzinger, 'Vom Nutzen und Nachteil der DDR-Literatur', in *Die Abwicklung der DDR*, ed. by Heinz Ludwig Arnold and Frauke Meyer-Gosau (Göttingen: Göttinger Sudelblätter, 1992), pp. 76–81 (p. 80).
23. Becker, p. 364.
24. Karen Leeder, '"Nachleben": Volker Braun and the Death and Afterlife of the GDR', *German Life and Letters*, 63 (2010), 265–79. While Leeder is not alone in referring to the 'afterlife of the GDR', her emphasis on the literary form of this afterlife is unique. For alternative interpretations of the term, see Mary Fulbrook, *A History of Germany 1918-2008: The Divided Nation*, 3rd edn (Malden, MA: Wiley-Blackwell, 2009), pp. 299–301; and Jonathan Bach, 'Vanishing Acts and Virtual Reconstructions: Technologies of Memory and the Afterlife of the GDR', in *Memory Traces: 1989 and the Question of German Cultural Identity*, ed. by Silke Arnold-de Simine, Cultural History and Literary Imagination, 5 (Berne: Lang, 2005), pp. 261–80.
25. Leeder, '"Nachleben"', p. 265.
26. Ibid., p. 279.
27. Ibid., p. 268.
28. Ibid., p. 265.
29. Ibid., p. 279.
30. Ibid. Elsewhere, Leeder has suggested that the preoccupation with spectrality in the literature of many former East German writers can be regarded as a feature of 'late work', a reflection prompted by the conjunction of biographical and epochal decline. See Karen Leeder, 'Dances of Death: A Last Literature from the GDR', in *Twenty Years On: Competing Memories of the GDR in Postunification German Culture*, ed. by Renate Rechtien and Dennis Tate (Rochester, NY: Camden House, 2011), pp. 187–202.
31. Peter Buse and Andrew Stott, 'Introduction: A Future for Haunting', in *Ghosts: Deconstruction, Psychoanalysis, History*, ed. by Peter Buse and Andrew Stott (Basingstoke: Macmillan, 1999), pp. 1–20 (p. 9).
32. See Terry Castle, *The Female Thermometer: Eighteenth-Century Culture and the Invention of the Uncanny* (New York: Oxford University Press, 1995), pp. 7–9.
33. Nicholas Royle, *The Uncanny: An Introduction* (Manchester: Manchester University Press, 2003), p. 51.
34. Irina Liebmann in conversation with Catherine Smale, 21 July 2009.
35. Anne Fuchs, *Phantoms of War in Contemporary German Literature, Films and Discourse: The Politics of Memory* (Basingstoke: Palgrave Macmillan, 2008), p. 48.
36. Elisabeth Bronfen, *The Knotted Subject: Hysteria and its Discontents* (Princeton: Princeton University Press, 1998), p. 384.
37. Peter Thompson, '"Die unheimliche Heimat": The GDR and the Dialectics of the Home', *Oxford German Studies*, 38 (2009), 278–87 (p. 284).
38. Ibid., p. 278.
39. Nicholas Abraham, 'Notes on the Phantom' (1975), in Nicholas Abraham and Maria Torok, *The Shell and the Kernel: Renewals of Psychoanalysis*, trans. by Nicholas Rand (Chicago: University of Chicago Press, 1994), pp. 171–76.
40. Fuchs, p. 1.
41. Sigrid Weigel, *Genea-Logik: Generation, Tradition und Evolution zwischen Kultur- und Naturwissenschaften* (Paderborn: Fink, 2006), p. 90.
42. Abraham, p. 166.
43. Ibid., p. 171.

44. Ibid.
45. Esther Rashkin, *Unspeakable Secrets and the Psychoanalysis of Culture* (Albany, NY: State University of New York Press, 2008), p. 94.
46. Nicholas Rand, 'Introduction: Renewals of Psychoanalysis', in Abraham and Torok, *The Shell and the Kernel*, pp. 1–22 (p. 17).
47. Abraham, p. 174.
48. Gabriele Schwab, *Haunting Legacies: Violent Histories and Transgenerational Trauma* (New York: Columbia University Press, 2010), p. 54.
49. Abraham, p. 175.
50. Ibid., p. 173.
51. Ibid., p. 175.
52. Abraham, p. 188. On the deceptive nature of the phantom, see Colin Davis, *Haunted Subjects: Deconstruction, Psychoanalysis and the Return of the Dead* (Basingstoke: Palgrave Macmillan, 2007), pp. 76–83.
53. Abraham, p. 188.
54. Ibid., p. 174.
55. Liebmann in conversation with Smale, 21 July 2009.
56. Ibid., p. 174.
57. Ibid.
58. Ibid., p. 189.
59. Ibid., p. 176.
60. Davis, *Haunted Subjects*, pp. 2–3.
61. Jacques Derrida, *Specters of Marx: The State of Debt, the Work of Mourning and the New International*, trans. by Peggy Kamuf (London: Routledge, 1994), p. 10.
62. See Jodey Castricano, *Cryptomimesis: The Gothic and Jacques Derrida's Ghost-Writing* (Montreal: McGill-Queen's University Press, 2001), p. 23; and Colin Davis, 'Hauntology, Spectres and Phantoms', *French Studies*, 59 (2005), 373–79 (p. 374).
63. Derrida, *Specters of Marx*, p. 6.
64. Ibid., p. 20.
65. Ibid., p. 11.
66. Davis, *Haunted Subjects*, p. 88.
67. Mattson, p. 96.
68. Derrida, *Specters of Marx*, p. xix.
69. Ibid., p. 54.
70. See Myra Love, *Christa Wolf: Literature and the Conscience of History*, East German Studies, 6 (New York: Lang, 1991), p. 77; and Mattson, pp. 129–30.
71. Derrida, *Specters of Marx*, p. 133.
72. Ibid., p. 135.
73. Andrew J. Webber, 'Topographical Turns: Casting Berlin in Contemporary Film', in *Debating German Cultural Identity 1989 to the Present*, ed. by Anne Fuchs, Kathleen James-Chakraborty, and Linda Shortt (Rochester, NY: Camden House, 2011), pp. 67–81 (p. 78).
74. Moritz Baßler, Bettina Gruber, and Martina Wagner-Egelhaaf, 'Einleitung', in *Gespenster: Erscheinungen, Medien, Theorien*, ed. by Moritz Baßler, Bettina Gruber, and Martina Wagner-Egelhaaf (Würzburg: Königshausen & Neumann, 2005), pp. 9–24 (p. 11).
75. On the mediation of individual and cultural memory, see *Mediation, Remediation, and the Dynamics of Cultural Memory*, ed. by Astrid Erll and Ann Rigney, Media and Cultural Memory, 10 (Berlin: de Gruyter, 2009), pp. 1–6.
76. As Baßler, Gruber, and Wagner-Egelhaaf write: 'Das Medium ist immer schon zu einem nicht eindeutig zu bemessenden Teil das, was es anscheinend nur vermittelt'. Baßler et al., p. 11.

77. As Elizabeth Hallam, Jennifer Hockney, and Glennys Howarth note, the medium experiences 'a loss of bodily boundaries as the spirit is allowed to enter. This effectively means a temporary loss of self'. Elizabeth Hallam, Jennifer Hockney, and Glennys Howarth, *Beyond the Body: Death and Social Identity* (London: Routledge, 1999), p. 156.
78. See Jill Galvan, *The Sympathetic Medium: Feminine Channeling, the Occult and Communication Technologies, 1859–1919* (Ithaca, NY: Cornell University Press, 2010), pp. 1–9; and Maria Warner, *Phantasmagoria: Spirit Visions, Metaphors, and Media into the Twenty-First Century* (Oxford: Oxford University Press, 2006), p. 300.
79. Baßler et al., p. 11.
80. Jeffrey Sconce, *Haunted Media: Electronic Presence from Telegraphy to Television* (Durham, NC: Duke University Press, 2000), p. 28.
81. Much has been written about the role of optical instruments in Hoffmann's tales. For a comprehensive overview, see Yvonne Holbeche, *Optical Motifs in the Works of E. T. A. Hoffmann*, Göppinger Arbeiten zur Germanistik, 141 (Göppingen: Kümmerle, 1975). For more recent studies, see Maik Müller, 'Phantasmagoria und bewaffnete Blicke: Zur Funktion optischer Apparate in E. T. A. Hoffmanns *Meister Floh*', *E. T. A. Hoffmann Jahrbuch*, 11 (2003), 104–21; and Anthony Vidler, *The Architectural Uncanny: Essays in the Modern Unhomely* (Cambridge, MA: MIT Press, 1992), pp. 33–35.
82. Mary Fulbrook, *Anatomy of a Dictatorship: Inside the GDR 1949–1989* (Oxford: Oxford University Press, 1995), p. 22.
83. Ibid., p. 22.
84. Ibid., p. 30.
85. Ibid., p. 23.
86. Andreas Glaeser has also analysed the Stasi as a mechanism of what he terms 'state paranoia'. Andreas Glaeser, 'Monolithic Intentionality, Belonging, and the Production of State Paranoia: A View through the Stasi onto the Late GDR', in *Off Stage/On Display: Intimacy and Ethnography in the Age of Public Culture*, ed. by Andrew Shryock (Stanford, CA: Stanford University Press, 2004), pp. 244–78.
87. As Jean-Philippe Mathy notes, 'the lost object keeps on living [...], but as a vision, a ghost, a shadow haunting the psyche'. Jean-Philippe Mathy, *Melancholy Politics: Loss, Mourning, and Memory in Late Modern France* (University Park, PA: Pennsylvania University Press, 2011), p. 39.
88. Nicholas Abraham and Maria Torok, 'Mourning or Melancholia: Introjection versus Incorporation' (1972), in *The Shell and the Kernel*, pp. 125–38 (p. 130).
89. Ibid., p. 130.
90. Ibid., p. 136.
91. Ibid., p. 148.
92. Jacques Derrida, *Béliers: Le dialogue ininterrompu: entre deux infinis, le poème* (Paris: Éditions Galilée, 2003), p. 74.
93. David Eng and David Kazanjian, *Loss: The Politics of Mourning* (Berkeley: University of California Press, 2003), p. 4.
94. Charity Scribner, *Requiem for Communism* (Cambridge, MA: MIT Press, 2003). Scribner diagnoses a 'collective sorrow' which has 'motivated a proliferation of literary texts and artworks, as well as a boom of museum exhibitions that survey the wreckage of socialism and its industrial remains' (p. 3).
95. *Diagnostic and Statistical Manual of Mental Disorders*, 4th edn (Washington, DC: American Psychiatric Association, 1994), pp. 296–97.
96. On the role of suspicion in paranoid thinking, see David W. Swanson, Philip J. Bohnert, and Jackson A. Smith, *The Paranoid* (Boston: Little, Brown & Co., 1970), pp. 14–15.
97. John Farrell, *Freud's Paranoid Quest: Psychoanalysis and Modern Suspicion* (New York: New York University Press, 1996), p. 43.

98. David Trotter, *Paranoid Modernism: Literary Experiment, Psychosis and the Professionalisation of English Society* (Oxford: Oxford University Press, 2001), p. 127.
99. Ibid., pp. 1–2.
100. Ibid., p. 68.
101. Ibid., p. 5.
102. Julian Wolfreys, *Victorian Hauntings: Spectrality, Gothic, the Uncanny and Literature* (Basingstoke: Palgrave, 2002), pp. xii.
103. See Wolfgang Müller-Funk, *Die Farbe Blau: Untersuchungen zur Epistemologie des Romantischen* (Vienna: Turia & Kant, 2000), pp. 7–8.
104. Andrew J. Webber, 'The Afterlife of Romanticism', in *German Literature of the Nineteenth Century: 1832–1899*, ed. by Clayton Koelb and Eric Downing, Camden House History of German Literature, 9 (Rochester, NY: Camden House, 2007), pp. 23–43 (p. 25). Webber argues that 'the Romantic itself may have a constitutional tendency toward repetition' (p. 27).
105. 'Klassisch ist das Gesunde, romantisch das Kranke'. Johann Wolfgang Goethe, 'Maximen und Reflexionen', in *Werke*, ed. by Erich Trunz, 14 vols (Munich: Beck, 1981), XII, 487.
106. See Patrick Baab, 'Die Mitwelt hat Anspruch auf Auskunft: Konzeptuelle Wandlung der Rezeption des "negativen" romantischen Erbes in der DDR am Beispiel von Christa Wolf', *die horen*, 29 (1984), 49–61 (pp. 50–51); Hanne Castein, 'Arbeiten mit der Romantik heute: Zur Romantikrezeption der DDR', in *Deutsche Romantik und das 20. Jahrhundert*, ed. by Hanne Castein and Alexander Stillmark (Stuttgart: Heinz, 1986), pp. 5–24 (p. 5–6); and Joachim Lehmann, *Die blinde Wissenschaft: Realismus und Realität in der Literaturtheorie der DDR* (Würzburg: Königshausen & Neumann, 1995), p. 183.
107. Georg Lukács, *Kurze Skizze einer Geschichte der neueren deutschen Literatur* (Darmstadt: Luchterhand, 1975), p. 83.
108. On the perceived relationship between Fascism and Romanticism, see Ursula Heukenkamp, 'Diskurse über den Irrationalismus in der SBZ/DDR zwischen 1945 und 1960', in *Neue Ansichten: The Reception of Romanticism in the Literature of the GDR*, ed. by Howard Gaskill, Karin McPherson, and Andrew Barker, GDR Monitor Special Series, 6 (Amsterdam: Rodopi, 1990), pp. 98–113 (pp. 100–05).
109. Hans-Georg Werner, *E. T. A. Hoffmann: Darstellung und Deutung der Wirklichkeit im dichterischen Werk*, Beiträge zur deutschen Klassik, 13 (Berlin: Aufbau, 1971), pp. 25–28.
110. Hans-Georg Werner, 'Romantische Traditionen in epischen Werken der neueren DDR Literatur', *Zeitschrift für Germanistik*, 4 (1980), 398–416 (p. 398).
111. Perhaps the most significant of these publications was the series *Märkische Dichtergarten*, edited by Gerhard Wolf and Günter de Bruyn, which focused on works by forgotten or disdained authors such as Ludwig Tieck and Friedrich de la Motte Fouqué. One such volume contained fantastic tales by E. T. A. Hoffmann. See *E. T. A. Hoffmann: Gespenster in der Friedrichstadt. Berlinische Geschichten*, ed. by Günter de Bruyn (Berlin: Der Morgen, 1986).
112. Baab, p. 51.
113. Franz Fühmann, *Fräulein Veronika Paulmann aus der Pirnaer Vorstadt oder Etwas über das Schauerliche bei E. T. A. Hoffmann* (Rostock: Hinstorff, 1979), p. 112. In the second half of the 1980s, Fühmann also created a film script based on Hoffmann's tale, 'Das öde Haus', although the film itself was never actually produced. See Dennis Tate, *Franz Fühmann, Innovation and Authenticity: A Study of his Prose-Writing*, Amsterdamer Publikationen zur Sprache und Literatur, 117 (Amsterdam: Rodopi, 1995), pp. 219–20.
114. Hans Kaufmann, *Versuch über das Erbe* (Leipzig: Reclam, 1980), pp. 31–32.

115. Ibid., p. 32.
116. Webber, 'The Afterlife of Romanticism', p. 24.
117. Two of the works in question — *Was bleibt* and *Stille Mitte von Berlin* — were produced several years before their publication. The book considers them in order of their genesis rather than their publication date, as this highlights their influence on texts written after them.
118. Irina Liebmann, blurb for *Die freien Frauen*.

CHAPTER 1

~

Phantom Images: Christa Wolf's *Was bleibt*

The title of this chapter, which refers to a recurrent image in the writing of Christa Wolf, is intentionally provocative. Wolf herself has denied the presence of the phantom as a thematic motif in her texts, actually expressing bafflement that her work might be seen to contain such a figure. In a letter to the author in 2010, she suggested: 'Was übrigens die Figur des "Phantoms" in meinen Texten tun soll, ist mir nicht verständlich'.[1] Given the vilification which Wolf experienced at the hands of the press during the early years of the 1990s, along with her subsequent efforts to re-establish her literary reputation, it might indeed seem understandable that she should baulk at the idea of such figures playing a significant role in her work. Phantoms tend to be unwelcome phenomena, appearing where they are least wanted and working to interrupt the life of the beholder. Their ability to signal the return of repressed realities or estranged areas of the human subject means that they resist closure, working against any attempts to establish a coherent sense of self. Wolf's inability — or unwillingness — to understand what such figures might be doing in her own writing therefore suggests a reluctance to expose herself to the disruption which they generate; it seems to imply an understanding that these phantoms would, if laid bare, undermine the fragile identity which she cultivated for herself in post-*Wende* Germany. This chapter, however, seeks to counter Wolf's expression of perplexity by highlighting the references to phantoms and other ghostly apparitions which can be found in her writing. It argues that her repertoire of the uncanny is closely bound up with her preoccupation with the legacy of the Romantic imagination and its influence on her literary project. Rather than being out of place in her work, such images reveal the pathological after-effects which haunt Wolf's writing, and illustrate the dystopian prospect lurking behind her seemingly utopian vision.

The main focus of this chapter is Wolf's *Erzählung*, *Was bleibt*, whose narrative details the surveillance operation against a female writer living in a flat in Berlin's Friedrichstraße. As Wolf's published diaries reveal, the text is in part based on her own experience of being watched by the Stasi in the period following the sensational expatriation of Wolf Biermann in 1976. In an entry written on 27 September 1977, she describes the negative consequences of this period of observation:

> Die Berliner Wohnung ist mir noch nicht wieder geheuer geworden, seit sie überwacht wurde, seit man in sie eingedrungen ist. Der kalte, öde und schmutzige Hausflur. Die Straße, auf die hinauszutreten ich mir einen Ruck geben muß, weil immer noch der Reflex da ist, daß ich beobachtet werde. Die dunkle Oranienburger.[2]

The boundaries of the home are shown here to have been violated by the invasive presence of the Stasi, which has rendered it strange and uninhabitable. Even after the surveillance operation has finished, its effects persist, altering how Wolf perceives her environment and instilling in her a kind of self-observation which inhibits her thoughts and causes her to question her behaviour. Particularly striking is the way in which Wolf adopts the vocabulary of haunting to describe this experience. The flat itself has become 'nicht [...] geheuer'; its eeriness might recall that of a haunted house, a home which has become fundamentally unhomely because of the unwanted presences which it hosts. And the 'öde[r] [...] Hausflur' seems to resonate with the qualities of Hoffmann's 'ödes Haus', whose desolate state lends it the appearance of being 'ganz unbewohnt' (H III, 166). Above all, the unrelenting after-image of the Stasi officers is transformed into a kind of phantom, appearing to Wolf in the form of 'Gespenster, die wir selbst heraufbeschworen, die uns Angst machen'.[3] Their external presence has been internalized by the subject, who responds instinctively to their existence; they become ghostly images formed in the mind's eye, involuntarily summoned by the individual who is in turn terrorized by them.

Was bleibt recalls this journal entry, both in its personal tone and use of the diary form,[4] and in its highly stylized depiction of the haunting effects of surveillance. In particular, Wolf draws on the notion of the 'phantom image' in her description of the Stasi agents outside her flat: 'an jenen Tagen, an denen die Autos nicht in Wirklichkeit, nur als Phantombild auf meiner Netzhaut vorhanden waren, die Angst nicht von mir wich, nicht einmal geringer war als an Tagen der offensichtlichen Observation' (CW X, 233). The protagonist's home is shown to have been spooked by the presence of the spies, whose gaze penetrates its boundaries. The phantom image is depicted here as a remainder, a trace which lingers after the physical presence of the Stasi men has disappeared; it signals the fact that 'etwas bleibt', a continuing reminder of the mechanism of observation which structures the protagonist's existence. As an after-image, it denotes not only a persistent optical impression of a past event, but also forms a kind of 'visual palimpsest',[5] a process of layering by means of which a mental image or fantasy is superimposed onto the subject's perception of reality. It illustrates the way in which the protagonist's past experience of being observed, having become ingrained on her retina, continues to affect and alter her view of the present. And this in turn instils such fear in the subject that she begins to observe herself, developing a form of internal surveillance which proves to be just as effective as the 'offensichtliche Observation' carried out by the Stasi agents. As the reality of these external figures becomes increasingly distant, the protagonist assumes a more active role in surveying and judging her thoughts and actions. This transition from object to subject, from observed to observer, points to a further connotation of the term 'Phantombild': namely that of a police identikit picture, a visual likeness of a wanted criminal whose culpability has not yet been proved in a court of law, but one which is so visually powerful that it often convinces the viewer that the person depicted must be guilty. The use of the image in *Was bleibt* can therefore be viewed in conjunction with the many references to guilt and wrongdoing which are found throughout the text.[6] It refers primarily to the culpability of the Stasi officials; and yet the incorporation of the image into the mind of the protagonist, together with her engagement in the act of self-observation, lends it an accusatory function which operates against the subject herself. She becomes haunted by a sense of guilt that is more powerful than any legal charge that could be brought against her. In watching herself, Wolf's protagonist is shown to act in accordance with the unspoken demands of the Stasi, and in doing so, she too becomes implicitly culpable.

Interpretation of *Was bleibt* continues to be influenced by the arguments of the *deutsch-deutscher Literaturstreit* of the early 1990s,[7] which focused primarily on questions regarding the autobiographical authenticity of the text.[8] Wolf was accused of hypocrisy in fashioning herself as a victim of the GDR regime when in reality she failed to speak out against it and, it was argued, even appeared to have benefited from her role as a State writer.[9] A second wave of accusations emerged when it was revealed that Wolf herself had, between 1959 and 1962, worked under the cover name 'Margarete' as an *inoffizielle Mitarbeiterin* for the Stasi.[10] Although Wolf was ultimately deemed to be of little use as an informant,[11] the fact that she kept quiet about her involvement with this organization served to heighten the negative reception of *Was bleibt*: the text was viewed by many as the self-serving, opportunistic expression of a woman who cared more about establishing her own reputation than about doing justice to the 'true' victims of the Stasi. While the *Literaturstreit* has now been reappraised as being 'part of a larger agenda, namely the "ideological shaping of reunified Germany"',[12] critics of *Was bleibt* have nevertheless tended to depict the text as 'eine Geschichte des schlechten Gewissens' (CW x, 238) and view Wolf's silence about her Stasi engagement as an example of 'die Sprachlosigkeit des Gewissenlosen' (CW x, 238). In tracing the significance of the phantom in Wolf's texts, this chapter seeks to challenge such reception of the *Erzählung*: it will be argued that her creative engagement with this essentially literary figure reveals an underlying preoccupation with the boundary between conformity and culpability. The phantom signals an uncertainty in the relationship between subject and object; it destabilizes the logic of self-scrutiny and in turn raises the possibility of destructive actions being carried out against the self. Above all, it reveals the way in which Wolf's commitment to Socialist ideals is always already shadowed by the possibility of their betrayal.

Unwahrscheinliche Geschichten

Although *Was bleibt* was published in 1990, Wolf first completed a version of the manuscript in 1979.[13] Thus, as Anna Kuhn points out, the *Erzählung*, 'by virtue of its genesis alone', can be seen to 'fall [...] within the periphery of Wolf's work on the Romantics'.[14] The text, Kuhn argues, can be read alongside *Sommerstück* and *Kein Ort. Nirgends* as part of a 'trio of "Künstler" narratives' written in the wake of the Biermann affair which allude — both directly and indirectly — to Romanticism in their exploration of 'the function of writing in sociopolitically repressive times'.[15] Wolf's preoccupation with alienation, and in particular with the exclusion of the writer from society, together with her exploration of different forms of community, can be understood as a response to the Romantic models which she so values.[16] However, *Was bleibt*, with its uncanny imagery and Gothic repertoire, can also be read as bearing traces of the more unlikely or improbable aspects of the Romantic imagination; in other words, it engages with precisely those elements which characterize her *Unwahrscheinliche Geschichten* of the early 1970s, and in particular the dream-narrative of 'Unter den Linden'.[17] On a thematic level, *Was bleibt* takes up unfinished business from this earlier tale.[18] The article written by Jürgen M. against his professor (CW x, 247) recalls the conflict between Peter and the university professors in 'Unter den Linden' (CW III, 398), while the young writer in *Was bleibt*, who has the courage to speak out about her political conviction, shares many characteristics with the figure of the girl in the earlier tale, who risks banishment to the countryside because of her unwillingness to compromise her beliefs.[19] On a formal level, too, *Was bleibt* shares both the imagery and the circular structure of 'Unter den Linden',[20] which implies that the common aesthetic of the two texts is not merely coincidental.

From the outset of 'Unter den Linden', Wolf cultivates a mode of narration which counters the Realist techniques favoured in her earlier novels and draws instead on the mode of the fantastic. The dream-like narrative offers her the possibility of overcoming the aesthetic restrictions posed by official cultural policy, and can in some respects be read as a defiant reaction against critics' negative response to the use of dream sequences in the otherwise conventional narrative of *Der geteilte Himmel* (1963).[21] On a thematic level, the protagonist experiences a liberation from the limits of temporality, materiality, and rationality; her wristwatch becomes illegible, preventing her from discovering the time of day; at times she seems to float through the streets, experiencing a weightlessness which frees her from the constraints of her corporeal existence; and events often defy logic, appearing to happen for no particular reason. Wildly improbable events appear to her to be entirely normal occurrences, while ordinary details in her everyday life strike her as bizarre and improbable. On a formal level, too, Wolf adopts a fragmentary style, juxtaposing unusual details and suspending chronological progression in order to eliminate 'die Übergänge zwischen dem Glaublichen und dem Unglaublichen' (CW III, 393). Her preoccupation with the genre of the fantastic relies on the technique of depicting reality in an altered manner, rendering it strange in order to encourage the reader to view the world in a different light. It challenges him/her to look beyond the bounds of what is plausible or reasonable in order to perceive new possibilities and potential in the present.

Wolf explained her intentions in appropriating the mode of the fantastic in an interview with Hans Kaufmann in 1974, where she made the following assertion:

> Ich hoffe, die 'Unwahrscheinlichkeit' dieser Geschichten, ihre Verlegung in Traum, Utopie, Groteske kann einen Verfremdungseffekt in bezug auf Vorgänge, Zustände und Denkweisen erzeugen, an die wir uns schon zu sehr gewöhnt haben, als daß sie uns noch auffallen und stören würden. Sie sollten uns aber stören, wiederum in der Zuversicht gesagt, daß wir ändern können, was uns stört. (CW IV, 432–33)

Her stylistic preoccupation with improbable or unlikely scenarios is shown here to have an apparently Brechtian intention. By juxtaposing the credible and the incredible, Wolf creates a form of alienation effect which encourages the reader to think critically about aspects of reality which (s)he has previously taken for granted. Seemingly natural processes, situations, and attitudes are all rendered strange in order to make them visible and potentially disturbing to the onlooker. And this in turn opens them up to the possibility of change, since it is only when something is perceived as abnormal or odd that the desire to alter it is evoked. Viewed in this light, 'Unter den Linden' can be seen 'to harness techniques derived from Romanticism to a particular social purpose'; it seeks to destroy the superficial ways in which the world is perceived, in order to 'take the reader behind everyday reality' and cultivate a creative relationship with the present.[22]

This form of productive alienation becomes apparent in the opening paragraphs of 'Unter den Linden', as Wolf creates a possible intertextual connection to the fantastic narrative of E. T. A. Hoffmann's *Das öde Haus*. The physical reality of Berlin's famous street — its popularity with tourists and its politically significant position as an 'Ost-West-Achse' (CW III, 383) — is juxtaposed here with its function as a place of fantasy; it becomes a 'Traum-Ort' in which the protagonist's subjective experiences converge with the images of the street which exist in the cultural imagination of the city. Like the central character of Hoffmann's tale, whose strolls down Unter den Linden lend him a very different view from the one enjoyed by other visitors to the city, so too is Wolf's protagonist engaged in a kind of *flânerie* which offers her a new, dynamic, and highly subjective experience of the urban landscape. While Hoffmann's characters debate the possibility of perceiving 'das Wunderliche' in everyday experiences (H III, 163–65), the protagonist of 'Unter den Linden' is preoccupied with the quest for a subjective experience of the world, a 'Wahrheit jenseits der wichtigen Welt der Fakten' (CW IV, 270). Towards the end of the second paragraph, for example, she writes: 'Nicht mehr bin ich an die Tatsachen gekettet. Ich kann frei die Wahrheit sagen' (CW III, 383). Her liberation from factual reality, from the bland way of perceiving the world without the influence of the imagination, is experienced as a release; it offers her a new means of articulating the truth of human existence, since she no longer has to conform to existing social norms and prescribed forms of expression. Her adaptation of the techniques of the *fantastische Erzählung* therefore marks an attempt to develop alternative forms of expression capable of capturing the depth of human experience and raising the possibility of freeing the subject from the inevitability of certain historical processes (CW IV, 432–33).

Through her productive engagement with reality, Wolf's protagonist assumes a visionary capability reminiscent of the 'Sehergabe' possessed by Theodor in Hoffmann's tale (H III, 164). This ability to see the world in a new light recalls a description of the writer's task which Wolf outlines in her essay 'Lesen und Schreiben'. She describes how she attempts to peel back the layers of meaning inscribed in a particular place, 'So daß ich nun, an demselben Platz vor derselben Landschaft stehend [...] alles anders *sehe*' (CW IV, 240). This clichéd phrase, she continues, is one which we often use, 'ohne ihm "auf den Grund" zu gehen'; it demands that we look beyond its superficial overtones, searching instead to find the meaning which lies at its base. In order to do this, she writes, one would have to have the courage, 'die Augen zu schließen, sich loszulassen' (CW IV, 240). The writer must have the audacity to adopt a different kind of perception, a second sight which involves seeing what cannot normally be seen. And this is precisely what the dream narrative of 'Unter den Linden' seeks to achieve. The title of the tale assumes a double meaning, referring not only to the name of the street, but also to the protagonist's ability to probe 'under' its surface, to see beneath the façade which it presents to the world. She is able to look beyond the superficial resemblance between the dream street and its existence in reality (CW III, 383). And, aware as she is of 'die Gewalt von Blicken' (CW III, 407), she finds she can see through any attempts to deceive her (CW III, 415). It is through her visionary capability that she seeks to reveal the historical grounding ('Grund') of the city, to uncover the questions, associations, and memories which lie at its base ('zugrunde liegen'), and explore the reasons ('Gründe') behind its potential ruination ('zugrunde gehen').[23]

Dystopian Prospects

Just as the second sight of Hoffmann's characters proves to be ambivalent, often leading them to witness sights which are disturbing or threatening, so too are the visionary powers of Wolf's protagonist inherently duplicitous. Through her concern with uncovering events and processes which usually remain 'verborgen' or 'verheimlicht' (CW III, 387), the protagonist assumes the uncanny role of bringing to light that which ought to have remained hidden. The streets of Berlin assume an uncanny quality, as their present existence is shadowed by the haunting legacy of the city's past and the troubling prospect of a dystopian future. Familiar surroundings are rendered unfamiliar and potentially threatening (CW III, 391), and people and objects are shown to be out of place, recognizable yet strangely out of keeping with the landscape in which they are found (CW III, 403). While the narrator asserts that dreams provide a retrospective means of catching up with what one has missed (CW III, 385), the text itself offers brief glimpses of the city's history, fleeting echoes of traumatic moments which have resisted incorporation into the official narratives of the nation's identity. The street can therefore be seen to harbour the threatening possibility of a return of the repressed, an unsettling encounter with these inassimilable fragments of the past, which carry the potential to disrupt the external appearances of the city and its everyday existence.

This preoccupation with the shadowy underside of Unter den Linden, a street which, the narrator notes, always leads her 'in die Tiefe' (CW III, 391), emerges primarily through Wolf's fascination with slippages and doublings in the visual apparatus of her protagonist. In particular, she employs the imagery of Hoffmann's *Das öde Haus*, with its reflective windows and mirror-images, as a means of mediating ghostly images and revealing 'other' prospects, alternative views of the city and its inhabitants. The classic urban topos of the 'Schaufenster' (CW III, 402), with its connotations of spectacle and spectatorship, is characterized here by its propensity to become opaque (CW III, 402) or specular (CW III, 403). It works to block the gaze of the onlooker, projecting it back on itself and in doing so affording a passing glimpse on an aspect of reality which is normally hidden from view. The glassy surface of the window thereby becomes a vehicle for projecting images of what lies beneath the city, for bringing to light what has been concealed in its depths. These revelatory moments often highlight the corruption and decadence lurking behind the ideal promulgated by official propaganda. Towards the middle of the tale, for example, the passers-by are subjected to the surreal vision of a magic goldfish, an intertextual *revenant* from Hoffmann's tale of Unter den Linden, whose reflection in the shop window has the effect of scaring people away (CW III, 402).[24] The fish interrupts their materialist fantasies, introducing a utopian dimension which is so foreign to their everyday lives that they cannot acknowledge it.

A similar criticism of the reality of the GDR emerges a couple of paragraphs later, when the protagonist views the reflection of the 'Lindenhotel' in the window panes of the bookshop (CW III, 403). The image, which represents the illusion of grandeur created by the GDR government, is tainted by its associations with Western materialism, which have been cultivated by its intended rivalry with the American Hilton Hotel in the West (CW III, 404). In offering us this image obliquely, as a reflection, Wolf dismantles the elegant façade of the street and opens up a view of the 'other' Berlin, a space which can only be experienced indirectly through various mediated representations. The image is superimposed onto the view of the interior of the shop, which can be seen through the pane of glass; like the ghostly double-exposure of a photograph, it draws together two different visual realities, enabling them to be viewed in a single instant and within a single spatial frame. On one level, the different possibilities signalled by such a technique form part of Wolf's 'Spiel mit offenen Möglichkeiten' (CW IV, 255), her desire to cultivate a flexibility of thinking based on the unexpected co-incidence ('Zufall' — CW III, 395) of different scenarios. They indicate the way in which the spaces of the city are occupied by other prospects which, though uninhabitable, offer an alternative perspective on the reality with which one is familiar.

At other points in the tale, however, the productive intention of these images is shown to be an illusion. The street becomes a 'Zufallsstraße' (CW III, 432) in a negative sense, a place which is prone to the destructive experience of collapse or fall. In the following paragraph, the same shop window is shown to display an image of the ruined city, a vision of devastation which counters the utopian prospect signalled by the reflection of the magic fish: 'Da ist in einem unbewachten Moment in der blitzenden Scheibe anstelle des Lindenhotels eine Trümmerlandschaft aufgetaucht, winddurchpfiffen, unkrautbewachsen, von einem Trampelpfad überquert, auf dem drei Figuren gehen, die mir bekannt vorkommen' (CW III, 404). The unguarded moment suggests that the protagonist's psychological mechanisms protecting against the intrusion of repressed memories have for a brief instant been dropped, enabling her to be confronted with this image from the past. At the same time, the possibility of the adjective 'unbewacht' to refer back to the image of the guardsmen outside the 'Neue Wache' also implies that the history being witnessed here is not normally included in official narratives. The image of the 'blitzende Scheibe', signalling the uncanny illumination of that which is usually kept concealed, might recall Walter Benjamin's description of the way in which the true essence of history can only be recognized belatedly, as a fleeting image which 'blitzt auf' in the mind (WB I.2, 695).[25] The scene of rubble reflected in the window can therefore be understood as a kind of 'after-image' or 'phantom image', since it comes in the wake of a past occurrence. It cannot be grasped or retained, but rather disappears at the moment of its recognition (CW III, 404), thus pointing to the inevitability of its own disappearance.[26] It disrupts what Wolf describes as 'die lineare Ausdehnung der Zeit' (CW IV, p. 242) by rendering the image of the past synchronous with the present and in turn signalling the dystopian potential of the future. This bustling shopping street, haunted by the image of its past destruction, is also shadowed by the possibility of once more dissolving into ruin.

The reflected image in the shop window also resembles a 'Phantombild' in the juridical sense of the term, since it shows the protagonist and her two friends on their way to deliver propaganda leaflets in the West, where their activities are soon branded as 'illegal' (CW III, 405) and they are taken away for questioning by the police officer. In the East, too, the protagonist's actions bring her into conflict with the enforcers of the law, as she unwittingly crosses the road on a red traffic light (CW III, 405). The encounter with the phantom image estranges the protagonist from herself, confirming her sense of being a wanted criminal, 'ein Missetäter [...], der seine Untat tief im Verborgenenen zu halten suchte und sich plötzlich von Zeugen umringt sieht' (CW III, 418). As a vehicle for revealing the offences of the individual, the apparition of the phantom image becomes linked with the repressive apparatus of a State which subjects its citizens to its authoritarian rule (CW III, 393) and permits no appeal against its judgements (CW III, 422).[27] It works to instil passive acquiescence into its subjects and reveals the streets of the city to be the scene of a crime whose details are kept secret (CW III, 393). Moreover, it leads the protagonist to collude with the ambivalent figure of the 'Traumzensor' (CW III, 409), an externalized projection of her internal self-censor, which works to pre-empt external criticism from the State, yet in doing so leads her to adopt its point of view and cooperate with its repressive measures. Signalling her potential loss of autonomy and her capacity to act on behalf of the regime which rules over her, the phantom image lodges itself inside her, cultivating a pervasive sense of culpability which shapes her identity, informing her actions and even flowing over into her waking life.[28] It creates a kind of existential guilt which alienates her from herself and ultimately resists the possibility of recuperation offered by the final paragraph of the tale.

Ghosts of Surveillance

In *Was bleibt*, the dystopian vision which shadowed the city of 'Unter den Linden' is shown to have become a reality. The 'Ort' of Berlin has been transformed into a 'Nicht Ort' (CW x, 241), a negation of the representative place of that earlier tale. And the protagonist's concern with uncovering what lies at the base of the city is transformed here into an exploration of 'what remains' of it once it succumbs to ruination: 'Was bleibt. Was meiner Stadt zugrunde liegt und woran sie zugrunde geht' (CW x, 289). This is a desolate, unredeemed space (CW x, 241), a realm which laments the departure of its 'gute Geister' (CW x, 287).[29] Its inhabitants are no longer 'Menschen aus Fleisch und Blut' (CW x, 241); suspended in a state of living death, they become ghostly presences whose 'gläserne Blicke' (CW x, 232) serve as indications of their spectral existence. Like the unseeing gazes of its inhabitants, the city itself is shown to be 'ohne Vision' (CW x, 241), lacking in foresight and therefore bound to remain in its present, ill-fated state. The visionary capability of the protagonist, which is emphasized in 'Unter den Linden', is shown here to be redundant, out of place in a city which has been spoiled by the effects of 'Gier, Macht und Gewalt' (CW x, 241). In this bleak depiction of a fallen Berlin, founded on 'Nichtswürdigkeit', the dream-like state of 'Unter den Linden' has been transformed into a nightmare (CW x, 241), in which the previously familiar streets and surroundings have become alien (CW x, 240) and buildings are transformed into eerie monstrosities (CW x, 241). The city has lost its previous life-spark (CW x, 241), and instead holds its citizens in a deceptive trance (CW x, 241), which enslaves them and renders them cold and lifeless. Above all, this uncanny setting is shown to have been internalized by the protagonist, so that it has become part of her mental landscape; her imagination is inhabited by 'schattenhafte Fledermäuse', shadowy *revenants* from Berlin's Gothic heritage, which appear to her as an 'unheimlicher Schwarm' (CW x, 264) and threaten to overwhelm her capacity to think clearly and act independently.

The transformation of the city into this unsettled haunting-ground, a desolate non-place inhabited by ghostly traces and remainders, is closely bound up with its role as a surveillance space.[30] The landscape of Berlin is now shown to be governed by the paranoid regimes of looking and watching represented by the emblematic image (CW x, 241) of the Stasi officials outside the protagonist's flat. In particular, the 'Phantombild' (CW x, 233) which shadows the protagonist's view from her window is associated with a covert form of observation, one in which the protagonist feels herself being watched despite not being able to see those who are actually observing her. Even on the days when no obvious surveillance operation can be detected, she nevertheless senses that she is under observation and consequently adjusts her own behaviour in order to conform to what is expected of her. In this respect, the presence of the Stasi agents, whether real or imagined, assumes a ghostly quality, recalling Jacques Derrida's assertion that 'the ghost, always, is looking at me'.[31] Derrida explains:

> The specter first of all sees *us*. From the other side of the eye, *visor effect*, it looks at us even before we see *it* [...]. We feel ourselves observed, sometimes under surveillance by it even before any apparition. Especially [...] it sees us during a *visit*.[32]

Derived from the Latin 'spectrum', meaning 'apparition', 'image', or 'spectacle', the term spectre refers normally to the object of viewing, to an image which appears before the human eye. Here, though, Derrida highlights its privileged status in the dynamics of observation, revealing its ability to watch without being watched, to behold others while also remaining concealed. The spectre's capacity for surveillance is therefore effective, precisely because it pre-exists our consciousness, seeing us before we see it and thereby cultivating an asymmetrical gaze which cannot be returned. Above all, it instils in us a perpetual state of paranoia, since it is always capable of presenting itself to us during an unexpected visitation, an apparition which would destabilize our sense of self by confounding the distinctions between presence and absence, self and other, visible and invisible.

In *Was bleibt*, then, the image of the Stasi agents becomes a kind of absent presence, a spectral apparition which continues to haunt the protagonist in a surreptitious fashion on days when there is no obvious surveillance, and whose potential visits instil in her a crippling fear. The appearance of these figures is from the outset uncertain, resisting the protagonist's attempts to see them clearly, to look into their eyes and be met by their gaze. They assume the identity of 'Abgesandte des anderen' (CW x, 232), emissaries from another world which are fundamentally different from the protagonist and whose existence is always inaccessible (CW x, 232). Throughout the narrative, the logic of their operation remains imperceptible, 'undurchsichtig' (CW x, 226), and the motives of their actions are perpetually concealed. At times, the protagonist experiences their attendance as though they are not actually there (CW x, 228), doubting their existence and calling into question her own perception of them. Although she repeatedly tries to gain a clearer view of them, she can never be sure whether or not her eyes are deceiving her, as she is uncertain whether or not the image of the officials is real (CW x, 225). Her faculty of vision is revealed to be unreliable, as her eyes have been touched by an alien hand (CW x, 241), and at times her sight fails her completely, forcing her to run 'blindly' through the city, aware of her observation by the Stasi yet unable to perceive those who are watching her (CW x, 250).

While the protagonist's view of the security agents is markedly restricted, however, the gaze of the Stasi agents purports to be all-seeing. Their 'gläserne Blicke' (CW x, 232), which appear to have taken on the glassy quality of the car windscreen, belong to an apparatus of perception which transcends the human, a system of observation which subordinates the individual to its totalizing control. These figures engage in a kind of 'sur-veillance' or 'Über-wachung' whose purpose is to gain an 'over-view' of the lives of those whom it observes. Unlike the 'vision' emphasized in 'Unter den Linden', which sought to delve 'underneath' the surface of reality, this form of observation is more concerned with recording overall impressions of a situation than with penetrating what lies beneath its façade. It prioritizes superficial details, the 'menschliche Schwächen der observierten Objekte' and 'abstruse Liebesaffären' (CW x, 234), which can be catalogued as a list of external actions and conversations and preserved on paper as an objectified record of human existence.[33] And it seeks to discover 'alles über eine Person' (CW x, 253), to gain total knowledge of his/her life. Crucially, such observation demands '[daß] man sich als Wissender über die Masse der Unwissenden erheben wolle' (CW x, 250); the preposition 'über' refers not only to the possibility of gaining an overview of these people, but also signals the sense of superiority which is required for such a task. Together with the verb 'erheben', it implies the sensation of being raised up onto a higher plane, from which one can look down on the inferior beings below. Unlike the writer, who seeks to enliven the objects of her creative world, the Stasi official attempts to become 'Herrn und Meister seiner Objekte' (CW x, 253); he seeks to gain complete mastery over people by transforming them into deadened, lifeless objects.

The 'phantom image' of the Stasi agents therefore exercises a particular power over the protagonist, which arises from its ability to observe her. As Derrida explains:

> The specter [...] is someone by whom we feel ourselves watched, observed, surveyed, as if by the law: we are 'before the law' [...], without reciprocity, insofar as the other is watching us, concerns only us, we who are observing it (in the same way that one observes and respects the law) without being able to meet its gaze.[34]

The ghostly figures of the surveillance officers assume the function of an absolute authority; they demand obedience to their law, since their gaze can catch and forestall any attempts to cross it. Moreover, they cannot be challenged, because they are fundamentally inaccessible; they resist identification and thereby foreclose any possibility of appeal. Like the protagonist of 'Unter den Linden', who is unable to locate any authority which will listen to her demands, the narrator of *Was bleibt* finds herself subjected to a law which she cannot dispute. She is bound to an authority which presumes her guilt without it being proven, and from whom there is never any chance of gaining pardon (CW x, 226). Such an authority tries to trick those whom it observes by causing them to carry out ill-considered actions which might then serve as evidence for the necessity of the surveillance operation (CW x, 232). And it instils a pervasive sense of guilt and lack of conscience in the protagonist; she stands accused in the eyes of the Stasi agents, and yet she also fails to live up to her own standards, berating herself for failing to oppose the oppressive regime in which she lives. She is drawn to what she describes as the 'Reiz der Gewissenlosen' (CW x, 244), the desire not to be morally implicated in events, and yet at the same time she expresses her sense of shock at experiencing such thoughts (CW x, 258).

Towards the middle of *Was bleibt*, these experiences of guilt and powerlessness combine in a revelatory moment of recognition. The narrator writes:

> Nie würde ich den Augenblick vergessen — blicklos stand ich gerade vor dem Schaufenster einer gewöhnlichen Drogerie — als, wie ein Blitz, die Erkenntnis mich traf, daß es der Schmerz war, der mich umtrieb. Ich hatte ihn nicht erkannt. Der rasende blanke Schmerz hatte von mir Besitz ergriffen, sich in mir eingenistet und ein anderes Wesen aus mir gemacht. (CW x, 240)

The image recalls the ghostly reflections which appear in the shop windows in 'Unter den Linden'. The revelation 'flashes up' before the protagonist, striking her 'wie ein Blitz', a sudden bolt of lightning which alters her perception of reality. It occurs in an instant, and yet its effects are revealed to be long-lasting, an incident which the protagonist will never forget. As an uncanny apparition, it interrupts the everyday appearance of the 'gewöhnliche Drogerie', rendering the ordinary street strange, and it involves the recognition of something which was not previously evident: namely, the realization that the protagonist is driven by a feeling of pain stemming from her permanent state of observation by the Stasi. The fact that the image appears to the protagonist's sightless gaze as the disclosure of something which is not normally seen lends it the quality of a spectral visitation; what was once invisible to her is now fully revealed as the controlling force behind her actions. And this force is shown to inhabit her, taking possession of her and alienating her from herself. Through her contact with its ghostly image, she is transformed into another being, one whose potential for autonomous action is undermined and whose freedom of expression is called into question.

Self-Scrutiny

The experience of being under constant surveillance engenders in the protagonist a feeling of estrangement reminiscent of that described by Derrida as 'absolute alienation'.[35] It brings about an 'alienation of self'[36] that renders the subject unfamiliar to herself, making her speak a language that is not her own and ensuring that she views herself and the world from a position of alterity. In particular, the 'Phantombild' of the Stasi officials, having become etched on her retina, becomes a psycho-physiological mark of this alienation; it signals the way in which the other, along with its ulterior way of perceiving the world, has been incorporated into her internal landscape. As the ghostly residue of a previously external authority, this image becomes an intrinsic part of the protagonist's psychic mechanism, estranging her gaze and altering her perception of reality. The internalization of the phantom image, of 'this spectral someone other [who] looks at us',[37] generates a form of self-scrutiny on the part of the protagonist; the act of watching the self is shown to be a function of being watched by the other. This in turn reveals the protagonist's encounter with the Stasi agents to be inherently reflexive; the encounter with the phantom image works to project her gaze back on itself and reveals her to be both an agent and a victim in the surveillance operation carried out against her.

Such reflexivity becomes particularly apparent in Wolf's depiction of the mechanism of observation. As the text develops, the protagonist's behaviour becomes increasingly furtive as she comes to adopt the features of the figures watching her. From the window of her flat, she is able to 'look over' ('überblicken') the city, assuming a position of surveillance which enables her to gain an 'overview' of what is happening in her street (CW x, 265). And she describes how she obsessively watches the car park where the Stasi agents usually wait: 'So stand ich also [...] hinter der Gardine, die dazu angebracht worden war, daß ich mich hinter ihr verbergen konnte, und blickte, hoffentlich ungesehen, hinüber zum großen Parkplatz, jenseits der Friedrichstraße' (CW x, 225). The image of the curtain at the window anticipates the later description of the metaphorical 'Vorhang' (CW x, 244) which closes over the eyes of one of the men outside. In both cases, the material serves as a screen which separates these figures from reality, while the protagonist hopes that her concealment behind it will enable her to observe the men in the car park without being seen by them.[38] She intends to cover her tracks, to disguise her behaviour in the hope that it will remain invisible to those whom she watches. Like the Stasi agents outside, she seeks to be inaccessible, a figure whose gaze cannot be met by others. And, like them, she conceals herself behind a series of glass screens which serve to mediate her perception of reality, while also adopting a cold, glassy stare which signals her embodiment of the apparatus of surveillance.

As the text progresses, the protagonist's mediated gaze becomes increasingly reflexive, turning back on itself as she begins to watch and censor her own behaviour. It becomes an 'innerer Blick', whose role is to survey and control the thoughts which are being played out on her internal stage (CW x, 263). Striking here is the way in which the protagonist, in her acts of self-observation, begins to adopt the perspective of the Stasi agents, taking note of her actions and altering them in anticipation of criticism. Her gaze originates from inside her, and yet its coincidence with that of the men outside lends it an alien quality, so that it appears to be externally generated. She is at once observer and observed, living a 'tief verschwiegene[s] Doppelleben' (CW x, 244) in which the distinction between self and other, perpetrator and victim, is uncannily blurred. Her double existence is experienced as a kind of 'Fremdheit' which alienates her from other people and, above all, from herself (CW x, 266). Her own actions are experienced as being at once familiar and strange, while her thoughts are perceived to be both intrinsic to the subject and also the internalized form of an ulterior power. The feeling of self-estrangement is reflected on a formal level by the 'hesitant' and 'torn' language of the text,[39] which repeatedly generates ideas only subsequently to call them into question, and which ultimately splits into a wavering dialogue with the protagonist's self-censor. As an intertextual visitant from 'Unter den Linden', the figure of the 'Selbstzensor' appears in *Was bleibt* as a constant companion to the protagonist (CW x, 256), challenging her repeatedly and preventing her from entertaining any thoughts or words without the possibility of these turning against her (CW x, 261).

The self-alienation felt by the protagonist culminates in an out-of-body experience towards the end of the text, where she loses contact with herself and reality (CW x, 271). The episode begins with the observation that something strange has happened to the protagonist. She writes: 'Irgend etwas ging mit mir vor, mit meinem Sehvermögen, oder, genauer, mit meinem gesamten Wahrnehmungsapparat. Verkehrstüchtig blieb ich, das war es nicht; ich sah nicht mehr richtig. Ich sah nicht mehr, was ich sah' (CW x, 270–71). The experience of estrangement is shown here to be predominantly visual, operating on the protagonist's faculty of perception. Even though she remains fit to drive, and insists that she can still see the houses, streets, and people around her, she is nevertheless aware that she is viewing them in a new light. The reference to her 'Wahrnehmungsapparat' recalls the official vocabulary of 'Apparate, Strahlungen, Gewalt' (CW x, 264), which the protagonist associates with the Stasi, and which she has gradually appropriated as a means of expressing her own thoughts. As she becomes increasingly detached from reality, she is characterized by an overwhelming 'Fühllosigkeit' (CW x, 271), an indifference which resembles the cold, dispassionate attitude of the Stasi towards their subjects. It is from this position of disinterest that the protagonist ultimately watches herself: 'Mühelos fädelte ich mich aus dem Verkehr, sah mich selbst aus einer gewissen Höhe nicht ohne Anerkennung dabei zu. [...] [Ich] sah mir aus einer gewissen Höhe dabei zu, sah mich lächeln' (CW x, 271–72). The emotion which causes her to smile, rather than being felt directly, is observed here as though it were happening to someone else; her own behaviour is rendered strange because she perceives it from the perspective of the other. Finally, the protagonist's sense of hovering above herself and looking down on her actions renders literal the term 'Überwachung'; she is shown to have internalized the superior position of the Stasi agents, watching over herself and directing an operation of surveillance against her own actions.

Visitations

Throughout *Was bleibt*, the reflexivity of the protagonist's gaze and her growing identification with the Stasi officials is played out against the backdrop of the protagonist's apartment. Through the regimes of looking and watching, the boundaries of the home are rendered permeable, recalling Anthony Vidler's assertion that surveillance renders living space uncanny. He writes:

> Private space is revealed as infinitely public, private rituals publicized to their subjects and these in turn connected to the public matrix. No longer sheltered from the public surveillance by a well-defended private realm, the space of the domestic will now become [...] an agent of self-surveillance.[40]

In a society characterized by surveillance, the home is no longer sheltered from the intrusive presence of the State. Its walls are always capable of being violated and private space is transformed into an extension of the public realm. At the same time, however, such political systems engender a form of self-surveillance which relocates the threat to the individual; no longer does the danger stem from outside the home, but rather it is located inside the domestic sphere. Rather than offering shelter from an external danger, the home is now shown to be playing host to this negative force; and in doing so, it ceases to be homely, instead becoming an uncanny space whose inhabitants are displaced and ultimately dispossessed.

Wolf's protagonist lives in perpetual fear of being visited by the phantom figures which guard her house. Their potential for crossing the boundaries of her home and violating her living space haunts her waking existence and also appears to her at night in her dreams. At one point, for example, she recalls a nightmare in which these men invade her apartment, having forced their way into her kitchen. She writes: '[die Männer], die sich, was ich schon immer so sehr gefürchtet hatte!, durch die todsichere Hintertür Einlaß in unsere Küche verschafft hatten, sich nun auf der Schwelle drängten' (CW x, 227). The urgency of the men's actions is revealed by the dynamic verb 'drängen', while the fact that they have forced their way through the 'todsichere Hintertür' signals the brutality of the intrusion. The uncanny dimension of this unexpected visitation is heightened by the reference to 'Tod' hidden in the adjective 'todsicher', which implicitly relates the doorway at the threshold of the home to the boundary between life and death. Although the men urge the protagonist to forget their presence and behave as though they were not there, she perceives their existence as an intrusion; her kitchen, the centre of her home, has been taken over by these figures, and she in turn experiences a sense of homelessness in her own space, a feeling that she is 'nicht mehr zu Hause' (CW x, 237). The intrusion of the 'spooks' into the home is therefore associated with a fundamental act of displacement. In entering the protagonist's living space, these figures are shown to take possession of it, taking over the role of the host and casting out the original owner, who in turn assumes the characteristics of an unwelcome visitor.[41]

Such an intrusion recalls the spectral 'visitation' described by Derrida, in which the ghost '*appears* to present itself', yet remains physically absent from the scene.[42] In Wolf's text, the protagonist never directly encounters the Stasi agents in her home. They appear to her as a phantom image, invading her dreams and her waking moments. Even when they do visit the house in reality, she becomes aware of their invasion by means of the traces which they have left: the footprints left in doorways and on the dark carpet in one of the rooms, and the shards of glass left after the men have smashed the mirror in the bathroom (CW x, 236). This trail of destruction, like that left in the wake of a poltergeist, was apparently created intentionally as a means of making her aware that the Stasi officials had visited her home: 'Wir mußten also davon ausgehen, daß die jungen Herren ihren Besuch in unserer Wohnung gar nicht verheimlichen wollten' (CW x, 237). The fact that these men have smashed the mirror might be seen as an attempt to obliterate any trace of the image which the mirror might preserve, thereby destroying all evidence of their visit and retaining the asymmetry which characterizes their observation of the protagonist. It might convey an unwillingness on the part of the Stasi to behold the reflection of themselves as intruders in the domestic sphere, indicating a reluctance to engage in this crucial moment of self-recognition. At the same time, however, these physical traces serve as indicators of 'the visibility of the invisible';[43] they paradoxically form a concrete sign of the unseen presence of the Stasi, a residue which is left behind after their sudden apparition. Their existence therefore serves to indicate the uncanny revelation of that which ought, professionally, to have been 'verheimlicht'.

These concrete remainders of the Stasi officers' visit therefore function in the same way as the 'Phantombild' on the protagonist's retina, signalling the fact that a criminal 'Tatbestand' (CW x, 237) has taken place and at the same time working as a kind of control mechanism, reminding her that she is being watched and warning her to act appropriately. In the next paragraph, the protagonist wonders whether the act of breaking the mirror might be understood as a form of intimidation: 'Einschüchterung nenne man das, sagte ein Bekannter, der genau Bescheid zu wissen vorgab, aber waren wir eingeschüchtert?' (CW x, 237). She confirms that she does react to these visible reminders of the presence of the Stasi, detailing how she unplugs the telephone when certain guests visit, and how she turns up the radio when sensitive topics come up in conversation (CW x, 237). Bound up with the threat of physical violence, which the protagonist fears, is a reference to a more subtle form of aggression: namely, the technique of 'Zersetzung' or subversion. As Paul Cooke and Andrew Plowman note, this 'psychological [...] subversion of an individual' was used by the Stasi 'to terrorise their victims', and often instigated 'a process of fragmentation and disintegration through which the role and identity of the [individual] is called into question'.[44] It sought to destroy the lives of potential enemies by undermining their self-understanding and destabilizing their relationships with others, and it aimed to cultivate a paralysing sense of anxiety or paranoia in its victims. Above all, it often marked 'a fissure in the [individual's] [...] relationship to the state and the realm of politics', calling into question his/her identity as a political subject.[45]

Viewed in this context, the image of the shattered mirror in the protagonist's apartment can be seen to represent the way in which the violence of the Stasi distorts and disrupts her understanding of her identity. The fragments of glass signal her experience of estrangement, her division into the multiple beings which make up her sense of self: 'Das, das sich kennen wollte? Das, das sich schonen wollte? Oder jenes dritte, das immer noch versucht war, nach derselben Pfeife zu tanzen wie die jungen Herren da draußen vor meiner Tür' (CW x, 255–56). In encountering these visible remnants and being exposed to the fear which they provoke, the protagonist is shown to have become increasingly like the Stasi figures which haunt her. She is tempted to dance to their tune and follow their commands, and she comes to think like them, extending their present power into the future and thereby enabling herself to be possessed by them (CW x, 264). The threat to herself is now revealed to be an internal one, arising primarily from her own fragmented identity and locating itself within the boundaries of her own home. Her transition from observed to observer, victim to perpetrator, is marked by the image of the broken mirror at the end of the novel, when the protagonist gazes at her own reflection 'in den Spiegel [...], den ich nicht zerschlagen konnte, weil sie ihn vor mir zerschlagen hatten' (CW x, 288).[46] The shattered mirror bears testimony to the violent actions of the Stasi agents. In expressing her own desire to smash it, the protagonist unwittingly echoes the thoughts of these figures who looked in the glass before her. Her own identity comes to be shaped by her specular relationship with these men. And yet the broken glass signals the destruction inherent in such a relationship. Located at the centre of her apartment, the mirror preserves the fragmented reflection of the protagonist, revealing her to be a stranger, an intruder in her own home. Ultimately, its shattered pane signals the way in which her identity has become a ghostly trace of its past self, a phantom image of what remains.

— * —

Towards the end of *Was bleibt*, the protagonist browses through her record collection and unexpectedly discovers a recording of Schubert's *Die Winterreise*, which then prompts her to recall the opening lines of the song-cycle: ' "Fremd bin ich eingezogen". Fremd zieh ich wieder aus' (CW x, 287).[47] Read in the context of Wolf's narrative, the lines can be understood as a signal of the profound alienation at the heart of the protagonist's condition. Their reference to acts of arrival and departure, which serve in the song-cycle to introduce the theme of lost love, are used here to indicate the instability inherent in the domestic realm, revealing it to be a space inhabited by a form of alterity. Throughout Wolf's tale, the boundaries of the home are open to penetration and invasion by external forces, and yet, crucially, these forces are shown to originate within the protagonist herself. It is she who poses a threat to the stability of the domestic realm. And it is she who renders the living space uncanny through her existential 'Fremdheit' (CW x, 266). The fact that her alienation is depicted as a constitutive part of her identity confounds the principle of cause and effect which appears to govern the protagonist's relationship with the Stasi. No longer can her complicity with the Stasi agents be regarded as a simple consequence of her observation; rather, her duplicitous status, her potential to collude with the regime, is always already inscribed into her existence. As a result, her inability to recognize the extent to which these lines from Schubert's song-cycle resonate with her own situation (CW x, 287) is telling; chiming to some degree with Wolf's own unwillingness to perceive the phantoms in her work, this inability highlights both the fundamental split in her identity and the vulnerability which it engenders. Confronted with the potential fragmentation of her sense of self, the subject of *Was bleibt* attempts to shore up her own identity, externalizing the perceived threat to her existence and regarding the world around her with paranoid hostility.

Notes to Chapter 1

1. Christa Wolf in correspondence with Catherine Smale, 27 October 2010.
2. Wolf, *Ein Tag im Jahr*, p. 228.
3. Ibid., p. 247.
4. On the significance of the diary form for Wolf, see Georgina Paul, 'Text and Context: *Was bleibt* 1979–1989', in *Geist und Macht: Writers and the State of the GDR*, ed. by

Axel Goodbody and Dennis Tate, German Monitor, 29 (Amsterdam: Rodopi, 1992), pp. 117–28 (pp. 118–20).
5. Joan Ramon Resina, 'The Concept of the After-Image and the Scopic Apprehension of the City', in *After-Images of the City*, ed. by Joan Ramon Resina and Dieter Ingenschay (Ithaca, NY: Cornell University Press, 2003), pp. 1–22 (p. 21).
6. Matthias Konzett points out that 'political guilt and its individual psychology [...] become the main focus of Wolf's literary self-investigation'. Matthias Konzett, 'Christa Wolf's *Was bleibt*: The Literary Utopia and its Remaining Significance', *Monatshefte*, 85 (1993), 438–52 (pp. 442–43). See also Ricarda Schmidt, 'Religiöse Metaphorik im Werk Christa Wolfs', in *Christa Wolf in Perspective*, ed. by Ian Wallace, German Monitor, 30 (Rodopi: Amsterdam, 1994), pp. 73–106 (pp. 97–103).
7. As Anna Kuhn observes: 'Discussions of Christa Wolf's *Was bleibt* have been driven by reactions to the *ad feminam* attack launched on her by the West German press in June 1990. Critics who felt compelled to defend Wolf against [...] an unfair attack failed to treat *Was bleibt* as a fictional text, thereby perpetuating the biographical fallacy of which Wolf's detractors are guilty.' Anna Kuhn, 'Zweige vom selben Stamm? Christa Wolf's *Was bleibt*, *Kein Ort. Nirgends* and *Sommerstück*', in *Christa Wolf in Perspective*, ed. by Wallace, pp. 187–225 (p. 187). See also Christopher Colton, '*Was bleibt*: eine neue Sprache?', ibid., pp. 207–26 (p. 207).
8. For documentation of the main contributions to the *Literaturstreit*, see '*Es geht nicht um Christa Wolf'*: *Der Literaturstreit im vereinigten Deutschland*, ed. by Thomas Anz (Munich: Spangenberg, 1991); and *Der deutsch-deutsche Literaturstreit oder 'Freunde, es spricht sich schlecht mit gebundener Zunge': Analysen und Materialien*, ed. by Karl Deiritz and Hannes Krauss (Hamburg: Luchterhand, 1991).
9. As Ulrich Greiner commented in his review of *Was bleibt*: 'Die Staatsdichterin der DDR soll vom Staatssicherheitsdienst der DDR überwacht worden sein? Christa Wolf, die Nationalpreisträgerin, die prominenteste Autorin ihres Landes, SED-Mitglied bis zum letzten Augenblick, ein Opfer der *Stasi*?'. Ulrich Greiner, 'Mangel an Feingefühl', *Die Zeit*, 1 June 1990, p. 53.
10. Whereas the Stasi files covering the years when Wolf was under observation total twenty-two volumes, there are only two folders detailing her work as an *IM*. See Joachim Walther, *Sicherungsbereich Literatur: Schriftsteller und Staatssicherheit in der Deutschen Demokratischen Republik*, Analysen und Dokumente, 6 (Berlin: Links, 1996), p. 21.
11. Ibid., p. 21.
12. Anna Kuhn, '"Eine Königin köpfen ist effektiver als einen König köpfen": The Gender Politics of the Christa Wolf Controversy', in *Women and the Wende: Social Effects and Cultural Reflections of the German Unification Process*, ed. by Elizabeth Boa and Janet Wharton, German Monitor, 31 (Amsterdam: Rodopi, 1994), pp. 200–15 (p. 206).
13. The manuscripts of *Was bleibt* are held in the Akademie der Künste in Berlin. However, Wolf asked for them to be placed under restricted access, and in response to my request for permission to view them, she replied:

> Ich möchte Sie bitten, auf eine Einsicht in meine Manuskripte im Archiv zu verzichten. [...] Ich glaube nicht, dass Sie für Ihr spezielles Anliegen da etwas finden würden, und nicht absichtslos habe ich die Einsicht in die Vorarbeiten zu meinen Büchern gesperrt. (27 October 2010)

14. Kuhn, 'Zweige vom selben Stamm', p. 187.
15. Ibid., p. 189 and p. 194. Astrid Köhler makes a similar point, suggesting that all three texts share a focus on 'das Scheitern einer gesellschaftlichen Utopie und vor allem des individuellen Anspruchs, Teil der Gesellschaft zu sein [...] sowie als Dichter gehört und ernst genommen zu sein'. Köhler, *Brückenschläge*, pp. 23–24.

16. *Sommerstück* and *Was bleibt* are also linked through their references to the final line of Hölderlin's poem, 'Andenken', which reads: 'Was bleibet aber, stiften die Dichter'. See Friedrich Hölderlin, *Sämtliche Werke und Briefe*, ed. by Jochen Schmidt, 3 vols (Frankfurt a. M.: Deutscher Klassiker, 1992), I, 360–62 (p. 362). Although the line is not directly quoted in *Kein Ort. Nirgends*, its sentiment is frequently echoed in the exchange between the figures of Kleist and Günderrode. See Köhler, *Brückenschläge*, p. 28.
17. As Brigitte Peucker argues, 'Unter den Linden' contains a Romantic 'literary subtext', which is not made explicit because attempts by writers to rediscover the Romantic heritage were not officially permitted in the GDR until 1972. Brigitte Peucker, 'Dream, Fairy Tale, and the Literary Subtext of "Unter den Linden"', in *Responses to Christa Wolf*, ed. by Marilyn Sibley Fries (Detroit: Wayne State University Press, 1989), pp. 303–11 (p. 306).
18. Astrid Köhler suggests that *Unter den Linden*, *Was bleibt* and *Kein Ort. Nirgends* can be read as 'Teile eines Gesamtwerks, Sätze einer Sinfonie'. Astrid Köhler, 'Begegnungen unter den Linden: Der etwa tausendste Versuch zum Thema Christa Wolf und die Romantik', *Weimarer Beiträge*, 52 (2006), 587–601 (p. 594).
19. This also recalls the self-banishment to the countryside which is undertaken by the characters in *Sommerstück*.
20. Sonja Hilzinger notes in her afterword to *Was bleibt* that the structure of the *Erzählung* remains fairly consistent throughout the various reworkings of the manuscript (CW X, 322). Such consistency might suggest that Wolf always intended *Was bleibt* to possess a structural link to 'Unter den Linden'.
21. See Philip Manger, 'Auf der Suche nach dem ungelebten Leben: Christa Wolf — *Unter den Linden*', in *Wissen aus Erfahrungen: Werkbegriff und Interpretation heute: Festschrift für Herman Meyer zum 65. Geburtstag*, ed. by Alexander von Bormann (Tübingen: Niemeyer, 1976), pp. 903–16 (p. 903).
22. Beverley Hardy, 'Romanticism and Realism: Christa Wolf's "Unter den Linden": The Appropriation of a Hoffmannesque Reality', in *Neue Ansichten*, ed. by Gaskill, McPherson, and Barker, pp. 73–84 (p. 74).
23. On the significance of Wolf's word-play using the phrases 'Grund', 'Abgrund', 'zugrunde gehen' and 'zugrunde liegen' in 'Unter den Linden', see Andrew J. Webber, *Berlin in the Twentieth Century: A Cultural Topography* (Cambridge: Cambridge University Press, 2008), pp. 240–45.
24. See ibid., p. 244.
25. As Sigrid Weigel points out, Benjamin's image also 'refers […] to the instant of the readability of memory traces which Freud described as the flickering-up (*Aufleuchten*) of consciousness in apperception'. Sigrid Weigel, *Body- and Image-Space: Re-reading Walter Benjamin*, trans. by Georgina Paul (London: Routledge, 1996), p. 115.
26. Resina, p. 13.
27. On the vocabulary of crime and punishment, and a reading of the possible references to Kafka's *Der Proceß* in Wolf's narrative, see Hans-Georg Werner, 'Unter den Linden: Three Improbable Stories', in *Responses to Christa Wolf*, ed. by Fries, pp. 279–302 (pp. 282–83).
28. Andrew Webber writes:

> The waking or the guarded language that frames the narrative is also readable as though it had spilled out of the dream narrative: the realization that 'hits' her and fills the body 'cell by cell' […] is ominous language for this text concerned with justice and force.

Webber, *Berlin in the Twentieth Century*, p. 245.
29. Renate Rechtien likens this image of the city to a vision of Hell. Renate Rechtien, 'From

a Topography of Hope to a Nightmarish "Non-Place": Chronotopes in Christa Wolf's "June Afternoon", "Unter den Linden" and *What Remains*', in *The Politics of Place in Post-War Germany: Essays in Literary Criticism*, ed. by David Clarke and Renate Rechtien (Lewiston, NY: Edwin Mellen, 2009), pp. 261–84 (p. 283).

30. As John McGrath points out, 'surveillance space' is inhabited by 'death', and 'our relation to death's aporia' is written into 'the structures of surveillance'. John McGrath, *Loving Big Brother: Performance, Privacy and Surveillance Space* (London: Routledge, 2004), pp. 17 and 211–14.
31. Derrida, *Specters of Marx*, p. 134.
32. Ibid., p. 101.
33. Stephen Brockmann suggests that this focus on recording external details means that the Stasi can be viewed as a 'Socialist realist author par excellence', a 'modern novelist, transforming life into literature'. Stephen Brockmann, 'Preservation and Change in Christa Wolf's *Was bleibt*', *The German Quarterly*, 67 (1994), 73–85 (p. 81).
34. Jacques Derrida and Bernard Stiegler, *Echographies of Television: Filmed Interviews*, trans. by Jennifer Bajorek (Cambridge: Polity Press, 2002), p. 120.
35. Derrida, *Specters of Marx*, p. 119.
36. Ibid.
37. Ibid., p. 6.
38. Her pose might also recall the episode in Walter Benjamin's *Berliner Kindheit*, where the child, hiding in the curtain and watching the world around him, comes to view himself as a ghost, a 'Gespenst in d[er] Gardine' (WB 4, p. 253).
39. Paul, 'Text and Context', p. 120.
40. Vidler, *The Architectural Uncanny*, p. 163.
41. On the etymological relation between the words 'ghost', 'host', and 'guest', see Peter Schwenger, *Fantasm and Fiction: On Textual Envisioning* (Stanford, CA: Stanford University Press, 1999), p. 18.
42. Derrida, *Specters of Marx*, p. 101.
43. Ibid., p. 125.
44. Paul Cooke and Andrew Plowman, 'Introduction', in *German Writers and the Politics of Culture: Dealing with the Stasi*, ed. by Paul Cooke and Andrew Plowman (Basingstoke: Palgrave Macmillan, 2003), pp. xv–xxi (pp. xvii–xx).
45. Ibid.
46. For an alternative reading of this passage, see Marilyn Sibley Fries, 'When the Mirror is Broken, What Remains? Christa Wolf's *Was bleibt*', *GDR Bulletin*, 17 (1991), 11–15 (p. 12). Fries regards the broken mirror as a symbol of the way in which Wolf's project of 'subjektive Authentizität' has been betrayed by the repressive interventions of the Socialist State.
47. Nikolaos-Ioannis Koskinas chooses this quotation for the title of his study of Christa Wolf's work, but he does not analyse its significance in relation to *Was bleibt*. See Nikolaos-Ioannis Koskinas, '*Fremd bin ich eingezogen, fremd ziehe ich wieder aus*': *Von Kassandra, über Medea, zu Ariadne: Manifestationen der Psyche im spätesten Werk Christa Wolfs* (Würzburg: Königshausen & Neumann 2008), p. 11.

CHAPTER 2

'Abschied von Phantomen'? Christa Wolf's *Leibhaftig*

The previous chapter outlined the role played in Wolf's writing by the 'Phantombild', that ghostly after-image of a past event which lingers as a spectral impression in the mind's eye. As we saw, the image serves in her work to distort the protagonist's perception of the world around her, highlighting a slippage between self and other, subject and object, and in turn pointing to her potential to comply with a regime of which she nevertheless feels herself to be a victim. The phantom image was shown to reside at the boundaries of the subject, calling into question the protagonist's capacity for autonomous action in the world and undermining her sense of independent selfhood. It illustrates the way in which the protagonist, under observation, comes to embody the surveillance apparatus of the State, submitting herself to its demands and acting as an agent on its behalf. The present chapter examines the way in which this elusive boundary between victimhood and complicity is developed in Wolf's more recent post-*Wende* work. Focusing above all on the essays and speeches in her collection, *Auf dem Weg nach Tabou* (1994), and on her *Erzählung*, *Leibhaftig* (2002), it argues that her preoccupation with phantoms and other figures of the uncanny in these texts forms part of her exploration of the collective legacy of the German past. At the same time, her recourse to such images can be seen to mark a more personal act of facing up to the past, which signals both her efforts to work through the loss of the GDR and her less public attempts to come to terms with the ambiguity of her role in it. The autoscopic logic of Wolf's narrative, which reinvigorates versions of the writer's past selves in order to examine their actions, is shown here to possess an autopsic dimension, penetrating her decaying body and uncovering traces of the duplicity which contributed to her demise.

Wolf's use of the phantom as a metaphor for the haunting effects of the recent German past emerges clearly in a lecture which she gave on 27 February 1994 at the Staatsoper in Dresden. Entitled 'Abschied von Phantomen: Zur

Sache Deutschland', her speech has at its centre a bold call to arms, in which Wolf appeals to the new Federal Republic to exorcise its phantoms and face up to the reality of its history. She states: 'Ich finde, es ist an der Zeit, im Osten wie im Westen Deutschlands von dem Phantom Abschied zu nehmen, welches das je andere und damit auch das eigene Land lange für uns waren. Zur Sache, Deutschland!' (CW XII, 532). Wolf's words refer to the situation of newly unified Germany and its efforts to come to terms with the double legacy of National Socialism and the former GDR government. Such attempts at engaging with the past, she argues, have been hampered by the distorted views which West and East Germans still hold of each other and each other's State. These misguided attitudes resemble a phantom, since they lack a basis in reality and they distract from the task in hand: namely, that of accessing the facts associated with historical experience. Like the 'Phantombilder' in *Was bleibt*, which cloud the protagonist's view of the world and warp her perceptual apparatus, such erroneous views serve to mislead and confuse; the phantom is thus shown to be the ultimate purveyor of myths and falsehoods. Wolf's injunction, 'Zur Sache, Deutschland!', might seem surprising, since its emphasis on factual authenticity appears to be at odds with her long-held belief in the importance of subjective experience.[1] And yet, throughout her career, even in the experiment with Socialist Realism in her early *Moskauer Novelle*, Wolf has endowed her literary protagonists with visionary powers, with the ability to see through the deceptions and illusions which society has built up around them. Her injunction to focus on the reality of Germany's situation therefore ties in with one of her central aims as a writer: the revelation of experiences which have been excluded from conventional social and historiographical narratives.

In the same speech, Wolf goes on to link the image of the phantom with the existence of a repressed historical reality. Speaking of the guilt of the wartime generation, for example, she argues that parents' refusal to speak to their children about their experiences conceals a double repression — first, of the existence of any guilt or complicity, and second, of the sense of unease evoked by this unacknowledged guilt. This pervasive silence, she argues, creates a phantom, which works to undermine any attempts made to come to terms with the past. The figure of phantom functions as a distraction, masking and forestalling the revelation of the secret which the subject is striving to conceal. So, rather than signalling a return of the repressed in the Freudian sense, Wolf's conception of the phantom depicts it as a psychological device whose main purpose is to divert attention away from the existence of a repressed event or emotion. And, like the phenomenon described by Nicholas Abraham in his 'Notes on the Phantom', the phantom in Wolf's lecture, along with the silence which accompanies it, is shown to be intergenerational. It is cultivated in families, and comes to signal the way in which a particular historical event can influence those who were born after it and never lived through it. The phantom is therefore doubly deceptive; not only does it try to conceal the history which it masks, it also acts as a kind of false memory for the generation which inherits it, transmitting a version of history which is dangerously distorted. As Wolf writes: 'Wir wissen ja, wohin geleugnete, verdrängte Wirklichkeit gerät: Sie verschwindet in den blinden Flecken unseres Bewußtseins, wo sie Aktivität, Kreativität schluckt, aber Mythen hervortreibt, Aggressivität, Wahndenken' (CW XII, 533). The phantom functions like a blind spot in the consciousness of the individual, whose existence can only be perceived indirectly, by means of the destructive effects which it generates.[2] It surreptitiously works to destroy creative impulses and instead cultivates aggression and fanaticism, while its identity as the instigator of such action remains fully inaccessible to the conscious mind.

Wolf's post-*Wende* writing seems above all to be motivated by the realization that the history of the GDR is also in danger of falling victim to this kind of silencing. Thus in her 'Rede für Hans Mayer', she writes: 'Wir müssen auf Konkretheit bestehen und aufpassen, daß uns nicht das Leben genommen wird, das wir wirklich geführt haben, und uns statt dessen ein verzerrtes Phantom untergeschoben wird' (CW XII, 357). Similarly, in another speech, she criticizes the superficial fraternity which exists between East and West, arguing that this 'äußerliche Annäherung' (CW XII, 227) conceals a process of repression and denial, through which the real history of the GDR is being erased from official historical accounts of the post-war period. The phantom therefore comes to operate on a collective level, signalling a form of public silencing which works against the development of a cultural memory capable of doing justice to the multifarious past it seeks to commemorate. Above all, it brings about a generalized sense of alienation, a shared feeling of 'Entfremdung' (CW XII, 227), which distances the post-war generation from its own past. Unlike the stylistic 'Verfremdung' emphasized in Wolf's *Unwahrscheinliche Geschichten*, whose purpose was to bring about a productive relation to the world, this feeling of estrangement is experienced on an existential level as a destructive force, challenging people's ability to relate to the world around them and undermining their quest for self-realization. It conveys what Wolf perceives as a common sense of dissatisfaction and unease felt by all those whose lives are being rewritten by authorized versions of history. Wolf's efforts to challenge this collective silencing nevertheless operate on a more private level, calling on individuals to engage personally with their knowledge of the GDR and encouraging them to reflect on 'what remains' (CW XII, 533) of this former State. Following her concept of 'subjektive Authentizität', which focused on the individual experiences which constitute the collective, Wolf's injunction to Germany to 'take leave of its phantoms' can be read as an appeal to reassess private experiences in the wake of the *Wende*; it suggests that any official engagement with German history must in fact be based on more personal acts of mourning and honest self-judgement, whose combined force creates a more differentiated approach to the country's recent past than that offered by conventional narratives.

'Ein fremder Mensch tritt mir gegenüber'

Wolf's essays on the collective legacy of the GDR need to be read in conjunction with her own response to the opening of the Stasi files and the revelation in 1993 that she had worked briefly as an *inoffizielle Mitarbeiterin* in the early phase of her career. Crucially, Wolf tailors her discussion of this disclosure to fit with the rhetoric and imagery which characterizes her description of Germany's collective phantoms. In a key interview with the journalist Günter Gaus conducted in 1993, shortly after the news of her complicity broke, she maintained that she had 'repressed' all knowledge of her possible involvement with the Stasi: 'Was ich nicht mehr wußte; daß ich einen Decknamen hatte, daß ich selbst einen Bericht geschrieben habe. Daß heißt, ich hatte sehr wirksam verdrängt, daß es sich um einen Vorgang handelte, der zu einer IM-Akte führen konnte' (CW xii, 454). Her claim to have 'forgotten' or 'repressed' these aspects of her past might, as some commentators have noted, be viewed as highly suspect.[3] However, her use of such vocabulary clearly situates her own experience within the narrative of repression which she has developed in her theoretical work. She implies that her unspoken engagement with the Stasi has been hidden in her unconscious mind, concealed by a kind of phantom whose existence haunts her in the form of a distorted or partial memory of the events which led to her being classed as an *IM*. The Stasi file itself functions as a distraction, turning her life into a caricature through its one-sided account of her life and thereby masking the full depth of her experiences (CW xii, 459). And yet her own memories prove to be just as unreliable, offering her a flawed version of her actions and preventing her from gaining access to the reasoning which lay behind her behaviour. These distorted recollections, she argues, forestall the possibility of an emotional engagement with her past, rendering false any display of remorse and undermining the validity of any public admission of guilt (CW xii, 460–61).

In the same interview, Wolf goes on to describe the pervasive feeling of self-alienation which overcomes her when she realizes that her hitherto unchallenged memory of her actions does not match that described in the Stasi files. She explains:

> Als mir klar wurde, daß es diese Akte gibt, und als ich sie kurz gesehen hatte und sie jetzt nun wirklich lesen konnte, ging etwas ganz anderes in mir vor.

> Ein fremder Mensch tritt mir da gegenüber. Das bin ich nicht. [...] Wer war ich eigentlich damals? Es ist ein schreckliches Entfremdungsgefühl, was mich überkommt, wenn ich das lese. (CW XII, 460–61)

Like the 'Entfremdung' which separates the wartime generation from their former lives, this sense of estrangement renders Wolf other to herself. It creates a split within her, a division between her self-understanding as an autonomous subject and her perception of herself as an alien being. On one level, this divide recalls the fragmented subject of *Was bleibt*, whose ambivalent relationship with the State leads to the fragmentation of her identity into a series of disparate, multiple beings. Just as the protagonist of that tale regards herself as a figure who is torn apart by the conflict between self-protection, complicity, and resistance, so too does Wolf come to see her sense of self as being threatened by the realization that her behaviour was governed by such contradictory impulses (CW XII, 461). And, while the protagonist of *Was bleibt* increasingly mirrors the actions of the Stasi agents, observing herself and echoing their thought patterns, so too does Wolf find herself speaking in the language of the Stasi and conforming to their characterization of her (CW XII, 461). Particularly striking is the fact that she acknowledges her cooperation with them — 'Ja, ich habe mich mit denen eingelassen' (CW XII, 457) — in the very terms which she uses in *Was bleibt* to describe the way in which the Stasi gain entry ('Einlaß' — CW X, 227) into the protagonist's home and life. In admitting that she worked for the Stasi, Wolf implies that she gained entry to their world, making herself at home there and adopting their system of surveillance. She suggests that she began to act like the agents observing her, and in doing so, became transformed into an alien being, one who was no longer recognizable to herself.

In order to work through this period of her past, Wolf realizes that she must learn to recognize herself in the ulterior figure which confronts her. In the same interview, she describes the process of self-examination necessary for such an act: 'Ich muß einfach versuchen, noch mal in diesen Schacht runterzusteigen, und mir das anzugucken, mich selbst angucken und im einzelnen fragen, wie ist es dahin gekommen, auch, wie ich davon wieder weggekommen bin' (CW XII, 461). The image of the body as a mineshaft is a recurrent motif in Wolf's writing, often used to highlight an attempt to uncover the depths which lie beneath the surface of human experience and thereby attain a form of self-actualization.[4] Here, the metaphor indicates Wolf's preoccupation with revealing the causes of her engagement with the Stasi and the reasons why it became buried in her unconscious. At the same time, it points to her quest for self-knowledge, her desire to understand why she behaved in such a way and to develop a subjective connection to her own past, no matter what pain it may cause (CW XII, 463). Viewed in this context, the shift from 'das' to 'mich' indicates a crucial moment of self-recognition; rather than viewing herself as an other, Wolf must be able to reconcile herself with the object of her gaze, incorporating this external figure into her experience as a subject and thereby coming to regard it as a part of herself. Her emphasis on the need to be a subject, to be a person in her own right rather than an object at the disposal of others (CW XII, 466), can only be fulfilled if she is prepared to integrate her other selves into her identity. It is only by empathizing with this estranged figure, by acknowledging its role in her life, that she can hope to obtain the self-identification necessary to overcome her feeling of alienation. And it is only by accepting her repressed past as her own that she stands any chance of coming to terms with the misleading phantoms which haunt her.

In her efforts to incorporate her past life into her present self, Wolf's post-*Wende* writing can be read as continuing a process of self-discovery which she first explored in *Kindheitsmuster*. In that novel, the protagonist strives to unite the different selves within her, which are signalled by the repeated shifts in narrative perspective and the alternation between 'du' and 'sie'. While the narrator does succeed in employing the pronoun 'ich' on the final page of the book, however, this apparent assertion of a unified identity actually serves to leave open the question of whether the ghostly voices of her past selves have been laid to rest.[5] In the closing paragraph, the narrator appears to abandon her attempts to assert a coherent sense of self by slipping into a kind of 'waking dream': 'Nachts werde ich — ob im Wachen, ob im Traum — den Umriß eines Menschen sehen, der sich in fließenden Übergängen unaufhörlich verwandelt, durch den andere Menschen, Erwachsene, Kinder, ungezwungen hindurchgehen' (CW V, 594). Initially, this passage appears to reinforce the split between the narrator and her past self, since the vision is primarily autoscopic: in her dream-like state, the protagonist views herself projected as other, depicted as an outline whose identity is not immediately recognizable. And yet, whereas the rest of the novel is concerned with the past, this final vision is shown to be forward-looking; the abrupt shift to the future tense might recall Ernst Bloch's definition of the 'waking dream' as a psychological state which optimistically reveals the prospect of change.[6] Wolf highlights the way in which several different time-frames converge in this rêverie; in a single instant, the protagonist witnesses different historical versions of herself as they are projected onto the figure before her.[7] In escaping from the constraints of temporal continuity, she becomes able to engage simultaneously with the various beings inside her; in a precise moment she finds that she can embrace various past and future versions of the self. And she comes to acknowledge that these different selves can all exist within her at any one given time, offering her multiple perspectives on the present and challenging the dominance of her present character.

Wolf's suggestion that she must descend inside herself in order to understand her complicity with the Stasi (CW XII, 461) recalls the dream-like state at the end of *Kindheitsmuster* through the challenge it poses to linear temporality; in both descriptions, the past is evoked in order for it to be understood more thoroughly and therefore accepted into the identity of the subject. The writer adopts a mediating role, conjuring up the phantoms of the past and staging an encounter with them in the present. Wolf explains this task further in a passage in *Kindheitsmuster*. Analysing the double meaning of the verb 'vermitteln', she writes: 'Schreibend zwischen der Gegenwart und der Vergangenheit vermitteln, sich ins Mittel legen: Heißt das: versöhnen? Mildern? Glätten? Oder: Eins dem anderen näherbringen? Der heutigen Person die Begegnung mit jener vergangenen möglich machen, vermittels geschriebener Zeilen' (CW v, 241). The writer stands at the intersection of past and present, and seeks by means of the creative process of writing to mediate between the two. Unlike the 'Medaillons' of memory which Wolf describes in 'Lesen und Schreiben' (CW IV, 255–58), fragmented remnants of the past which have become fossilized and disconnected from the present,[8] this encounter with earlier events and figures is shown to rest on a form of vivification. By invoking a historical event or figure and bringing it into the present, the writer seeks to enliven it and thereby offer a new perspective on it. By seeking out its connections with the present, she can view it from a position which was originally inaccessible to her and in doing so can breathe new life into it. As Michelle Mattson has observed, this act of conjuring up the past necessarily 'alters, embellishes and reconfigures that past'.[9] It enables particular details to be analysed from a position of hindsight, while also diminishing the importance of factors which were previously considered important. At the same time, the activity of the writer also has the capacity to alter our view of the present, by ensuring that we consider it in conjunction with past events.

For Wolf, then, the text becomes a realm in which temporal boundaries are collapsed. It opens up a space in which the voices of her previous selves can speak and be acknowledged, lending her the possibility of reacquainting herself with these elusive figures and coming to understand the motives and desires which once governed her actions. And it offers her the chance to develop connections between her thoughts and behaviour in these different time periods, perceiving correlations between the two and thereby making possible the process of self-assertion, the 'Zu-sich-selber-Kommen des Menschen' (CW XII, 461), which has driven her creative activity since the writing of *Nachdenken über Christa T.* However, this encounter between past and present is shown to be highly ambivalent. The protagonist's experience of the present is founded upon the very past which now casts doubt on the morality of her current existence, while her efforts to engage with that past are simultaneously facilitated and called into question by the gaps which exist in her present knowledge. In addition, the words which the writer uses prove to have a 'Doppelsinn' (CW v, 241), a double meaning which is at once enriching and potentially misleading, and this duplicity serves to highlight the way in which her attempts to narrate the past are always shadowed by the risk of falsifying or misrepresenting it (CW v, 396). Wolf's depiction of the writer's intermediate position highlights the personal costs of this encounter between past and present. In mediating between these different temporal realms, in placing herself between the two ('sich ins Mittel legen'), the writer exposes herself directly to phantoms which haunt her and risks succumbing to their deception. The encounter with a repressed past is effected corporeally, operating on and through the apparatus of the writer's body, and this renders her particularly vulnerable to the destructive effects of the history that requires mediation.

The Spirit Medium

Wolf's Erzählung, Leibhaftig, thematizes her relationship with the GDR and the process of coming to terms with her ambiguous role in it.[10] The narrative is set in 1988, shortly before the fall of the Berlin Wall, and depicts the illness and subsequent recovery of a woman writer submitted to hospital with a ruptured appendix. As she floats in and out of consciousness, the protagonist is subjected to a series of nightmarish visions, finding herself transported through layer upon layer of German history into the labyrinthine network of tunnels, cellars, and wartime air raid shelters beneath Berlin. On these journeys, she encounters various phantoms and other ghostly figures, which she describes as 'diese Seelen, die sich auf der Grenze bewegen, nicht mehr lebend, noch nicht ganz tot' (L, p. 178). In depicting such forms, Wolf renders literal her metaphorical depiction of the writer as a medium: here, the protagonist assumes the role of a spirit-medium, channelling the spirits of the dead and making possible an encounter with the past. Embodying the classic, projective predicament of the medium, she becomes the apparatus of mediation while also assuming the characteristics of the phantoms themselves.[11] Her body acts as an interface between past and present, yet it also comes to resemble the ghosts which she invokes: she becomes 'gespensterhaft' (L, p. 53), and her movements assume an ethereal quality as she glides (L, p. 25) and hovers (L, p. 57) above the streets of Berlin. These ghostly figures are linked with the history of the GDR through their particular connection to the topography of divided Berlin. While the Friedrichstraße station, the main transit point between East and West Berlin, becomes a gateway to the spirit world (L, pp. 25–26), the metaphysical 'Grenze' upon which these phantoms move recalls the geographical boundary which has been an indirect presence throughout Wolf's oeuvre. And the protagonist is able to pass, unhindered, through various 'Übergänge'; unlike the checkpoints which in reality sought to constrain her freedom of movement, these clear the way for her to engage with the legacy of the GDR and offer her the opportunity to confront her role in it.

As a medium, Wolf's protagonist comes to exist in a 'Zeitlücke' (*L*, p. 69), an intermediate realm in which the distinction between past, present, and future is collapsed. Her experience of this gap in temporality is highlighted directly towards the middle of the *Erzählung*, where the narrator introduces an associative reflection on the concept of time,[12] prompted by the memory of a boy who died from an illness similar to the one afflicting the protagonist. The passage contrasts the regimented division of her normal life into 'Zeitabschnitte' and 'Zeiträume' (*L*, p. 68) with the absence of temporal boundaries experienced during her illness. Her usual routine is structured by the passage of time, by the 'Tage, die aus Morgen und Abend werden' (*L*, p. 69); it is characterized by the separation of her actions into distinct units which, as discrete fragments of experience, bear little relation to one another. By contrast, the protagonist's illness is marked by the disruption of this schedule, by the realization that her experience of 'Zeitlichkeit' has been replaced by a sense of 'Zeitlosigkeit' (*L*, p. 69). Like the dream-like state in 'Unter den Linden', where the suspension of temporality enabled the narrator to perceive the world in a new light, the protagonist's illness is here experienced as a liberation, a 'Befreiung vom Zeitgeschehen' (*L*, p. 69), which enables her to observe more clearly the connections between past, present, and future. Because she is no longer 'subjected' ('unterworfen' — *L*, p. 69) to the ordering of time, nor trapped by the metaphorical 'Zeitgitter' (*L*, p. 68) which normally constrains her perception of reality, she is free to pursue the ghostly visions which appear before her without feeling bound to assign them to a particular place in the temporal 'Ordnung' (*L*, p. 69) of her waking hours. This liberation ultimately creates a sense of release, since she is no longer compelled 'an der Zeitgeraden entlang vorwärts [zu schleppen]' (*L*, p. 70) or to cling to the 'schmale[r] Mauersims' (*L*, p. 70) — another implicit reference to the topographical division of the city — which restricts her temporal existence.

At the same time, however, this experience of 'Unzeit' (*L*, p. 69) is also revealed to be highly disorientating for the protagonist. Although she is no longer caught in the 'Zeitnetz' of her everyday life, her escape from this is described as a fall (*L*, p. 70), an unbridled descent which plunges her into a state of powerlessness. Unable to control her experience of time, she is subjected to a series of ominously prophetic visions of the future which cause her to lose her way and call into question her position in the present. Towards the middle of the narrative, for example, she registers with alarm the sign 'MAUERDURCHBRUCH' (*L*, p. 112). The abrupt penetration of this spatial barrier widens her horizons in a manner which is frightening, rather than liberating, while the implicit anticipation of the events of 1989 is shown to take over the protagonist's experience of the present, causing her to panic and lose her way. Later in the novel, past and future appear to converge in a vision of the Friedrichstraße, which is 'aufgerissen' (*L*, p. 142), bearing its 'Eingeweide' (*L*, p. 143) to the world in a manner which resembles the wounded body of the protagonist (*L*, p. 137). The 'tiefe Gräben' (*L*, p. 142) which run along the street recall the bomb damage done to the city during the war; at the same time, however, the vision of monstrous diggers and cranes seems to anticipate the prolific building work and regeneration which emerged in this area following the *Wende*. The concurrence of these different temporal layers forms what the narrator describes as the 'Unterwelt' of the city (*L*, p. 143). It reveals the urban unconscious, which Wolf first explored in 'Unter den Linden', to be an uncanny realm, emitting a 'geisterhaftes Licht' (*L*, p. 143) which threatens to draw the protagonist into its depths. While the 'ditches' ('Graben' — *L*, p. 143) in the road risk becoming 'graves' ('Gräber' — *L*, p. 142), the protagonist faces the danger of losing her way and unintentionally stumbling into the hellish realm which they contain (*L*, p. 162).

At other points in the *Erzählung*, the protagonist's disorientation arises from the irruption of past events and people into the present. Often, these figures are intertextual *revenants* from her earlier works; the young writers whom she mentors in *Was bleibt* haunt this text, as does the figure of her Aunt Lisbeth, whose affair with a Jewish doctor in the 1930s was first described in *Kindheitsmuster*.[13] Each time they appear, more details about this couple are revealed, culminating with the revelation that she bore an illegitimate child in the face of persecution from the National Socialist regime. The figures are therefore connected with concealed memories and details about the past which have not previously been spoken about. Yet their presence is also perceived as threatening to the protagonist, who, upon their appearance, falls into a 'tiefe Verwirrung', triggered by the fact that 'die Zeitebenen einander heillos durchdringen' (*L*, p. 59). Her involuntary subjection to this temporal rupture, emphasized by the repetition of the adjective 'heillos', is illustrated further by the portrayal of the figures as uncanny intruders, who are out of place in the present. The fact that they appear in front of the *Tränenpalast* of the GDR marks them out as restless beings, whose existence is characterized by a lack of belonging, while the building's association with tearful acts of departure belatedly marks the grief caused by the couple's enforced separation in the Third Reich. Their attempt to cross over the 'Grenzübergang', which is not yet 'geschlossen' (*L*, pp. 59–60), signals their ability to traverse both geographical and temporal boundaries; their action is nevertheless described as futile, since they do not belong in the Germany of the 1980s (*L*, p. 60). As the past is drawn into the present and the protagonist becomes increasingly aware of the incongruity of the scene which she is witnessing, she voices the question: 'Wo leben die denn, und wo lebe ich, in welchem Zeitalter' (*L*, p. 60). The urgent outburst of rhetorical questions signals the protagonist's confusion regarding this suspension of temporality. Her encounter with the ghostly figures of Tante Lisbeth and her lover not only leads her to question the validity of their presence, but it also causes her to doubt her own sense of belonging in this epoch; in coming face to face with these outcast figures, she too is shown to be uprooted and fundamentally displaced.

Tricks of the Light

The protagonist's encounter with what one reviewer calls these 'Gespenster am Krankenbett'[14] can be viewed as part of her quest for historical truth. The figures play a crucial role, both in her attempts to trace the cause of the suffering which she is experiencing (*L*, p. 184) and in her efforts to get to the bottom ('auf den Grund [...] gehen' — *L*, p. 138) of her corporeal existence. More specifically, the protagonist's contact with them signals an engagement with the revelation of repressed memories and a desire to gain access to traces of historical experience which been omitted from conventional narratives. The ghostly figures which the protagonist meets are therefore portrayed as messengers from another realm, carrying 'Botschaften einer versunkenen Epoche' (*L*, p. 144), while their role is to point her in the direction of the 'Wahrheit' which is hidden from her (*L*, p. 148). The protagonist searches for the 'geheim[er] Sinn' (*L*, p. 128) which they bear, and seeks to find the 'Bedeutung' which is impregnated in their apparition (*L*, p. 97). Despite their connection with the repressed memories at the root of the protagonist's illness, however, these ghostly figures are also shown to be highly duplicitous figures. Like the deceptive phantoms which Wolf describes in her theoretical writing, these ghosts also serve as distractions, at times drawing the protagonist's attention away from the secrets which they guard. Their messages are sometimes countered by 'Antibotschaften' (*L*, p. 97), which call into question the veracity of their original content, while their ability to lead her to the 'Kern der Wahrheit' (*L*, p. 138) proves to be inseparable from their connection to the 'Kern der Lüge' (*L*, p. 138). Their role as harbingers of truth is therefore shown to be highly questionable, and this unreliability means that the protagonist's attempts to reveal repressed memories are fraught with the difficulty of separating truth from illusion.

The precarious position of the protagonist with regard to these deceptive phantoms is highlighted above all through Wolf's experiment with different lighting effects. While the writer's task is primarily one of enlightenment, bringing to light that which has been concealed from view, her quest is undermined by various tricks of the light which cast doubt on the veracity of that which they reveal. At the outset of the tale, the protagonist's loss of consciousness is likened to drowning and a descent into darkness: 'Untertauchen. Untergetauchtwerden. Dunkel. Stille' (*L*, p. 6). The shift from active to passive verb, and subsequently to the nominal form, highlights the relinquishing of herself as an active subject. Darkness is presented here as a realm of ignorance, an escape from the bombardment of details which the protagonist experiences in her waking life. This pattern is partially inverted a few lines later, as the protagonist is propelled abruptly back to consciousness: 'Sie wird hochgeschleudert, öffnet die Augen. Zuviel Licht' (*L*, p. 8). However, the passive verb here is unexpectedly violent, and the opening of the patient's eyes appears to be involuntary. The final resolution is undermined by the fact that the light is too much; because it temporarily blinds the protagonist, it becomes a kind of darkness. Wolf thereby collapses the distinction between light and dark in a manner which reflects the ambivalence wrought by the convergence of past and present. Light, despite its revelatory capacity, also has the potential to blind; similarly, darkness is at times shown to be a realm of insight, yet it is always haunted by the danger of not seeing, of not being able to distinguish the reality of what appears before one's eyes. The visionary capability of the writer which Wolf emphasized in her earlier work is shown to be complicated by the unreliability of that which she sees, while her task of seeing the connections between seemingly unrelated events is made difficult by the fact that she can so easily be deceived and misled.

The protagonist's journey into this 'Zwischenwelt' (*L*, p. 70) therefore suggests an attempt to negotiate her way between blindness and insight, ignorance and understanding, despite the realization that one so easily merges with the other. Her sick-room, a dimly lit space illuminated only by the 'matte[r] Schein' (*L*, p. 96) of a nightlight and by the 'bleiche[s] Licht des Mondes' (*L*, p. 58), is transformed into a ghostly realm, 'die von bleichem Zwielicht und Gesichten erfüllt ist' (*L*, p. 69). In this half-light, it becomes increasingly difficult for the protagonist to distinguish between the real people in her hospital room and the phantom figures which appear before her; both assume an ethereal quality which lends them the character of a hallucinatory vision. And while the real figures in the hospital keep the protagonist in the dark — both literally, by closing the curtains of the room, and metaphorically, by not telling her about the severity of her illness — the phantom figures of her visions are associated with uncanny lights which prove to be highly unreliable. In the middle section of the novel, for example, the protagonist hears an announcement on the radio about the discovery of a murdered infant in a Berlin cellar. This prompts a vision, in which she wanders through a network of underground tunnels in search of the dead child. Some of these rooms are completely dark, creating a sense in which the protagonist is trespassing in areas which are resistant to her presence. In others, she finds wobbly light switches and dusty light bulbs which emit 'ein trübes, schwankendes Licht' (*L*, p. 110); although they promise illumination, the uncertainty of this light merely serves to cast doubt on the reliability of that which it reveals. Towards the centre of the vision, the protagonist finds herself being guided by a Faustian homunculus, which emits an eerie blue glow (*L*, p. 107). Despite its apparently helpful efforts to lead her towards the secret which she is seeking to uncover, the homunculus soon assumes an accusatory function. As it begins to turn on the protagonist, its light becomes overwhelmingly bright, causing her to cry out, 'Es ist zuviel' (*L*, p. 113), an echo of the earlier reference to 'zuviel Licht' (*L*, p. 8).[15] The revelatory potential of the figure brings about a sensory overload which poses a fundamental danger to the protagonist and ultimately threatens to lead her towards her own death.

Wolf's protagonist has no control over these guiding lights, and she is therefore torn between her realization that they are often no more than deceptive *Irrlichter* and her total dependence on them as a means of pursuing the forgotten. At times, the ghostly figures themselves are revealed to be nothing more than illusory apparitions created from patterns of light, which the protagonist is nevertheless forced (*L*, p. 32) to confront as though they were real. Thus at one stage her aunt's face rises out of the darkness (*L*, p. 73), and she recalls her former friend, Hannes Urban, as a figure glowing in the half-light. Elsewhere in the novel she is compelled to look on as images of human suffering are played out on her 'innere Bühne' (*L*, p. 32). These projections of light at times recall the ghostly figures of early cinema, whose dematerialized bodies blur the distinction between actuality and illusion, calling into question 'the boundaries between diegetic representation and reality'.[16] The protagonist, as a spirit medium, is also shown to assume the qualities of a cinematic medium, transmitting moving images which have the appearance of reality and the capacity to deceive the protagonist. The fact that these figures are only projected when her internal 'Regisseur' is inactive (*L*, p. 32) lends them a particular link to the unconscious, thus recalling what Walter Benjamin saw as cinema's affinity to the 'Optisch-Unbewußte[s]', its capacity to circumvent the controls of the conscious mind and present aspects of experience which have not yet been fully registered by the human subject (WB II.1, 371).

Wolf's focus on moving images, on the cinematic interplay of light and shadow, can be read as a development of the exploration of photographic representation found in *Kindheitsmuster*. In that earlier text, Wolf draws on references to the photographic image as a means of lending validity to the narrator's memory. As Linda Rugg points out, 'real images' are shown to exist 'on the same plane as imagined images'.[17] She continues: 'In framing her memories as if they were photographs, the narrator calls upon the testimonial power of photography'.[18] At the same time, however, Wolf insists upon 'the necessity to regard static images [...] with suspicion',[19] since photographic stasis can signal the reification of memory and in particular the objectification of the past and its exploitation for political purposes.[20] In *Leibhaftig*, memories also appear to the protagonist in the form of photographs (*L*, p. 44), which are then filed in her internal archive (*L*, p. 49). And yet the referential function of such images is called into question, as these memories are merely shown to resemble photographic stills, assuming their characteristics without actually being grounded in reality. In a similar vein, Wolf's efforts to counter the stasis of the photographic image by animating memories in the manner of a filmic sequence are also highly problematic.[21] The projections of moving images which confront the protagonist are shown to be artificial; these ghostly figures possess bodies which are insubstantial, and their apparent movement is illusory and able at any moment to slip back into an arrested state. Their documentary potential is undermined by their precarious connection to the reality of the protagonist's existence; although they appear to be linked to events in her waking life, their actual relation to her historical existence remains elusive and incomprehensible.

Gothic Bodies

While the phantoms which Wolf invokes never directly allude to her complicity with the Stasi, the imagery which she uses to describe her protagonist's role resonates with the vocabulary of her earlier interview with Günter Gaus, in which she admitted to having worked as an *inoffizielle Mitarbeiterin*. At one point in the narrative, Wolf depicts the process of revealing the repressed through the image of her protagonist as a miner, burrowing her way through the cells and arteries of her own body with the aid of a miner's lamp to illuminate her path: 'Mein Körper als Bergwerk. Das Kopflicht des Bergmannes, das voranleuchtet. Das einen matten Schein gibt, mikroskopisch klein, das jede Körperzelle zur Höhle vergrößert, jede Ader zum Flußbett und das Blut zu einem Strom, der pulsierend einem weitverzweigten Stromnetz folgt' (*L*, p. 97).[22] The image of her body as a mine shaft assumes an ominous character through its potential allusion to the classic scenario of Gothic undeadness found in E. T. A. Hoffmann's *Erzählung*, 'Die Bergwerke zu Falun' (H IV, 208–41). In that tale, the eponymous mine, which promises hidden treasures to those who enter it, is inhabited by spectral figures, whose function is to mislead and ultimately destroy the protagonist. The narrative creates a disturbing analogy between the personified body of the mine, with its 'jaws', 'mouth', and 'veins', and the petrified corpse of his protagonist at the end of the *Erzählung*. Whereas for Hoffmann, the uncanny blurring of the boundary between the animate and the inanimate illustrates the dangers faced by the writer who becomes too involved in his creation, Wolf's use of the image serves to highlight the personal risks associated with the task of revealing repressed memories. The protagonist's body becomes the site of an encounter with phantoms which is at once enlightening and potentially destructive. It stands at the centre of a process of remembering which promises to transform the protagonist's understanding of herself while also threatening to lead her towards ruination.

Wolf goes on to link the image of the mine more explicitly with the task of remembering events which have previously been forgotten: 'Das Bewußtseinslicht, das hier innen und unten nur geduldet wird, solange es nicht störend eingreift, es schleust mich weiter, durch Sperren, Netze, Widerstände hindurch' (*L*, p. 97). Just as the figure in Hoffmann's tale feels compelled to enter the mine despite the dangers of losing himself in it, so Wolf's protagonist is propelled by an unstoppable force. The miner's lamp which guides her becomes a 'Bewußtseinslicht'; it belongs to her conscious mind, while the barriers and resistances which stand in its way are reminiscent of those which, according to Freud, are placed around memories in the unconscious. The protagonist's autopsic journey inside her body therefore becomes a voyage into her mind, an attempt to shed light on the repressed experiences which are concealed there. In adopting such an image, Wolf calls into question the Cartesian dualism of mind and body, the notion that the mind, as an immaterial essence, is distinct from the physical substance of the body.[23] In Wolf's text, the protagonist's mental processes are shown to be inseparable from her corporeal existence.[24] The materialistic understanding of her soul as a kind of appendix, 'ein bleiches gekrümmtes Stückchen Hautschlauch' (*L*, p. 130), is recalled here by the 'Blinddarmschmerzen' (*L*, p. 131) through which her psychic pain is made manifest. Her nocturnal wanderings inside her own body transport her into the 'Bereich des kaum noch Körperhaften' (*L*, p. 97), into a realm 'in dem die Unterschiede zwischen Geistigem und Körperlichem schwinden' (*L*, pp. 97–98).[25] Physical processes are shown to be experienced mentally, as 'Empfindungen' in the 'Gehirn' (*L*, p. 95), while immaterial thoughts and emotions are perceived as corporeal sensations (*L*, p. 98). The protagonist's psychic distress manifests itself in physical scars which, in the Kafkaesque fashion of 'literalizing the metaphor', are written like a text onto her body (*L*, pp. 132–33), while her physical symptoms are shown to be an expression of immaterial questions which cannot be formulated in words (*L*, p. 17). And her encounters with the ghostly figures in her nightmarish visions are experienced as a form of corporeal torment; these immaterial images penetrate (*L*, p. 32) her body and are burned (*L*, p. 20) into her memory.

Wolf's depiction of the human body as the site of a corporeal encounter with the phantoms of German history resonates with Kelly Hurley's understanding of the 'Gothic body' as an arena in which 'a crisis in the epistemology of human identity' is 'obsessively' staged and re-staged.[26] For Hurley, Gothic texts offer a space in which conceptions of human identity are challenged and renegotiated. On the one hand, they can be read as a *'productive* genre', creatively exploring 'new representational strategies' as a means of 'imagin[ing] [...] human realities' and offering a vibrant depiction of the 'plasticity' of the human form.[27] Evolving out of 'a collective psychological demand' at moments of radical social and ideological change within a culture, Gothic writing offers an instrumental means of 'negotiat[ing] the anxieties that accompany social and epistemological transformations and crises'.[28] According to Hurley, such texts frequently betray a fascination with the process of 'becoming', with the tantalizing promise of a new existence which emerges through their remodelling of human identity.[29] They provide ways of exploring the 'morphic possibilities' of the human subject, delighting in 'the variety and sheer exuberance of the spectacle'.[30] In doing so, they seek to 'reconfigure the known world',[31] recasting the familiar in a new light and revealing aspects of human existence which had not previously been perceived.

On the other hand, Hurley suggests that such renewal is also founded on the abrupt fragmentation and disintegration of the human being. Gothic texts, she argues, undermine any construction of the human subject as 'stable and integral' by offering 'the spectacle of a body metamorphic and undifferentiated'.[32] Presenting violent and often repulsive images of 'gross corporeality',[33] these texts challenge 'the meanings of human identity'[34] by revealing the radical disintegration and fragmentation of the body. In particular, Hurley reads the Gothic 'ruination'[35] of the physical form as a grotesque literary response to the writings of nineteenth-century materialist philosophers, which negated the possibility of human transcendence by reducing all mental and psychological processes to the level of material phenomena. Because, in the context of such philosophy, 'no transcendent meaningfulness anchors the chaotic fluctuability of the material universe', any efforts to 'stabilize the meanings of "human identity"' are merely 'provisional', unsatisfactory measures taken to shore up the integrity of the individual in the face of its impending disintegration.[36] This reduction of the human being to the status of matter is reflected in Gothic texts by the depiction of 'liminal, admixed, nauseating [and] abominable' bodies, which are 'without integrity or stability'.[37] Such bodies are no longer precisely defined beings, but rather 'Thing[s]', 'anomalous entit[ies]' which serve to 'evacuat[e] [...] the "human" of its meaningfulness'[38] and strip it of its identity. They become expressions of 'estrangement',[39] signalling a consciousness which is permanently 'entrapped within a body [...] in danger of becoming-Thing'.[40]

Wolf's text reveals the ambivalence associated with the 'Gothic body' through its exploration of the protagonist's rootedness in her corporeal existence. On the one hand, her sick body, which has been viewed by several critics as a metaphor for the decaying State of the GDR,[41] becomes the site of a productive reworking of the protagonist's identity in the light of the historical events through which she has lived. It enacts a process of transformation, a dynamic overcoming (L, p. 126) of her previous existence, which offers her the chance to live on (L, p. 129) despite the political changes around her. Paradoxically, her experience of physical illness is described as a form of 'Heilung' (L, p. 93); it is shown to be a liberating state in which the mind can pursue the memories which have been hidden as pathogens in the body.[42] The prerequisite for such healing, Wolf suggests, is an 'Entdeckung' (L, p. 93), an experience of psychic revelation which will act as an 'Entgiftung' for her body (L, p. 93). And indeed, the protagonist's illness becomes associated with various instances of 'Erkenntnis' (L, p. 53), 'Einsicht' (L, p. 158), and 'Bloßlegung' (L, p. 137), moments of insight which alter her perception of what lies before her eyes (L, p. 146) and illuminate (L, p. 164) her view of reality. These experiences of enlightenment are apprehended corporeally, as moments of realization which 'grip' the protagonist's heart (L, p. 146), and yet these physical changes also serve to highlight the psychic alteration which the protagonist is undergoing.

At the same time, these discoveries are explicitly linked with images of the ruination or 'Zusammenbruch' (L, p. 127) of the protagonist's body. Wolf's text recalls the Gothic manipulation of the material basis of the human being by depicting the protagonist's body as a kind of prison. Exploiting the double resonance of the title, Leibhaftig, with its connotations of both 'having a body' and 'becoming the prisoner of it',[43] Wolf reveals her protagonist to be trapped inside her corporeal existence and subjected directly to the physiological aftereffects of the German past. Her body at times seems to take on an uncanny life of its own, staging (L, p. 13) its physical symptoms as a means of controlling the protagonist, who is in turn forced to ask, 'was mein Körper mit mir vorhat' (L, p. 132). And while her corporeal sensations assume the function of communicating enigmatic messages to the protagonist (L, p. 133), she is often revealed to be entirely at the mercy of her body, which appears to be turning against her ('Ob er sich gegen mich auflehnt' — L, p. 132). Her speech organs are overpowered by the violent shivering to which she is subjected (L, p. 80), thus undermining her capacity to talk about the guiles of her body (L, p. 84). As the protagonist increasingly fails to master the pain in her wound (L, p. 80), she begins to realize that she is no longer in control of herself ('es gibt keine Selbstbeherrschung mehr' — L, p. 80). Her 'Seele', her 'Bewußtsein', in its defenceless state (L, p. 137), proves to be involuntarily consigned to the experience of manipulation ('der Manipulation ausgeliefert' — L, p. 137), while her body becomes estranged from her, an alien presence in this 'Zone der dritten Person' (L, p. 66). It becomes an object, 'das Ding' (L, p. 101), which threatens to undermine her ability to act independently and overturn her identity as an autonomous individual.

Ghosts in the Machine

During the course of her illness, Wolf's protagonist becomes alienated from her own body. At times, she describes the existence of 'jemand [...] in mir' (*L*, p. 150), an ulterior being which seems to have taken control of her thoughts and actions, and she seems to be inhabited by an unnameable 'Etwas' (*L*, p. 5), whose foreign presence is felt but not seen. Moreover, the protagonist's relation to herself often assumes an autoscopic perspective, as she comes to observe her body as other. Towards the opening of the tale, for example, she watches as rows of prisoners ('Züge von Gefangenen' — *L*, p. 23) parade past her. These ghostly figures are not described as people, but rather as 'Leiber' (*L*, p. 19), corporeal entities with whom the protagonist is unable to identify. Their presence seems to torture her (*L*, pp. 19–20), as she is unable to comprehend the meaning of such an apparition. As the vision develops, however, the protagonist begins to realize that she is not only being presented with a general portrayal of human suffering, with what she describes as 'das Martyrium und Untergang der Leiber' (*L*, p. 20), but that she is also seeing her own body, 'mein Leib mitten unter ihnen' (*L*, p. 20). The central position of her body in the midst of these figures recalls her role as a medium, whose purpose is to transmit between past and present, self and other; in this case, her body is both a participant in this parade of suffering figures and the stage on which it is taking place. Her revelatory experience is founded upon a crucial moment of recognition, as the protagonist comes to see herself among the strange figures appearing before her. Like the 'fremder Mensch' of Wolf's earlier self (CW XII, 256–57), which is at once unknown and potentially unknowable, the protagonist is confronted with an estranged version of herself, one whose thoughts and motives are apparently inaccessible.

As the narrative of *Leibhaftig* develops, Wolf increasingly adopts vocabulary which implicitly relates the protagonist's self-alienation to the experience of observation and self-observation which she describes both in *Was bleibt* and in the aforementioned interview with Günter Gaus. While the protagonist of that earlier tale becomes the 'Objekt' of a Stasi investigation, thus becoming reified and alienated from herself, here the patient is subjected to the surveillance of the medical team in the hospital, whose constant monitoring of her intimate physical functions transforms her body into an object of inquiry. In particular, she becomes connected to various medical 'Gerät[e]' (*L*, p. 14) and 'Apparate' (*L*, p. 17), which, like the State apparatus in *Was bleibt* (CW X, 264), monitor her most private physical functions and record the signals being emitted by her body. The rays of the hospital scanner ('Strahlen' — *L*, p. 86) in which the protagonist undergoes diagnostic tests are described using similar vocabulary to the laser beams ('Laserstrahl'; 'Strahlungen' — CW X, 264) which are associated with the world of the Stasi in *Was bleibt*. The 'Kabel' (*L*, p. 17) and 'Drähte' connecting the patient to the outside world (L, p. 118) resemble the cables and wires of the Stasi bugging device in the protagonist's central vision (L, pp. 108–09), which in turn recalls the electronic 'Abhörgeräte' with which the Stasi officials monitor the apartment in Wolf's earlier tale (CW x, 231). Above all, the medical controls ('Kontrolle' — L, p. 86) which objectify the patient's body recall the checks and controls carried out on the protagonist's flat in *Was bleibt*, and this parallel is emphasized further by the fact that these health checks initially take place in a 'Haus', a homely space whose 'Steintreppen' and 'abgetretene[s] Linoleum' (L, p. 86) resemble the domestic setting of the surveillance operation in that earlier text.

While the doctors in *Leibhaftig* and the Stasi agents in *Was bleibt* both seek to gain 'wichtige Auskünfte' (L, p. 43) about the respective protagonists, their presence is repeatedly shown to be uncomfortable and intrusive. In the earlier tale, the protagonist resists the gaze of those watching her by hiding behind the curtain at her window (CW x, 225); in *Leibhaftig*, the patient admits her embarrassment at betraying her inner situation and breaking down 'vor aller Augen' (L, 9), and describes her reluctance, 'sich unverhüllt zu zeigen' (L, p. 148). The experience of 'bloßlegen, bloßgestellt werden' (L, p. 137) — where the shift to the passive implies a relinquishing of control on the part of the protagonist — is regarded as an invasion of her privacy, a form of exposure which is uncomfortable and somehow indecent. While the Stasi agents in *Was bleibt* gain forced entry to the protagonist's home (CW x, 227), thus invading her private space, the protagonist of *Leibhaftig* complains that 'Der Arzt läßt nicht nach, in sie zu dringen' (L, p. 9). His attempts to probe inside her body and manipulate (L, p. 137) the physical processes taking place deep inside her are shown here to resemble the Stasi agents' attempts to invade the life of the protagonist of *Was bleibt* and take control of her thoughts and feelings. Both parties are experienced as an unwanted presence, disrupting the integrity of the respective protagonists and challenging their ability to assert their own subjecthood. The observers' desire to gain complete mastery over those in their control undermines the protagonists' potential for autonomous action, transforming them instead into lifeless objects.

Such objectification appears to be related to the impersonal methods of surveillance and data collection adopted by the respective observers. The protagonist of *Was bleibt* is struck by the sense that she is closer to the Stasi agent than his own wife (CW x, 229); and yet the familiarity of their relationship is countered by her realization that he is only interested in recording banal details from her life (CW x, 234). Similarly, the narrator of *Leibhaftig* emphasizes this blend of intimacy and banality in her description of 'die Intimität der Situation, die durch ein ausgeklügeltes Ritual versachlicht wird' (L, p. 137). Like the prosaic manner in which personal information is collected and recorded by the Stasi, the doctors' access to the patient's inner life is rendered mundane by means of an elaborate ritual. While the Stasi report, which purports to capture an objective record of human life, risks overlooking the subjective dimension of experience, so too is the doctors' observation 'versachlicht' (L, p. 137); it focuses on recording quantifiable, physical details to the detriment of the protagonist's innermost feelings. Wolf's use of this term might allude to the technique of 'Versachlichung' which was adopted by the Stasi as a means of objectifying the people whom they were observing. As Christian Bergmann writes, this linguistic process 'vollzieht sich dadurch, dass mit einem etwas Gegenständliches oder Abstraktes bezeichnenden Substantiv eine Person benannt wird oder dass eine Personenbezeichnung als Kontextpartner eines Verbs auftritt, das in der Regel Sachbezeichnungen an sich bindet'.[44] People under observation were, for example, described as '*Objekt*[e]' and '*Quelle*[n]', or in bureaucratic terms as '*angefallene* Personen'.[45] This technique, Bergmann argues, betrayed a mindset, particularly common in totalitarian regimes, in which 'die Individualität der Persönlichkeit mit dem Status eines Objekts gleichgesetzt wird'.[46] Based on an overriding principle of dehumanization, it sought to repress any expression of individuality and cultivate an attitude of total conformity towards the regime.

In Wolf's case, this principle of dehumanization emerges primarily through her preoccupation with the fluctuating boundary between the animate and the inanimate. On the one hand, she reveals the doctors in the hospital to be depersonalized by the monstrous machines which they operate. At two points in *Leibhaftig*, the protagonist is sent down to the basement of the hospital, to an underworld (L, p. 38) reminiscent of the 'Untergrund' (CW x, 240) inhabited by the Stasi officials in *Was bleibt*. Here she is placed inside an MRI scanner, a 'große Machine' or 'Übermonster' (L, p. 40), whose purpose is to gather details about her illness, which it then translates into a 'grünflimmernde Grafik auf dem Bildschirm' for the doctors to read (L, p. 47). From her position inside this machine, the protagonist is shown to be separated from the medical personnel by a glass screen, a 'dicke Glasscheibe' (L, p. 43), which enables her to be surveyed from a distance. Like the glass window in *Was bleibt*, which separates the central figure from the Stasi agents (CW x, 224), this screen is not fully transparent; it reveals the world beyond ('jenseits' — L, p. 43; CW x, 225) to be an unknown realm, a 'dunkle[r] Raum' (L, p. 43) whose inhabitants can never be seen clearly. Because of the opacity of this window, the voice of the radiographer becomes increasingly impersonal (L, p. 43). Transmitted by the speakers inside the scanner (L, p. 43), this disembodied voice appears to stem from the machine itself, becoming a 'leicht verzerrte technische Stimme' (L, p. 44), whose mechanical quality renders it inseparable from the apparatus as a whole. Like the 'Institution' of the State in *Was bleibt* (CW x, 232), whose agents are machine-like and inhuman, the hospital here is characterized by medical workers who assume the features of the equipment in their control.

On the other hand, Wolf reveals the way in which these medical devices also serve to dehumanize the protagonist, as she is increasingly subjected to their invasive procedures. Under this observation, she is obliged to conform to the expectations of the medical personnel (*L*, p. 43), whose control she experiences as a form of 'Ausgesetztsein' (*L*, p. 48). While the protagonist initially tries to resist their commands, stealing a quiet cough when she thinks that they are no longer watching (*L*, p. 44), she soon becomes aware that they miss nothing ('Es entgeht ihnen nichts' — *L*, p. 44). Physically bound to obey their orders (*L*, p. 43) and mentally incapable of offering any resistance (*L*, p. 49), she finds herself beginning to behave as they would wish ('Ich versuche, mich [...] anzupassen' — *L*, p. 44). And as the protagonist increasingly begins to conform to their expectations, she starts to observe herself, censoring her own actions and ultimately ceasing to think for herself (*L*, p. 48). She is subjected, not only to the investigations of the doctors, but also to her own investigation, regarding herself as an object which needs to be governed and held in check. Like the protagonist of *Was bleibt*, whose experience of observation leads to a split in her conception of herself, revealing a potential slippage between victimhood and agency, the central character of *Leibhaftig* is shown to alternate between being a passive object of the doctors' surveillance measures and actively participating in their implementation. She becomes a duplicitous figure, whose acts of conformity are easily transformed into expressions of culpability.

This unstable boundary between victimhood and agency becomes particularly apparent in Wolf's depiction of the machine-like quality of the protagonist's body. As she begins to conform to the expectations of the medical personnel, her physical processes increasingly assume the characteristics of the machine in which she is placed. She finds herself breathing mechanistically ('ganz mechanisch' — *L*, p. 44), adapting the rhythm of her body to that of the scanner (*L*, p. 44) and becoming part of the 'verfluchte Maschine' (*L*, p. 49) which is observing her. Her body is gradually incorporated by the apparatus, adopting its features and thereby becoming increasingly inhuman. At other points in the narrative, Wolf draws on the Hoffmannesque image of the body as an electrical apparatus, describing the protagonist's blood as a current ('Strom' — *L*, p. 97), which is connected to electricity via a pulsating 'Stromnetz' (*L*, p. 97). The 'Netze' and 'Widerstände' (*L*, p. 97) through which the protagonist is driven in her visions suggest a form of electric circuit, which is developed further through her reference to an 'Impuls' which nevertheless lacks the energy to charge it ('der ihn aufladen müßte' — *L*, pp. 7–8). As the protagonist begins to observe herself, so too is her faculty of vision shown to be connected to this electrical apparatus: images are projected onto her retina, her 'Netzhaut' (*L*, p. 106), which is linked to the 'Stromnetz' and 'Netze' inside her body. The sights which she encounters often have the effect of an electric shock (L, p. 98), or form part of a sensory overload which creates a short-circuit, causing the protagonist's visual apparatus to shut down briefly (L, p. 8), and the consequences of this overload sometimes recall the effects of electrocution: at one stage, for example, the protagonist is abruptly propelled upwards ('hochgeschleudert' — L, p. 8) from her semi-conscious state, while at other points these revelations are described as a form of 'Schock' (L, p. 98) which overcomes her body and alters her perception of herself.

As Andrew Webber observes, the image of the body as an electric circuit serves in the tales of E. T. A. Hoffmann 'to galvanize fictional life'.[47] While 'the eye takes on the function of electric contact' and 'will power is manifest as lightning in the eyes', the narrator is able to enliven his fictional subjects by means of 'electric conduction'.[48] 'By operating the right levers', Webber writes, Hoffmann's narrators 'contrive [...] to induce live currents into the narrative machinery and to vivify the automaton'.[49] The electric circuit can be regarded in this context as a metaphor for the way in which Hoffmann's tales breathe life into inanimate characters, lending them the status of the living dead. In Wolf's text, the image of the protagonist's electric body serves to illustrate the writer's capacity to animate the phantoms of her past. Her body becomes an uncanny apparatus through which the return of the repressed is effected, mediating a productive encounter with the past while also subjecting her to its violent after-effects. The mechanistic quality of the protagonist's body reveals her double agency as both observer and observed: on the one hand, she is continuously watched by this monstrous apparatus, which invades her space and records her most intimate physical processes; on the other, she submits herself to this apparatus, providing it with information and ultimately becoming an integral component in its controlling machinery. The legacy of Wolf's ambivalent relationship with the Stasi is therefore revealed to be a ghost in the machine of her protagonist's body, a persistent remainder of her previous actions which is shown to inhabit and govern the mechanical apparatus of her sick frame.

— * —

In his study, *Shifting Perspectives*, Dennis Tate raises the possibility that Wolf's protagonists can be viewed as alter egos of herself, suggesting that their resemblance to the author is tempered by 'a narrative gap' which 'leave[s] open the potential for the kind of "invention in the interests of truth" for which she had pleaded in "Lesen und Schreiben"'.[50] The autoscopic gaze of the patient in *Leibhaftig* can be regarded in this context as an illustration of Wolf's own relation to the project of autobiography. Viewing herself as other, she is able to reflect on her past actions, reanimating the ghosts of her previous selves in order to maintain a living connection to them. Yet this productive form of self-scrutiny is founded on a destructive alienation, which perpetuates the split in the writer's identity and continually estranges her from herself. Recalling the structural logic of her ambiguous relation to the apparatus of the State, it forecloses any possibility of achieving a unified sense of identity, and undermines the possibility, raised in her theoretical writing, of laying the phantoms of the past to rest. The nurse's warning to the protagonist in *Leibhaftig*, 'daß der Lebende nicht in die Augen der Toten blicken soll' (*L*, p. 179), can be read in this light as a self-conscious reflection on the risks posed by Wolf's autopsic examination of her past behaviour. The text's illustration of the seductive attractions of the 'Totenreich' (*L*, p. 179) might allude to Wolf's own reluctance to abandon her attachment to the State which fostered her creative activity, while its suggestion that the individual risks being cast out of the 'Reich der Lebenden' (*L*, p. 179) seems to refer to the author's rejection at the hands of the public following the events of 1989. Above all, the apparent closure offered by the novel's final lines is undermined by an allusion to Ingeborg Bachmann's poem, 'Enigma', which offers a bleak vision of a world in which 'nichts mehr wird kommen' and 'Frühling wird nicht mehr werden'.[51] While the protagonist cannot envisage a future without the insight offered by the ghostly figures of her dreams, so too is Wolf unable to sustain the utopian vision which previously inspired her.

Notes to Chapter 2

1. A similar emphasis on factual reality can be found in Wolf's letter 'An eine Akademie', where she discusses the need to confront the 'wirkliche deutsche Geschichte' and not replace it with a 'Phantom' (CW XII, 317).
2. The destructive potential of Wolf's 'Phantom' also resonates with Nicholas Abraham's description of the phantom, which serves to 'wreak havoc, from within the unconscious, in the coherence of logical progression'. Abraham, 'Notes on the Phantom', p. 175.
3. See, for example, Peter Graves, 'The Treachery of St. Joan: Christa Wolf and the Stasi', in *Christa Wolf in Perspective*, ed. by Wallace, pp. 1–12 (p. 3).
4. See Martin Beyer, *Das System der Verkennung: Christa Wolfs Arbeit am Medea-Mythos*, Epistemata, 590 (Würzburg: Königshausen & Neumann, 2007), pp. 105–09. A discussion of the use of the image in *Leibhaftig* appears later in this chapter.
5. See Boa, 'Christa Wolf: Kindheitsmuster', p. 87.
6. Ernst Bloch, *Das Prinzip Hoffnung*, 3 vols (Berlin: Aufbau, 1954–59), I, 99–101.
7. Anna Kuhn suggests that this fluidity recalls Maxim Gorky's definition of the human subject, which was so influential to Wolf in the writing of *Nachdenken über Christa T.* Anna Kuhn, *Christa Wolf's Utopian Vision: From Marxism to Feminism* (Cambridge: Cambridge University Press, 1988), p. 137.
8. Several critics have commented on Wolf's understanding of memory, and in particular her theory of 'medallions' — the fragments of recollection which require perpetual reinvigoration in order to prevent them from becoming 'fossilized' remains — and its similarity to the writings of Walter Benjamin. See, for example, Felsner, pp. 51–52;

Klaus Schenk, 'Erinnerndes Schreiben: Zur Autobiographik der siebziger Jahren und ihren didaktischen Konsequenzen', in *Gedächtnis und kultureller Wandel: Erinnerndes Schreiben — Perspektiven und Kontroversen*, ed. by Judith Klinger and Gerhard Wolf (Tübingen: Niemeyer, 2009), pp. 19-32 (pp. 28-29); Sabine Wilke, *Ausgraben und Erinnern: Zur Funktion von Geschichte, Subjekt und geschlechtlicher Identität in den Texten Christa Wolfs*, Epistemata, 110 (Würzburg: Königshausen & Neumann, 1993), pp. 40-52.

9. Mattson, p. 98.
10. On the legacy of the *Literaturstreit* and its influence on *Leibhaftig*, see Cooke, '"GDR literature" in the Berlin Republic', pp. 57-58. See also Julia Hell, 'Loyal Dissidents and Stasi Poets: Sascha Anderson, Christa Wolf, and the Incomplete Project of GDR Research', *German Politics and Society*, 20 (2002), 82-118; and Hannes Krauss, 'Was ist geblieben? Rückblicke auf einen (Literatur-)Streit', in *Kulturpolitik und Politik der Kultur: Festschrift für Alexander Stephan*, ed. by Helen Fehervary and Bernd Fischer, German Life and Civilization, 47 (Oxford: Lang, 2007), pp. 175-90.
11. See Baßler et al., p. 11; and Warner, pp. 256-68.
12. This altered experience of time might be regarded in conjunction with the 'gründlich anderes Verhältnis zur Zeit' which Wolf describes in *Was bleibt* (CW x, 233).
13. In *Kindheitsmuster*, however, the figure's name is rendered as 'Liesbeth' (CW v, 122-26).
14. Beatrix Langner, 'Gespenster am Krankenbett. *Leibhaftig*: Christa Wolf lässt die Vergangenheit aufleben', *Neue Zürcher Zeitung*, 23 February 2002.
15. The phrase also suggests a possible reference to the infamous dying words of Goethe, thus linking it with the thread of Faustian references in the novel. For more detailed analyses of Wolf's allusions to Goethe, see Koskinas, pp. 219-20; and Christine Cosentino, '"Aus Teufels Küche": Gedanken zur Teufelsfigur in der Literatur nach 2000: Christoph Heins *Willenbrock*, Christa Wolfs *Leibhaftig* und Monika Marons *Endmoränen*', *Germanic Notes and Reviews*, 35 (2004), 121-27 (pp. 123-24).
16. Frances Guerin, *A Culture of Light: Cinema and Technology in 1920s Germany* (Minneapolis: University of Minnesota Press, 2005), p. 103. A similar point is made by William Paul, who argues that the uncanny quality of cinema rests upon its creation of 'a seeming physical reality contrived from a mere play of light and shadow'. William Paul, 'Uncanny Theatre: The Twin Inheritances of the Movies', *Paradoxa*, 3 (1997), 322-23 (p. 330).
17. Linda Rugg, *Picturing Ourselves: Photography and Autobiography* (Chicago: University of Chicago Press, 1997), p. 201.
18. Ibid., p. 214.
19. Ibid.
20. Ibid., p. 202.
21. As Friedrich Kittler observes, the montage effect of silent film can have a destructive impact on the observer, who becomes alienated through the flood of optical images: 'An die Stelle reflexiver Hinterfragungen treten neurologisch reine Datenflüsse, die immer schon Netzhautfilm sind. Zur Allmacht gelangte optische Halluzinationen können einen Körper überschwemmen, lostrennen und schließlich zum Anderen machen'. Friedrich Kittler, *Grammophon Film Typewriter* (Berlin: Brinkmann & Bose, 1986), p. 245.
22. Cheryl Dueck highlights the mythical resonance of this passage, arguing that the protagonist's internal landscape, with its 'Fluß' and 'Höhle', bears much resemblance to the Greek underworld. Cheryl Dueck, *Rifts in Time and in the Self: The Female Subject in Two Generations of East German Women Writers*, Amsterdamer Publikationen zur

Sprache und Literatur, 154 (Amsterdam: Rodopi, 2004), p. 162. Dennis Tate suggests that the references to the underworld in *Leibhaftig* can be understood as an allusion to the late work of Franz Fühmann, who is also evoked in the text as the 'Freund' (*L*, p. 23) who failed to survive a similar illness to the one experienced by the protagonist. Tate, *Shifting Perspectives*, pp. 234-35.
23. On Cartesian dualism, see John Cottingham, 'Cartesian Dualism: Theology, Metaphysics and Science', in *The Cambridge Companion to Descartes*, ed. by John Cottingham (Cambridge: Cambridge University Press, 1992), pp. 236-57.
24. The notion of psychosomatic illness has been a recurrent theme in Wolf's writing since the 1980s. See in particular her essays, 'Krankheit und Liebesentzug: Fragen an die psychosomatische Medizin' (CW VIII, 410-33) and 'Krebs und Gesellschaft' (CW XII, 326-51).
25. The intertwining of physical and mental processes can be read as a further continuation of the study of memory introduced in *Kindheitsmuster*. There, the function of memory is described as 'bioelektrische Vorgänge zwischen den Zellen' combined with 'eine Angelegenheit der Chemie', 'Gedächtnismoleküle' (CW V, 74-75). The images which are preserved in the brain are therefore inseparable from the physical processes which create and store them.
26. Kelly Hurley, *The Gothic Body: Sexuality, Materialism, and Degeneration at the fin de siècle*, Cambridge Studies in Nineteenth-Century Literature and Culture, 8 (Cambridge: Cambridge University Press, 1996), pp. 4-6.
27. Ibid., pp. 6-7.
28. Ibid., p. 5.
29. Ibid. p. 4.
30. Ibid.
31. Ibid., p. 20.
32. Ibid., p. 3.
33. Ibid.
34. Ibid., p. 8.
35. Ibid., p. 3.
36. Ibid., p. 9.
37. Ibid.
38. Ibid., p. 29.
39. Ibid., p. 19.
40. Ibid., p. 32.
41. See Dueck, pp. 160-61; Hell, p. 88; Martina Caspari, 'Im Kern die Krisis: Schuld, Trauer und Neuanfang in Christa Wolfs Erzählung *Leibhaftig*', *Weimarer Beitrage*, 49 (2003), 135-38 (pp. 136-37); and Charity Scribner, 'Von *Leibhaftig* aus zurückblicken: Verleugnung als Trope in Christa Wolfs Schreiben', *Weimarer Beiträge*, 50 (2004), 212-26. Carol Costabile-Heming suggests that Wolf's use of illness as a metaphor in *Leibhaftig* moves beyond the context of the GDR, forming part of her broader exploration of her role as a writer. Carol Costabile-Heming, 'Illness as Metaphor: Christa Wolf, the GDR, and Beyond', *Symposium*, 64 (2010), 202-19 (pp. 212-17).
42. Astrid Köhler reads this sentence in conjunction with the depiction of physical and psychological healing found in Wolf's earlier novel, *Der geteilte Himmel*. Both Rita and the protagonist of *Leibhaftig*, she argues, need to alter their utopian thinking in order to overcome their illness. Köhler, *Brückenschläge*, pp. 38-46.
43. For a more detailed analysis of the range of meanings evoked by the title of the *Erzählung*, see Rolf Michaelis, 'Krankengeschichten. Heilgeschichten. Wenn der (Staats-)Körper leidet: Christa Wolfs Erzählung *Leibhaftig*', *Die Zeit*, 28 February 2002.

44. Christian Bergmann, *Die Sprache der Stasi: Ein Beitrag zur Sprachkritik* (Göttingen: Vandenhoeck & Ruprecht, 1999), p. 24.
45. Ibid., p. 24.
46. Ibid., p. 25.
47. Andrew J. Webber, *The Doppelgänger: Double Visions in German Literature* (Oxford: Clarendon, 1999), p. 155.
48. Ibid.
49. Ibid.
50. Tate, *Shifting Perspectives*, p. 209.
51. Ingeborg Bachmann, *Werke*, ed. by Christine Koschel, Inge von Weidenbaum, and Clemens Münster, 4 vols (Munich: Piper, 1978), I, 171.

CHAPTER 3

~

Spectral Images: Irina Liebmann's *Stille Mitte von Berlin*

The previous two chapters have highlighted the way in which the imagery of ghostliness is used in Wolf's work as part of a self-conscious reflection on the mediation of memory and experience. By examining the way in which the texts depict the human body and its interaction with various forms of technological apparatus, they show how the spectral phenomena in these works create a slippage between the animate and the inanimate, revealing the individual to be at risk of becoming dehumanized through her encounter with the ghostly figures which she invokes. This chapter focuses on another example of technological mediation in its analysis of the photographs published in Liebmann's documentary volume, *Stille Mitte von Berlin*. It suggests that her recourse to the photographic medium is highly productive, since it enables her to view the city and its history in a different light; its ability to arrest the passage of time and estrange the scenes depicted ruptures established historical narratives and enables new connections to be perceived between past, present, and future. However, this positive alienation, recalling what Walter Benjamin describes as the revolutionary potential of the photograph, is shown to rest on a destructive principle, which threatens to shatter these arrested moments even as it seeks to salvage them. Liebmann's project attempts on the one hand to engage productively with the loss and destruction associated with German history, mediating repressed memories and uncovering traces of the city's past, but her photographs often block such efforts, refusing the work of mourning and foreclosing the possibility of progress.

The medium of photography has had a close relationship with the ghostly since its inception in the nineteenth century. While the camera was developed primarily as a rational tool to be used for scientific inquiry into the visible world, its capacity to conjure up unexpected apparitions and shadows soon became evident.[1] Often these apparitions were unintentional, created as the result of accidents or errors made in the photographic process. The long exposure times required by early cameras meant that anyone who moved in and out of the shot while only a portion of the exposure was completed would feature as a blurry silhouette. Moreover, various blunders in the process of developing and printing the photographs could create a series of unfocused forms, marks, and superimpositions which would appear on the image. To the untrained eye, however, such apparitions could seem enigmatic and 'suggestively supernatural'.[2] These two characteristics of photography, its rationality and its ability to invoke apparitions, merged in the genre of spirit photography, which sought to harness the perceived technical precision and scientific accuracy of the camera to the supernatural belief in spirits. Photography, with its apparent ability to create spirits, was used here as a means of proving their existence.[3] The lens of the camera came to be viewed as an artificial eye with the uncanny ability to perceive spirit forms invisible to unaided human perception; yet at the same time, it also seemed to play a role in the creation of these ghostly figures, whose existence was considered to depend upon the very technology of the medium.

This apparent erasure of the distinction between photography and spirit as medium and subject matter has been echoed in several canonical theories of photography. Rather than being seen as distinct entities, photography and spirit are treated as analogous and interdependent. Walter Benjamin, for example, likens the camera to a spirit medium in its ability to render visible scenes from the 'Optisch-Unbewußte[s]' (WB II.1, 371), that inner repository of images which are invisible to the unaided human senses. More recently, Roland Barthes adopts the language and imagery of spirit photography in his study *Camera Lucida*, where he comes to view the photograph as a 'ghost', as 'the ectoplasm of "what-had-been"'.[4] As in spirit photography, which was understood to create a record of the material manifestation of the dead, so too does Barthes see the photograph as a literal 'emanation of the referent' possessing a powerful physical connection to the subject before the camera.[5] The photograph is understood as bearing a direct, albeit mystical relation to reality; it is seen as 'a *magic*, not an art',[6] enabling some real trace of the photographic subject to reach the viewer, even if this process involves crossing different temporal and spatial boundaries.[7] For both Barthes and the earlier spirit photographers, this direct connection of the photograph to the 'what has been' lends it a particular ambivalence with regard to the passage of time. The photograph is caught between the desire to evoke the dead in order to facilitate the process of mourning, and the creation of a melancholic attachment to them; it is caught between the desire to conjure up what no longer exists in order to take leave of it, and the wish to remain emotionally invested in it. Above all, the photograph freezes its image, suspending it as a perpetual moment of life and foreclosing any attempt to release oneself from its hold.

Liebmann's documentary volume resonates with many of the questions raised by the legacy of spirit photography, particularly as expressed by Benjamin and Barthes. Taken in the 1980s, as an aide-memoire for her project on the history of this former Jewish quarter, the photographs depict the empty streets and neglected *Mietshäuser* around the Große Hamburger Straße in East Berlin. Many of these buildings bear visible reminders of the city's heterogeneous past: the signs of shops which no longer exist, for example, can still be seen, along with bullet holes in the brick work and the occasional Star of David in stairwells and on the entrances to buildings (SM, p. 6). The reflective essay which precedes these images seeks to uncover the little-known history of this area of Berlin through a wide range of sources, including photographs, interviews, and old town records. On the one hand, Liebmann repeatedly stresses the documentary nature of her photographic work, privileging its status as an authentic record of a particular historical moment, and emphasizing its ability to present a 'realistisches Bild' of the city.[8] She conceives of her photographs in factual terms, as 'Material' for her project (SM, p. 5), and values their ability to capture the appearance of the area as it was at the time of her research (SM, p. 61). On the other hand, however, Liebmann also reveals her desire to uncover various forms of 'Erinnerungslücken', gaps both in the official historiographical narratives of the GDR and in the personal memories of the people she meets, and to reveal what has been 'vergessen, vermieden oder sogar verboten' (SM, p. 6). In this respect, her photographs assume another, more uncanny function: that of revealing elements of the past which usually remain invisible. These images serve to mediate between the past and the present, and in doing so, they establish a particular connection to aspects of history which have been lost or erased from individual and collective memory. And they document the involuntary side-effects of her historical work, revealing the ghostly as that which emerges in the wake of her project of enlightenment.

'Allgemeiner Stillstand'

The front cover of the 2002 edition of Liebmann's volume bears a photograph of the historic *Postfuhramt* in Berlin's Oranienburger Straße (Figure 3.1).[9] The image is of poor quality, with faded colours and a slight blurring of the focus, which heightens the air of austerity and neglect conveyed by the scene. The perspective of the photograph, taken from an upper storey window on the opposite side of the street, overemphasizes the size of the buildings and correspondingly dwarfs the few pedestrians who populate the street, creating an impression of lifelessness which is characteristic of the collection as a whole. While the street itself is virtually empty, the few figures which do appear are rendered small and insignificant in the context of their surroundings. And

Fig. 3.1. Postfuhramt an der Oranienburger Straße, Ecke Tucholskystraße (1984)
© bpk — Bildagentur für Kunst, Kultur und Geschichte/Irina Liebmann

these surroundings are characterized by dilapidated architectural structures, marked by eroding stonework, boarded-up shop fronts and blind windows. In this respect, the photograph can be read as a programmatic illustration of Liebmann's project: documenting the way in which traces of the past are preserved on buildings and landscapes, it reveals the way in which remnants of Berlin's turbulent history continue to haunt the topography of the city, competing with each other for memory space in the face of imminent obliteration. At the same time, it alerts us to the existence of those memories which have not found expression, those historical experiences which have been silenced by a form of collective amnesia.

Liebmann's photograph is characteristic of her project as a whole, since it simultaneously comments on three different historical eras: the late nineteenth- and early twentieth-century history of the area, the time when the photographs were taken in the 1980s, and the early years of the twenty-first century, when the volume was assembled and published. As the once imposing nineteenth-century building suggests, the overt concern of the project is the pre-GDR history of this part of Berlin. The *Postfuhramt* dates back to the Age of Bismarck; completed in 1881, its ornate façades recall the self-confidence of the former imperial capital, while the decorative putti on the panels around the windows, reminiscent of the Italian Renaissance, lend the architecture an air of exoticism which is out of keeping with the unadorned style of the buildings opposite.[10] Significantly, the *Postfuhramt* has been described as the architectural partner of the *Neue Synagoge*, situated a little way down the same street, because their façades are built in the same style, with characteristic orange and yellow brickwork and tall, rounded archways, and because both buildings were originally crowned by a similar dome-like construction.[11] However, the two met quite different fates in the National Socialist period. Despite sustaining some war damage, the *Postfuhramt* was used by the East German postal service until 1973, whereas the *Neue Synagoge* was subjected to an arson attack in the November pogrom of 1938 and was then badly destroyed by air raids. By focusing on the intact, though dilapidated state of the *Postfuhramt*, Liebmann's photograph calls to mind the history of this other building; through the presence of the postal offices, it indirectly focuses our attention on the absence of the synagogue. Exploiting what Barthes describes as the unity between the photograph and the referent, the particular guarantee 'that what I see has indeed existed',[12] Liebmann paradoxically makes us aware of that which we do not see, the original form of the Synagogue which has been irrevocably lost. In doing so, she introduces an aesthetic which operates throughout her project. She explores the links between the positive image of Berlin, which the grandeur of such buildings suggests, and the darker side of this history, thus exposing the undercurrents of violence and loss which exist beneath the surface of the city.[13] Viewed in this light, the evacuated scenes of Liebmann's photographs repeatedly exploit the tension between presence and absence, thus obliquely focusing awareness on what is not there, on what has been permanently excluded from the image.

In addition to this concern for pre-GDR history, Liebmann's photographic study also exposes and criticizes elements of the GDR of the 1980s. While the image of the *Postfuhramt* might recall its former grandeur, when the photograph was actually taken it was in a state of disrepair, and the houses on the opposite corner of the street have been rendered almost uninhabitable through neglect. In her accompanying essay, Liebmann criticizes the poor living conditions faced by tenants of these houses, caused, she suggests, by shortages of money and building materials, and by the government's preferred policy of building new living quarters in the outskirts of the city rather than renovating these so-called 'Altbaugebiete' (*SM*, p. 11). In addition, she highlights an 'allgemeine[r] Stillstand', which she regards as characteristic of the GDR of the late 1980s (*SM*, p. 10), and which is evoked in the cover photograph: the street is marked by stasis, and the few human figures in the scene are halted, their movements suspended. The potential of the photographic medium to create 'the stasis of an *arrest*'[14] is used here to generate a sense of lifelessness, a despondency which might be seen to anticipate the demise of the GDR.

Finally, the very fact that we can read this demise into Liebmann's photograph lends it a further historical dimension. Her project was published after the *Wende*, in the context of the revival of *Mitte* as a fashionable neighbourhood, and this situates it among the various post-reunification debates about the memorialization of the GDR.[15] Her photograph of the *Postfuhramt* therefore resonates with what we know about the area today: the building has now been restored and houses art exhibitions,[16] while the neighbouring Synagogue has been rebuilt. The contrast between the Oranienburger Straße of the early twenty-first century, which is 'bunt, glänzend und voller Leben' (*SM*, p. 61), and its 'verwahrloste[r] Zustand' (*SM*, p. 11) of the 1980s raises questions about Berlin's relationship to its past: to what extent has this regeneration been shaped by what Brian Ladd describes as a 'destruction that is supposed to bring renewal'?[17] To what extent is this apparent revival of the area still haunted by the ghosts of the city's less attractive past? And to what extent is Berlin 'caught in a struggle between [...] forgetting, on the one hand, and preservation [...], on the other'?[18] Liebmann's condemnation of the way in which the established narratives of the GDR concealed certain aspects of Berlin's history can be read in this context as an indirect criticism of the way in which the trend of silencing has continued following the *Wende* with regard to elements of the GDR past.

Liebmann's exploitation of the ability of the photographic image to mediate between these different historical eras lends her work an uncanny dimension, since, in a single frame, we are presented with the convergence of past, present, and future. Recalling Benjamin's notion of the image world as a place in every photograph which encapsulates not only the character of a past moment, but also the future (WB II.1, 368–85), Liebmann's work seeks to utilize this potential in order to open up realms of possibility, leading us to consider what might have been and what might still be. Such a dynamic sometimes has positive overtones for Liebmann, who delights in focusing on the productive potential of ambiguities and creating suggestive allusions in her work. The ruined *Kolonistenhaus* in the Sophienstraße (Figure 3.2; *SM*, p. 97), for example, can either be viewed negatively as a figure of destruction, a 'cemetery of its own past',[19] or more positively as a space of potential, whose rubble resembles that of a building site, anticipating future construction. The image of a tree growing up out of the ruins seems to emphasize this positive view, suggesting that life can still flourish despite the chaos around it. Furthermore, Liebmann's photograph contrasts the rubble in the foreground with the image of an intact house behind it, whose status is once again ambiguous. Is this building too, like the *Kolonistenhaus*, destined to become rubble? Or are the remains in the foreground due to be restored to the state of this building behind? Significantly, the windows of this *Mietshaus* reflect the sky and the leaves of the tree, thus creating an apparently utopian prospect which opens up a new perspective

Fig. 3.2. Abriss des Kolonistenhauses in der Sophienstraße (1984)
© bpk — Bildagentur für Kunst, Kultur und Geschichte/Irina Liebmann

on the scene. This slippage between transparency and reflectivity enables Liebmann to depict the scene differently, to reveal the conditional, the image which might occur if reality were otherwise. Like the ghostly figures in her novels, which reveal the counterfactual possibilities inherent in the passage of time, so too do these photographs open up an alternative realm in which the inevitability of historical events can be called into question.

At other times, the temporal ambiguity of Liebmann's photographs assumes a darker tone, recalling what Roland Barthes describes as the camera's ability to reveal an 'anterior future'. Discussing a photograph by Alexander Gardner of the prisoner Lewis Payne waiting in his cell, shortly before his execution, Barthes is struck by the fact that the young man 'is going to die'. As a result, he claims, 'I read at the same time: *This will be* and *this has been*; I observe with horror an anterior future of which death is the stake'.[20] The photograph reveals both the past, the *'this has been'*, and the future, the *'this will be'*, of its subject. Yet, for Barthes, both of these revelations are bound up with death, since the execution of the man is imminent: 'By giving me the absolute past of the pose (aorist), the photograph tells me death in the future'.[21] Barthes then goes on to suggest that this logic operates in every photograph, regardless of whether or not the subject is already dead: historical photographs, he argues, are always

Fig. 3.3. Große Hamburger Straße mit Pfütze (1984)
© bpk — Bildagentur für Kunst, Kultur und Geschichte/Irina Liebmann

governed by a 'defeat of Time', a realization that '*that* is dead' and that '*that* is going to die'. This 'vertigo of time defeated'[22] can even be experienced in photographs where there is no human subject featured: in this case, the places depicted seem to evoke not only their own history, but also their potential alteration or destruction.

Liebmann's project transposes this notion of the 'future anterior' onto the scarred cityscape of Berlin: her photographs work to expose 'the place that is' along with 'the place that has been' and 'the place that will be'. This is strikingly apparent in her picture of the Große Hamburger Straße at its intersection with the Oranienburger Straße (Figure 3.3; *SM*, p. 78). Once again, the houses here are shabby, and a pile of rubble can be seen at the edge of the road. The colours are drab; the brightest thing in the picture is the yellow paintwork of one of the cars, and yet even this is dulled. The hunched shoulders of the pedestrians suggest an air of care-worn inertia, which resonates with Liebmann's description of the tired state of the GDR in the 1980s. At the centre of the image is a large puddle, which functions as a kind of mirror: reflected in it, the houses assume a brighter colour and their decaying condition is masked. The reflection offers another perspective on the reality of the scene: the present is transcended momentarily, and the image is opened up to the possibility of change. Not only does this mirroring suggest the former state of the buildings shown, it also points to their possible renovation in the future. However, the heap of rubble standing alongside this serves as a reminder of the fragility of this vision; it implies that the regeneration of the city is undermined by the threat that it could, at any instant, dissolve into rubble or ruin. Liebmann thereby shifts Barthes's description of the connection between photography and death onto the places which she captures: for her, the future depicted by the photograph is permanently overshadowed by the threat of 'Zerstörung' (SM, p. 5). The Berlin which features in her photographs therefore appears as a haunting ground, shadowed by the ghosts of past violence yet also anticipating the spectre of its future destruction.

'Dialektik im Stillstand'

Liebmann's exploitation of the potential of the photographic medium to create an 'allgemeine[r] Stillstand' serves to highlight the uncanny confluence of these different historical eras. The single instant at which the photograph was taken is captured and stilled, thereby rendering visible the various temporal axes which converge in it. The revelatory dimension of this moment of arrest might recall what Walter Benjamin terms 'Dialektik im Stillstand' (WB v.1, 578). In a fragment from his *Passagenwerk*, Benjamin describes the explosive collision which occurs when the past meets the present:

> Nicht so ist es, daß das Vergangene sein Licht auf das Gegenwärtige oder das Gegenwärtige sein Licht auf das Vergangne [sic] wirft, sondern Bild ist dasjenige, worin das Gewesene mit dem Jetzt blitzhaft zu einer Konstellation zusammentritt. Mit andern Worten: Bild ist die Dialektik im Stillstand. (WB v.1, 578)

The relationship between past and present is, he argues, essentially a dialectical one, and their collision in a single image is highly revealing: the past ('das Gewesene') sheds light on the present ('das Jetzt'), just as the present provides an understanding of the past. What is particularly important for Benjamin is the tempo at which such a constellation occurs. Although the convergence of the past and the present is 'blitzhaft', an adjective which might evoke the brief yet explosive flash of the camera, it is nevertheless brought to a standstill in the image. Like the arrested movement implied by Freud's definition of the uncanny as 'etwas, was [...] hervorgetreten ist' (SF IV, 264), this brief moment of stasis enables existing temporal relations to be reconfigured and consequently viewed in a new light.

According to Benjamin, such images offer the only possible means of capturing history (WB I.3, 1247). Past historical moments prove to be transitory, and yet their expression in stilled images enables them to create a lasting impression upon the observer. Although the past can never be 'brought back' in precisely the same way that it was experienced, such fleeting glimpses can enable certain aspects of it to be identified and preserved. For Liebmann, too, one of the main concerns of the historian is how to capture these short-lived encounters with the past. Her volume contains repeated references to the suddenness of these confrontations. Phrases such as 'mit einem Schlag', 'unerwartet', 'neu', and 'nun' create a sense of urgency, and yet she also emphasizes the need to maintain a continuing 'Verbindung' to the past (SM, p. 6), to grasp its consequences and ensure that they remain 'spürbar' (SM, p. 5). The potential of historical events to irrupt into the present is captured in the simile of ink penetrating a piece of blotting paper: 'Sind wir im Krieg [...]? Nein, aber wie ein Tintenfleck durch ein Löschblatt dringt die Vergangenheit' (SM, p. 27). Although the original writing is covered up by the blotting paper, its ink creates a stain; the past is thus shown to leave a haunting trace which interrupts the present. The ink stain functions as a transitional object between text and image, revealing the way in which the past and present converge in a visual mark which has the potential to override the written word. Such traces can be disturbing, since they present a different view of the past from that which we are used to seeing, and yet they also possess a more positive quality, enabling us to alter the way in which we perceive the connections between past and present and thereby change our understanding of historical circumstances.

The revolutionary potential of Benjamin's 'Dialektik im Stillstand' resides in the juxtaposition of images from different historical eras, which enables their underlying dialectical structures to be exposed.[23] It is only by bringing to consciousness the relationship between the different elements in an image that the individual can become aware of the true condition of his own time and be inspired to change this for the better. At the same time, however, the concept is characterized by ambivalence, since its revolutionary force is dependent on a destructive impulse. As Michael Jennings explains: 'Certain past moments can be "saved", liberated from the burial ground of history, but only through a double movement that destroys as it redeems them'.[24] The redemption of those images which might have a positive effect on the present can only occur through the 'mortification' of the cultural object, through the act of arresting or fragmenting it. The stilled image assumes emblematic status as a historical remainder which has resisted the destruction wrought by passage of time; yet this status is founded on its extrapolation from its original context and its preservation as a frozen, reified object. The photographic medium can be seen in this context to possess a revelatory power, a capacity to invoke what Benjamin terms 'die Erhellung des Details' (WB II.1, 379), to liberate individual moments and isolated minutiae from the whole and enable them to be perceived in a new light. This focus on fragments and details brings about the 'Beschriftung' or 'Literarisierung' of the image (WB II.1, 385), a literary or semiological inscription which enables the viewer to gain access 'zu einer Bedeutung jenseits von Bewußtsein oder Absicht'.[25] At the same time, however, it risks being transformed into a 'Hölle des Details' (WB II.3, 1136), a moment in which the visibility of hidden image-worlds becomes opaque and illegible. Resisting interpretation and narrativization, these details serve as persistent remainders of a history which cannot be fully apprehended.

This ambivalent relation to detail chimes with the fragmented structure of Liebmann's volume. Her photographs often focus on parts of buildings and disconnected details, leaving the reader to negotiate a path through them, comparing certain details and making his/her own links between them. One photograph of a structure on the Große Hamburger Straße (Figure 3.4; *SM*, p. 74), for example, depicts a section of a building, part of which is covered by scaffolding and a builder's placard, a detail which immediately points to the decaying state of the structure. The building itself is presented as a part whose whole is not shown, and it is in turn made up of a series of isolated details, whose significance in the picture is unclear and must be deduced through implied connections to other photographs. One of the window frames, for example, is supported by a stone pillar, topped by an ornamental filial decorated with a leaf-like pattern. In itself, this detail is unremarkable, if slightly out of keeping with the plain style of the rest of the building. Yet in the context of the other photographs, the decoration can be linked to the highly adorned architecture of some of the grander nineteenth-century structures which Liebmann portrays, such as the *S-Bahnhof Marx-Engels-Platz* (SM, p. 110) and the aforementioned *Postfuhramt* (SM, p. 112). Such a connection links this building, presumably a private house, with the more public history of these other edifices, thus exemplifying Liebmann's assertion that it is necessary to delve beneath what is officially known or acknowledged about the past.

In a similar vein, the wall of this building on the Große Hamburger Straße is marked by a curious circular shape, where the brickwork is lighter than that which surrounds it. In the centre of this circle is a square shape, lighter again, which looks as though it has once had a window in it. The shapes of this detail are inversely reflected in the manhole cover in the street below, which takes the form of a circle inside a square. These forms gain significance when they are considered in conjunction with the picture of the *Hofsynagoge* in the Brunnenstraße (Figure 3.5; *SM*, p. 94), which shows the remains of a former synagogue destroyed in the November pogroms of 1938 and used in the GDR by neighbouring businesses for storage.[26] At the top of the building, three large, circular holes are visible, framed by square shapes formed by the brickwork and the ivy which is climbing over the building. Moreover, since the restoration of part of the building in 2002, it is now possible to see that these circular windows

Fig. 3.4. Große Hamburger Straße (c. 1984)
© Berlin Verlag/Irina Liebmann

originally contained square, wooden frames. Viewed in this context, the figuring of these shapes in the building on the Große Hamburger Straße, along with their inversion in the manhole cover, might evoke the history of this other building; it recalls both the run-down state of the *Hofsynagoge*, along with the shadow of its past and future states. The connection encourages the viewer to think otherwise about these images, to be alert to the speculative and indirect links which emerge between them.

Liebmann's photographs thereby resist the imposition of a coherent narrative linking them through a consideration of historical cause and effect. Instead, the viewer is left to negotiate his/her way through them, concentrating on isolated details and allowing these to determine his/her overall encounter with the images. The montage form of the accompanying essay adopts a similar logic. At first sight, the essay appears to be an attempt to weave the various historical sources together, shaping them into a coherent order. However, the form of the text soon undermines this. Liebmann highlights the diverse sources in her essay by adopting different typographical conventions when citing them: extracts from her own diary entries are printed in italics (*SM*, p. 14), as are quotations from newspapers and records of her conversations with the inhabitants of the houses, while passages from encyclopaedias are printed in a smaller font

Fig. 3.5. Hofsynagoge in der Brunnenstraße (c. 1984)
© Berlin Verlag/Irina Liebmann

which is indented on the page. The use of these visual markers is, however, not always consistent. When discussing the responses of the inhabitants to her questions, some are placed in italics, while others, such as the phrases 'Ja, waren Juden' and 'Solche Leute waren auf einmal weg' (SM, p. 17), remain in Roman type.[27] Similarly, some of these responses are rendered in their own idiom, with Liebmann reproducing the characteristic features of the Berlin dialect, while others are quoted in a more standard form of German. While these inconsistencies highlight the diversity of the people and wealth of sources with which Liebmann engages in her study, they also appear to undermine the coherence of her essay, revealing its narrative to be a construct and drawing attention to its montage form.

This implicit questioning of the project's continuity becomes all the more apparent in the relationship between the essay and Liebmann's photographs. At first sight, there appears to be a complete separation between these two aspects of the volume: the essay occupies the first half while the photographs are placed together in the second, and there are two blank pages marking the division between the sections. Liebmann nevertheless sets up various cross-references between the images and her text. In her discussion of the photograph of a shop on the Große Hamburger Straße (SM, pp. 7, 67), for example, she recalls being captivated by the 'schöne Schrift' above the entrance. This 'Schrift' can be seen on the photograph, and is alluded to on a typographical level in the essay, as Liebmann cites the shop sign, 'GEMÜSE KONSERVEN KARTOFFELN' (*SM*, p. 7). Yet often such links prove to be misleading, as Liebmann describes photographs which are not to be found in the volume (*SM*, p. 7), and includes images in her collection which possess no corresponding descriptions in her essay. In particular, the technique of reproducing the font of the signs found in the pictures is sometimes deployed even when there is no photographic referent: thus the references to the 'CAFÉ EDWIN' (*SM*, p. 7) and to the '**Franz Pretzel | Maschinen Treibriemenfabrik**' (*SM*, p. 44) create the illusion of being based on a photographic source, where actually none is to be found.

While Susanne Lenné Jones argues that these inconsistencies 'harm her documentary intent, rather than support it',[28] Liebmann's technique of setting up unreliable links between her photographs and her text can be read as part of her desire to shed new light on certain aspects of the past by situating them in a different context. This is particularly apparent at one point in the text, where Liebmann creates a visual connection between the photograph of a poster which invokes the spectre of Marx through its motto, 'Im Karl Marx Jahr 1983: Jeder jeden Tag eine gute Tat für den Frieden!' (Figure 3.6; *SM*, p. 106), and the newspaper headlines from September 1983 which Liebmann cites in her essay: 'GUTE BILANZEN UND NEUE ZIELE, BEKENNTNISSE, VERPFLICHTUNGEN, WETTBEWERBE ZUR STÄRKUNG DER REPUBLIK' (*SM*, p. 41). These headlines, she suggests, served to mask the lack of reportage about a Korean aeroplane which, in September 1983, was shot down over the sea near the Soviet island of Sakhalin, having allegedly strayed into Soviet airspace. Though the incident was widely discussed in West German media from the outset, it was initially concealed by the GDR authorities; even when reports of the shooting began to emerge three days later, these made no mention of the 269 passengers who were killed in the incident (*SM*, p. 41). For Liebmann, this concealment signals an attempt on the part of the GDR government to disguise the true human cost of the event and ensure that the 'das Objekt sich im Dunkeln verloren hätte' (*SM*, p. 41). And yet, in discussing these headlines, Liebmann uncovers this act of suppression, and by creating a link to them through her photograph, she implicitly raises the question of what else might have been masked by the poster featured in the picture. Such hidden connections can be found repeatedly in Liebmann's work, and yet they are not stated directly. As a result, they rely on a different way of reading, one which pays more attention to images and visual patterns than to the overt content of the text. This technique might recall Benjamin's claim that 'Geschichte zerfällt in Bilder, nicht in Geschichten' (WB v.1, 596); his use of the prefix 'zer' underlines the destructive principle on which this new vision of history rests; it

Fig. 3.6. Rosenthaler Straße, Blick zum Hackeschen Markt (*c.* 1984)
© Berlin Verlag/Irina Liebmann

highlights the fragmentation of conventional narratives and their replacement by discrete images. For Liebmann, too, the revelation of new historical insights shatters the concept of historical progress which was taught her as a schoolgirl in the GDR (*SM*, p. 18). Aspects of the past, she suggests, are compelled to return (*SM*, pp. 5, 61), haunting the present in a ghostly manner and resisting efforts to incorporate them into teleological narratives. In order to acknowledge these spectral traces, we must learn to read between the lines, adopting an alternative form of vision and learning 'zu sehen, was man sieht'.[29]

The Scene of the Crime

Liebmann's emphasis on this altered form of perception forms part of a series of references in her work to the field of forensics. In many respects, the empty street scenes which she captures recall those of Eugène Atget, who between 1897 and 1927 photographed the vacant streets and architecture of Paris. Like Liebmann, Atget purposefully avoids capturing bustling scenes, often taking his photographs early in the morning, and he focuses in particular on doorways, stairwells, and idiosyncratic architectural details on the façades of buildings.

Several commentators have noted that Atget's images recall photographs of a crime scene. In an early printed edition of his photography, for example, the editor Camille Recht likens them to 'eine Polizeiphotographie am Tatort',[30] while Walter Benjamin famously observes: 'Sehr mit Recht hat man von ihm gesagt, daß er sie aufnahm wie einen Tatort' (WB I.2, 485). Through his forensic approach to the city, Atget's photographs appear to contain criminological indices which point to historical acts of violence. And this in turn lends them a particular resemblance to the spirit photograph: the scene of crime emerges as a haunted site, inhabited by the spectres created by past brutality.

Benjamin's discussion examines two main features of Atget's work, arguing that it is these in particular which lend his photography a forensic character. First, the emptiness of the images creates an air of desolation which recalls that of the crime scene; and second, he seems to focus on clues and traces, such that 'seine Aufnahme erfolgt der Indizien wegen' (WB I.2, 485). The photographic images assume the role of 'Beweisstücke im historischen Prozeß' (WB I.2, 485). For Benjamin, the crime is not simply an individual one, but rather, it has a more general character, associated with the passage of time. In this respect, he is developing the implications of an earlier allusion to Atget's photographs from his 'Kleine Geschichte der Photographie', where he suggests that every inch of our cities is a crime scene and every passer-by a culprit (WB II.1, 385). The twentieth century is reconfigured as an age of mass violence and trauma, and the photographer's task, like that of a detective, is to reveal guilt and point out the guilty (WB II.1, 385). Moreover, for Benjamin, Atget's photographs have a hidden political meaning which asserts itself by unsettling the observer and forcing him/her to consider the details before him/her in an alternative light. No longer is (s)he capable of 'freischwebende Kontemplation' (WB I.2, 485). Rather, the photographs produce an inherently political response, precisely because they provoke analysis and interpretation rather than simple aesthetic contemplation.

Towards the outset of her essay, Liebmann links her photographs with the work of a detective by describing a new perspective which she discovered while she was undertaking research for her project: 'Diese Perspektive war neu für mich: Das Leben vom Ende her gesehen, das Drama, die Kriminalgeschichte, berlinisch verkürzt und auf den Punkt gebracht, makaber, aber doch auch amüsant' (*SM*, p. 16). Such a perspective is unsettling for Liebmann. The view of history as a detective story seems to provide a source of entertainment for the people she meets, who revel in its macabre details and unexpected revelations. And yet, for her, this realization has a more serious impact which comes to govern the overall aesthetic of her project: namely, the realization that she needs to view 'das Leben vom Ende her' in order to trace the reasons behind the crimes which have been concealed from memory. This realization introduces to Liebmann's project what Ralph Rugoff terms the 'aesthetic of aftermath'.[31] Images of crime scenes, he argues, always invite the observer to look backwards, to piece together 'a history of prior actions and motivations'.[32] The viewer is encouraged to adopt a forensic approach, scouring the scene for evidence and attempting to reassess or 'interpret the residue of events'.[33] Like the detective story, which adopts retrospective narration because the crime always takes place before the story has begun,[34] the scene of crime is always concerned with the aftermath of an event, with the remainder which is left behind after an act of violence.

Liebmann therefore combines her *flânerie* through the city with the occupation of a detective, recalling Benjamin's assertion that the disconnected details which the *flâneur* pursues inevitably lead to a crime (WB 1.2, 543). She concerns herself above all with conducting a search for traces, the 'Spurensuche' of her volume's subtitle, searching for 'Hinweis[e] auf die Geschichte des Ortes' (*SM*, p. 9). The buildings which she encounters seem to be full of 'rätselhafte Details' (*SM*, p. 8), appearing to her as a 'Nachricht aus einer längst vergangenen Zeit' (*SM*, p. 28), while her task is to look for the 'Verbindungsstück' (*SM*, p. 6) between all these clues, to reveal the secrets (*SM*, p. 8) which they signal. Crucially, the crimes which they indicate are at once general and specific. Liebmann's study concerns itself with the crime of historical repression, with the loss caused by the passing of time and the pain and injustices of a silenced past. More specifically, however, the traces point increasingly to the deportations of the Jews in the Third Reich; they lead Liebmann to focus on the very question which she was seeking to avoid when she began her study (*SM*, pp. 18, 61). In this context, the traces point to human lives which have been lost, functioning as ghostly indicators of the figures that once inhabited this ground.[35] On another level, such clues lead Liebmann towards a consideration of the division of Berlin, to the curtailment of individuals' freedom in the East and the painful separations of families and relationships which occurred as a result (*SM*, p. 22). Many of the buildings which she depicts appear to be cut off in the middle, recalling the houses on the Bernauer Straße which ended in the border, and whose windows were eventually blocked off to prevent people from jumping out in attempts to reach the West (*SM*, pp. 80, 90, 92, 98). Having pieced together these various clues, Liebmann finally acknowledges this double-edged focus of her investigation on the closing page of the study: 'Die Juden — waren sie das Thema der Gegend, hatte ich mich damals gefragt, oder war es der Westen? Die Juden *und* der Westen, denke ich jetzt' (*SM*, p. 61).

This acknowledgement encourages us to read Liebmann's photographs in the light of this 'Kriminalgeschichte' (*SM*, p. 16). The objects which she depicts take on a double identity; they are no longer defined by their 'inherent' characteristics, but depend instead on how they behave with regard to each crime.[36] Moreover, as Carlo Salzani points out, each item in a historical crime scene assumes a palimpsestic quality, on which 'every generation leaves a new set of scars or traces'.[37] The different implications of each object are built up in layers, while the historian as detective is encouraged to decipher the relationship between these strata, ultimately focusing on their connection to the visible surface of the present. This palimpsestic quality becomes particularly apparent in Liebmann's close-up photograph of the house on the corner of the Oranienburger Straße and the Tucholskystraße (Figure 3.7; *SM*, p. 95). The building featured is that opposite the *Postfuhramt* in the photograph discussed earlier; here, though, Liebmann focuses on the detail of the façade. The image depicts two boarded-up shop windows separated by a rusting grille, which appears to block the viewer's gaze, preventing it from penetrating deeper into the photograph. The stone work in the middle is potted with bullet holes, while the shop front on the right-hand side is covered by faded, peeling whitewash. Beneath this, the unusual combination of words advertising 'Dauerwellen', 'Rum', and 'Cognac', written in Gothic type, is faintly visible. On top of the layer of whitewash is an array of graffiti, of which the only legible section reads: 'Wissen ist Macht! Nichts wissen macht nichts'. This popular adaptation of Frances Bacon's famous assertion that knowledge is power might be read as an ironic comment on the collective amnesia which Liebmann is seeking to challenge in her work. The fact that these different layers of text are visible simultaneously means that they compete with one another for the viewer's attention, with each attempting to assert itself over the other.

The image of the palimpsest enables a particular 'dialectic of remembering and forgetting' to be played out in the space of the building as text.[38] Like the mystic writing pad described by Freud in his 1925 essay, which provides not only a receptive surface, like a slate, on which things can be written over and over again, but also holds permanent traces of the marks made on it, the palimpsest retains remainders of the past even if these have apparently been erased (SF III, 365–69). It can therefore be read as a way of figuring the operation of cultural memory. Although a society might seek to whitewash over the past in order to create a blank canvas on which to project its own ideas and ideologies, traces of this history always inevitably remain present and partly visible. This dynamic of forgetting and remembering also operates in a future-oriented manner, signalling how the inscriptions made by present and successive generations will be preserved and united by the retentive quality of the palimpsest.[39] In the context of Liebmann's photograph, the whitewashed shop front might be read as an allusion to the unwillingness of its inhabitants to face up to the National Socialist past, which Liebmann documents in her essay by describing the number of times doors are shut in her face and the evasive responses to her questions (*SM*, pp. 16–19). The fact that the old shop signs cannot be covered up, however,

Fig. 3.7. Detail Eckhaus Oranienburger Straße, Tucholskystraße (c. 1984)
© Berlin Verlag/Irina Liebmann

implies that the past cannot be erased, that it remains in a spectral form in the present, neither fully here nor there. Finally, the forward-looking dynamic of the study draws our attention to the state of the graffiti; will this reminder of the GDR past also be erased, so that only its ghostly trace remains?

For Liebmann, this dynamic of forgetting and remembering is closely bound up with the places which she photographs. At times, these places seem to be cut off from the rest of the city, thus recalling the notion of the crime scene as an 'anti-place', an eerie space separated from the bustle of everyday life through its associations with transgression, violation, and fatality, and through the more practical need to preserve the clues in such a way as to make them most readable.[40] Liebmann often focuses on the courtyards of buildings, which are part of the outside world, yet are nevertheless delineated from this by the walls of the surrounding houses (SM, pp. 70–72). In the photograph of the *Königliche Pfandleihe* on the Wilhelm-Pieck-Straße (SM, p. 85), a section of the ground is portioned off by means of a row of red and white railings, while the frame of the photograph creates the other side of this boundary; here, the camera itself participates in the ritual act of marking out the scene of the crime. Similarly, a picture of the Rosenthaler Straße has a section of

Fig. 3.8. Rosenthaler Straße (*c.* 1984)
© Berlin Verlag/Irina Liebmann

the image marked off by a temporary fence made of yellow builders' tape, and by the walls of two apparently disused buildings (Figure 3.8; *SM*, p. 91). These artificial boundaries demarcate an area of ground filled with rubble and debris, while the abandoned, dilapidated setting lends it the unsettling atmosphere of a crime scene. And yet the attempt to separate this space from its surroundings is nevertheless undermined by the fact that some of the rubble seems to have spilled out from the neighbouring building. Moreover, part of the stonework in the pavement outside the defined area has broken up, itself turning to rubble and thus mirroring the condition of the ground beyond the fence. The distinction between inside and outside, between the extraordinary space of the crime scene and the external world, is thus called into question.

This slippage marks a crucial feature of Liebmann's volume. On the one hand, she seeks to link specific historical events to particular places; on the other, she acknowledges that such attempts must be balanced by an awareness of space and history more generally, a realization that the past with which she is engaging at times transcends the limits which she seeks to place on it. The ghosts of Berlin's violent history are at once site-specific, bound to the places in which these crimes occurred, and itinerant, haunting the spaces of the city at large. As Anthony Vidler points out, modernity is increasingly characterized by a sense of doubt over the position of 'X' (that 'X' which marks the spot where a crime took place). 'Space', he writes, 'infiltrating and dispersing *place*, put the tangibility and thereby the veracity of the courtroom "exhibits" into doubt. The crime takes place in space, which in turn renders its exact position unstable'.[41] If, as Walter Benjamin suggests, history is itself a 'Prozeß', every inch of our cities is a crime scene and every passer-by in some way guilty, then any attempt to demarcate the scene of the crime, to limit the traces of the past to a particular spot, is fundamentally flawed. Viewed in this light, the photograph of the stone plaque marking the site of the *jüdisches Altersheim* and former collection point for the deportations in the Große Hamburger Straße seems to be out of keeping with the rest of Liebmann's images (Figure 3.9; *SM*, p. 77). The flowering magnolia and flourishing trees around the monument create a vibrancy which is at odds with the human mortality associated with the site, while the tidiness of the area contrasts with the disorderly scenes in her other photographs. The attempt here to fix the memory of the deportations to this particular site might appear to be problematic, since it seems to pave the way for other, less visible sites of violence and anti-Semitic measures to be overlooked. Situated in the context of Liebmann's volume, this particular image ultimately alerts the observer to the need to perceive the crimes of the past in everyday surroundings; her photographs serve to highlight the way in which the crime scene has exceeded the places of 'official memory' and come to be relocated in the streets and public spaces of the city.

'Living Dead'

Despite her emphasis on uncovering traces, those spectral 'Reste von etwas' which remain in the scenes which she captures (*SM*, p. 9), Liebmann rejects the detachment of the classical detective or investigator, seeking instead to cultivate a personal response to the history which she uncovers. She differentiates between the terms 'wissen' and 'wirklich wissen', suggesting that many of the details which she uncovers in her volume were somehow already known, but that they were not absorbed by the individual: 'Wir wussten es schon, aber es war irgendwie nicht angekommen, es war nicht wirklich gewusst, dieses Füßegetrappel von fünfzigtausend Menschen. Und wie soll man es eindringlich wissen [...]?' (*SM*, p. 58). Like the ink stain which 'dringt' through the paper, this type of knowledge is 'eindringlich': it penetrates the individual and encourages him/her to feel a personal connection to the events described. For her, the conventional forensic gaze comes to be associated with indifference and hard-heartedness; it forecloses any true understanding of the historical material and is therefore implicitly unethical: '"Historisch", das war mir damals ein Wort für

Fig. 3.9. Große Hamburger Straße. Gedenkstein für das jüdische Altersheim, ehemals Sammelstelle zur Deportation Berliner Juden (*c.* 1984)
© Berlin Verlag/Irina Liebmann

Gefühllosigkeit geworden. Ein Wort für Taubheit und Kälte. Ich spürte sie an mir selber bei dieser Recherche. Ich war so kalt wie meine Gegenüber' (*SM*, p. 18). Factual knowledge of historical events is not adequate; the individual is also required to have a subjective connection to them based on a kind of intuitive understanding.

For Liebmann, then, the observer is required to abandon his/her impartial stance and adopt instead the role of moral witness or judge. While the term 'forensisch', deriving from the Latin term 'forum', has implications of public discussion and debate,[42] her volume stresses the need to develop a private connection to the past beneath the official public narratives. Such a task involves acknowledging the contingency of any given viewpoint and the imperfect character of any piece of evidence. It also involves seeking to carry certain aspects of the past into the present, to bring them closer to the observer, as she explains: 'Man muss nach den Details suchen, die einem das Leben damals beschreiben, näher bringen'.[43] In particular, the task demands the ability to view the past, not as a frozen image, but rather as a living form, as a scene which was once vibrant and animated. In other words, it relies on what Liebmann describes as 'diese Vorstellung, das alles könnte einmal belebt gewesen sein, kleinteilig und vielfältig bunt' (*SM*, p. 11). This attempt to animate the inanimate, to enliven the scenes presented in the photographic stills through the dynamic power of the imagination, in turn has a reciprocal effect upon the observer: it prevents him/her from becoming too detached from the images and ensures that (s)he remains fully human.

Liebmann's emphasis on the reciprocity of this approach to history recalls Barthes's description of the *punctum* of the photograph as that which lends the photographic subject 'a whole life external to her portrait'.[44] In being struck by a particular detail of the picture, the viewer attempts to reanimate the subject, to shield him/her from a death which we know has already or is about to happen. The observer becomes aware of the photograph's capacity to bring the presence of the subject as 'a living, breathing being' closer to him/her,[45] to re-create the dead person in the present as 'a new being […]: a reality no-one can touch'.[46] At the same time, the *punctum*, as 'that accident which pricks me', is entirely personal to the individual observer, serving to engage and, significantly, to 'animate' him/her.[47] It is precisely this dynamic which lends the photograph a spectral dimension, presenting us with what Barthes terms 'the living image of a dead thing'.[48] The photograph suggests that what it depicts (the 'this-has-been') is already dead; its referent existed in the past and is therefore no longer living. But it also vouchsafes the reality of its subject, rendering this present and thereby endowing it with a life-like character of its own. The photographic subject is therefore shown to be alive and yet always already dead.[49] Moreover, thanks to the reciprocal relationship between the observer and the photograph, we are also implicated in this spectral existence: on the one hand, we are animated, rendered more alive through our encounter with the image; on the other, we can be fatally wounded by the piercing arrow of the *punctum*, 'arrested' by this direct encounter with the certainty of death.

For Liebmann, the ambivalence wrought by this personal engagement with the past is expressed in the rhetorical question, 'wie soll man es eindringlich wissen, warum auch es sich immerzu klar machen, wenn man doch leben will?' (*SM*, p. 58). Although on one level this intense, piercing connection to historical events prevents one from being overly disconnected, it nevertheless has the potential to arrest life, to deaden the observer. The sheer scale of the historical crimes addressed in her study threatens to become overwhelming, and it is perhaps for this reason that Liebmann abandoned her project in the 1980s, claiming that she ran away from it because the material was 'zu schwer' (*SM*, p. 9).[50] Moreover, it is precisely because of this dynamic that her photographs can be seen to oscillate between facilitating the work of mourning and cultivating a melancholic attachment to scenes which they portray. On the one hand, they encourage the observer to acknowledge the reality of loss by allowing him/her to gain a certain proximity to the lost object, while also withdrawing, preventing him/her from gaining full access to it. They evoke a 'flat' representation of the lost object[51] in order to make possible the recognition that this loss cannot be undone. On the other hand, photographs are incapable of 'transform[ing] grief',[52] plunging the observer instead into a melancholic silence[53] and threatening to freeze him/her in a state of 'living death' reminiscent of that diagnosed by Freud in his essay on mourning and melancholia (SF III, 198).

Liebmann's images often exploit this mortality of the medium, the capacity of the photograph to create a state of living death, both in its subject and in the observer. Several of her images focus on liminal realms such as graveyards and cemeteries, places which, for Benjamin, mark the primal site of photography through their facilitation of the passage between life and death (WB II.1, 373). One such picture shows a funeral taking place in the *Friedhof der Sophiengemeinde* (Figure 3.10; *SM*, p. 96), a graveyard situated on the edge of the Eastern sector of the city, and therefore a boundary space in both a literal and a metaphorical sense. The image depicts a group of mourners with their backs to the camera. In the foreground, four pall-bearers cross the photograph diagonally, pushing an empty bier. The photograph seems to be full of life, since, unlike many of the vacant scenes which Liebmann depicts, this one is occupied by a number of people. However, the picture is anything but vibrant: the pall bearers, dressed in black, and the bier, covered in dark velvet, dominate the scene. Strikingly, no human faces are visible to the observer: even though the pall-bearers appear to be facing the camera, the bright sunlight blanks out their facial features. While no actual corpse is present in this photograph, Liebmann seems to be dehumanizing or reifying the figures she depicts, rendering them half-dead through their lack of facial features. Our eyes cannot meet theirs, and this interrupted gaze therefore implicates us in this process of dehumanization; we are simultaneously drawn into and yet excluded from the image in a manner which apparently prevents us from identifying fully with the humans in it. The only face properly visible is that of a stone statue on the left of the picture: a figure of a Madonna, whose countenance is apparently animated by the events she witnesses. Liebmann's photograph thereby blurs the boundary between the animate and the inanimate, deadening the human beings so that they appear to be fully at home in the graveyard setting, and vivifying the lifeless statue, rendering it more life-like than the people themselves.

This slippage between the animate and the inanimate is most apparent in those photographs in Liebmann's volume which depict humans in relation to architectural structures. Particularly striking is her focus on frames, such as doors and windows, which mark points of human access to buildings. In her photograph of a corner house at the junction of the Große Hamburger Straße and the Krausnickstraße (Figure 3.11; *SM*, p. 73), the base of the image,

Fig. 3.10. Friedhof der Sophiengemeinde (c. 1984)
© Berlin Verlag/Irina Liebmann

corresponding to what Barthes would term the *studium*, is formed by the grey-brown wall of a building, with flecks of white paint daubed on it. The *punctum* of the photograph, the subjectively determined detail which 'rises from the scene',[54] might be indicated by a lattice window, with its shutter half down, recalling an eyelid. Evoking the traditional analogy between the building and the body, this detail lends the image the corporeal quality of a human face.[55] Alongside this window is a doorway, in which the figure of a man is half visible. The scale of the image is such that, in comparison with the frame of the door, the man appears to be tiny, and, once again, his face remains unseen; his human features therefore seem to have been overtaken by the corporeality of the frame. By linking thresholds, points of entry and exit, with the passage between the animate and the inanimate, Liebmann's photographs repeatedly evoke human absence.[56] And in focusing on the deadening of human life, she implicitly links her study to the 'jüdische Schicksale' (*SM*, p. 18) which have come to haunt the project. While the faces of the buildings which she depicts seem to suggest a longing for a return, a desire to revisit a past where human life flourished, the empty spaces in her photographs, which recall what Andreas Huyssen terms the 'voids of Berlin', generate a powerful sense of something missing, an 'invisible history' which has nevertheless left its mark on the city.[57]

Fig. 3.11. Große Hamburger Straße, Ecke Krausnickstraße (1984)
© bpk — Bildagentur für Kunst, Kultur und Geschichte/Irina Liebmann

— * —

Liebmann's photographs often evoke this sense of loss through their exploration of the interplay between light and shadow. While the sunlight is at times too bright, blanking out the faces of the people she captures and resulting in a curious ghosting effect through the overexposure of the image, other scenes are thrown into partial darkness by the shadows cast by absent objects. In her picture of the Auguststraße, for example, the houses in the frame are crossed by the shadows projected by the building opposite, which is not visible in the scene (Figure 3.12; *SM*, p. 86). The pattern formed by these shadows creates the impression of an absent presence, a ghostly effigy of an object which is excluded from the image. Recalling Freud's description of melancholia as a condition in which the bereft subject falls under the 'Schatten des Objekts' (SF III, 102), the shadow appears to project personal and collective losses from the past onto the urban scene in the photograph, indirectly evoking what is missing from the present while also foreshadowing the possible repetition of these losses in the future. Assuming a spectral quality reminiscent of the elusive 'Aura' described by Benjamin,[58] the shadow haunts these photographs as an oblique figuration of absence and departure, evoking places and figures which once

Fig. 3.12. Auguststraße (c. 1984)
© Berlin Verlag/Irina Liebmann

existed and revealing the present state of the city to be incomplete. At the same time, it defies limits and refuses to be contained by the aperture of the camera: spilling out beyond the bounds of the frame, it appears to fall onto the viewer of the image, projecting the effects of these historical losses onto his/her ego and plunging him/her into the arrested state of the melancholic individual. Through his/her contact with the ghostly images invoked by the photographic medium, the onlooker becomes a spectral figure, frozen in a condition between life and death.

Notes to Chapter 3

1. See Rolf Krauss, *Beyond Light and Shadow: The Role of Photography in Some Paradoxical Phenomena: A Historical Survey* (Munich: Nazraeli, 1995), p. 14.
2. John Harvey, *Photography and Spirit* (London: Reaktion Books, 2007), p. 114.
3. Rolf Krauss, p. 10; and Harvey, pp. 70–71.
4. Roland Barthes, *Camera Lucida: Reflections on Photography*, trans. by Richard Howard (London: Jonathan Cape, 1982), p. 87.
5. Ibid., p. 80. Marianne Hirsch explains this connection thus: 'The photograph of the footprint is the index par excellence, pointing to the presence, the having-been-there, of the past [...]. Pictures [...] "materialize" memory'. Marianne Hirsch, 'Surviving Images: Holocaust Photographs and the Work of Postmemory', in *Visual Culture and the Holocaust*, ed. by Barbie Zelizer (London: Athlone Press, 2001), pp. 215–46 (p. 224).

6. Barthes, p. 88.
7. As Barthes writes: 'From a real body, which was there, proceed radiations which ultimately touch me, who am here' (p. 80).
8. Interview with Susanne Lenné Jones, reproduced in the appendix to Susan Lenné Jones, 'What's in a Frame? Photography, Memory, and History in Contemporary German Literature' (unpublished doctoral dissertation: University of Cincinnati, 2005; abstract in *Dissertation Abstracts International*, 66 (2006), 4035–36), p. 250.
9. The same image can be found on p. 112 of the 2009 edition.
10. For a brief history of the *Postfuhramt*, see Laurenz Demps, *Die Oranienburger Straße: Von der kurfürstlichen Meierei zum modernen Stadtraum* (Berlin: Parthas, 1998), pp. 119–31 and 167–71.
11. See, for example, Georg Dehio, *Handbuch der deutschen Kunstdenkmäler: Berlin*, 2nd edn, rev. by Michael Bollé (Munich: Deutscher Kunstverlag, 2000), p. 89; and Wolfgang Feyerabend, *Durch das Scheunenviertel und die Spandauer Vorstadt: Vom versunkenen zum wiedererfundenen Stadtteil* (Berlin: Haude & Spener, 2004), pp. 27–28. Alan Balfour also claims that the architecture of the Synagogue 'influenced the design of the central post office'. Alan Balfour, *Berlin* (London: Academy Editions, 1995), p. 251.
12. Barthes, p. 83.
13. Liebmann initially claims that she was concerned with exploring 'die Mischung der vertretenen Religionen' in Mitte, highlighting her reluctance to regard 'die Juden' as 'das Thema dieser Gegend' (*SM*, p. 18). However, she devotes the next five pages of her essay to a detailed examination of the situation of the Jews in the Third Reich, and returns repeatedly to the question of anti-Semitism throughout the volume. While Susanne Lenné Jones suggests that Liebmann's research was 'taking on a direction of its own' (Jones, p. 171), I argue that this tension in Liebmann's volume results from the temporal gap between her initial research, and her completion of the essay in 2001; while her earlier self appears to be unable or unwilling to engage fully with the legacy of anti-Semitic violence, her more recent self laments this indifference and attempts to rectify it by returning to the 'jüdische Schicksale' from which she had initially distanced herself (*SM*, p. 18).
14. Barthes, p. 91.
15. See Marven, '"Souvenirs de Berlin-Est"', p. 223; Köhler, *Brückenschläge*, p. 110.
16. Details of exhibitions can be found on the website of the *Postfuhramt*: <http://www.postfuhramt.de/veranstaltungen/veranstaltungen_archiv.php> (accessed 30 April 2010).
17. Brian Ladd, *The Ghosts of Berlin: Confronting German History in the Urban Landscape* (Chicago: University of Chicago Press, 1997), p. 37.
18. Ibid.
19. Anthony Vidler, 'Air War and Architecture', in *Ruins of Modernity*, ed. by Julia Hell and Andreas Schönle (Durham, NC: Duke University Press, 2010), pp. 29–40 (p. 34).
20. Barthes, p. 96.
21. Ibid.
22. Ibid., p. 97.
23. Rolf Tiedemann terms this the 'revolutionärer Umschlag' of Benjamin's thinking. Rolf Tiedemann, *Dialektik im Stillstand: Versuche zum Spätwerk Walter Benjamins* (Frankfurt a. M.: Suhrkamp, 1983), p. 21.
24. Michael Jennings, *Dialectical Images: Walter Benjamin's Theory of Literary Criticism* (Ithaca, NY: Cornell University Press, 1987), p. 38.
25. Sigrid Weigel, *Literatur als Voraussetzung der Kulturgeschichte: Schauplätze von Shakespeare bis Benjamin* (Munich: Fink, 2004), p. 49.
26. A brief history of the Synagogue can be found on the following website: <http://www.anderes-berlin.de/html/synagoge__beth_zion_.html> (accessed 16 June 2010).

27. See Jones, pp. 177–79.
28. Ibid., pp. 177–78.
29. Liebmann in conversation with Smale, 21 July 2009. Liebmann emphasizes the necessity of this act of seeing: 'Die meisten Menschen sehen nicht, was sie sehen. [...] Ich habe ja alles vor Augen, und ich kann es nicht erkennen. Das ist ja [...] so ein Aufwachen, man muss ja nur sehen, was man sieht. [...] Das ist die allergrößte Verdrängung, die allerallergrößte Verdrängung, zu sehen, was man sieht.'
30. Introduction to Eugène Atget, *Lichtbilder: Photographe de Paris*, ed. by Camille Recht (Leipzig: Jonquières, 1930), pp. 18–19.
31. Ralph Rugoff, 'Introduction', in *The Scene of the Crime*, ed. by Rugoff (Cambridge, MA: The Museum in association with MIT, 1997), pp. 17–21 (p. 19).
32. Ibid., p. 18.
33. Ibid., p. 9.
34. See Ernst Bloch, 'Philosophische Ansicht des Detektivromans', in Ernst Bloch, *Verfremdungen*, 2 vols (Frankfurt a. M.: Suhrkamp, 1962), I, 37–63.
35. This recalls Benjamin's assertion that 'Wohnen heißt Spuren hinterlassen' (WB 5.1, p. 53).
36. See Ralph Rugoff, 'More than Meets the Eye', in *The Scene of the Crime*, ed. by Rugoff, pp. 59–108 (p. 82).
37. Carlo Salzani, 'The City as Crime Scene: Walter Benjamin and the Traces of the Detective', *New German Critique*, 34 (2007), 165–88 (p. 183).
38. Tony Bennett, *Pasts beyond Memory: Evolution, Museums, Colonialism* (London: Routledge, 2004), p. 89.
39. Josephine McDonagh, 'Writings on the Mind: Thomas De Quincey and the Importance of the Palimpsest in Nineteenth-Century Writing', *Prose Studies*, 10 (1987), 207–24 (p. 212).
40. See Peter Wollen, 'Vectors of Melancholy', in *The Scene of the Crime*, ed. by Rugoff, pp. 23–36 (p. 25).
41. Anthony Vidler, 'The Exhaustion of Space at the Scene of the Crime', in *The Scene of the Crime*, ed. by Rugoff, pp. 131–42 (p. 134).
42. See Rugoff, 'More than Meets the Eye', p. 73.
43. Liebmann in conversation with Jones, p. 243.
44. Barthes, p. 57.
45. Laura E. Tanner, *Lost Bodies: Inhabiting the Borders of Life and Death* (Ithaca: Cornell University Press, 2006), p. 111.
46. Barthes, p. 87.
47. Ibid., pp. 27, 20.
48. Ibid., p. 79.
49. 'For the photograph's immobility is somehow the result of a perverse confusion between two concepts: the Real and the Live: by attesting that the object has been real, the photograph surreptitiously induces belief that it is alive'. Barthes, p. 79.
50. This chimes with Marianne Hirsch's observation that photographs which allude in some way to the Holocaust necessarily 'resist the work of mourning' and 'cannot be redeemed by irony, insight or understanding'. See Hirsch, 'Surviving Images', pp. 234–35.
51. Barthes, p. 92.
52. Ibid., p. 90.
53. Ibid., p. 93.
54. Ibid., p. 26.
55. On the history of this analogy, see Vidler, *The Architectural Uncanny*, pp. 69–84.
56. As Marianne Hirsch notes, doors and gateways have an iconic status in the visual

culture of the Holocaust, where they assume both literal and figurative functions. Hirsch, 'Surviving Images', p. 244.
57. Andreas Huyssen, 'The Voids of Berlin', *Critical Inquiry*, 24 (1997), 57–81 (p. 65).
58. Benjamin describes 'Aura' as 'ein sonderbares Gespinst von Raum und Zeit: einmalige Erscheinung einer Ferne, so nah sie sein mag. An einem Sommernachmittag ruhend einem Gebirgzug am Horizont oder einem Zweig folgen, der seinen Schatten auf den Betrachter wirft' (WB I.2, 440).

CHAPTER 4

'Lebendige Bilder': Irina Liebmann's *In Berlin*

Irina Liebmann's first work to be published after the *Wende* bore the simple title *In Berlin* (1994). The text's complex narrative structure and lack of a clearly defined plot have prompted numerous interpretations, with critics reading it variously as a love story, an autobiography, a city novel, and as a form of 'Ortsbestimmung'.[1] This chapter, however, focuses on the way in which Liebmann's evocation of the ghostly is bound up with a series of intertextual and intermedial references, which allude both to her own earlier work and more indirectly to the *fantastische Erzählungen* of E. T. A. Hoffmann. While the previous chapter considered the way in which her photography exploits the potential of the camera to create a state of living death, it will be argued here that Liebmann's fiction is founded on the Hoffmannesque notion of the 'lebendiges Bild'.[2] Her text frequently makes reference to the frozen scenes of her photographs, and yet it seeks to enliven these as *tableaux vivants* through the dynamic principle of the narrative. At times, for example, her writing assumes a cinematic quality, engendering life in these images and lending them a seemingly unstoppable momentum, while the streets of Berlin are shown to stage a series of uncanny events as memories of the past come alive in the present. The temporal logic of Liebmann's photographs, their ability to mediate between past, present, and future, is thus transformed into a living encounter with the ghostly existence of the city and its history. And yet, for Liebmann, this animating principle is always shadowed by the threat of seizure, by the potential for these living images to return to a state of arrest. Despite seeking to evoke the vitality of the city, to recreate its movement and breathe life into its inhabitants, her narrative always risks returning to a series of static images; it remains bound by its attachment to various forms of stilled or deadened life.

Liebmann's preoccupation with the tension between the static image and the dynamic principle of the narrative can be viewed as part of a wider concern with the position of the human subject in relation to the passage of time. Her focus on points of slippage and fixation in the forward-flowing momentum of the narrative raises questions about the chronological progression of historical events. Such disruptions often signal a distorted perception of historical experiences, characterized by a compulsive repetition resulting from traumatic events or by a melancholic attachment to what has occurred; above all, they indicate a persistent refusal or inability to mourn what has been lost.[3] The protagonist of *In Berlin* is therefore shown to be haunted by a past, at once personal and collective, which doggedly refuses to be laid to rest, resurfacing instead in moments of disjuncture and disorder. In addition, she becomes a figure of displacement; like the moving images which have, in a ghost-like manner, stepped out of the time and place in which they belong, so too is Liebmann's protagonist 'out of joint' with the historical age and location in which she lives. Unable to feel at home in the Berlin of the late 1980s, she becomes a threshold figure, inhabiting both the temporal boundary of the *Wende* and the spatial border between East and West. As her living space is rendered increasingly uninhabitable, she forges a 'Gespensterweg' through the city, compulsively visiting and revisiting certain locations in search of a sense of belonging. Her existence is therefore shown to be a marginal one; she is at once *in* Berlin, and yet also paradoxically excluded from being at home in the city.

As Liebmann explained in a recent interview, this preoccupation with the passage of time is an overriding principle of both her documentary work and her fiction. Citing the prologue of the travel volume *Visum der Zeit* (1929) by the Russian author Ilja Ehrenburg, she renders literal the notion of chronography (time-recording, time-writing) through an analogy with maritime navigation. She explains:

> 'Der Seefahrer stellt mit Hilfe von Kompaß und Karte den Standort des winzigen Schiffleins inmitten des Überflusses und der Anonymität der Elemente fest. Wenn wir doch ebenso mit der Zeit zu verfahren wüßten, wenn wir doch unsere, sei es überpathetischen, sei es gewöhnlichsten Tage, auf der Karte der Epochen finden könnten! ... Dann wäre es leicht, alle Grübeleien der nachfolgenden Seiten durch die eine alltägliche Frage zu ersetzen: "Verzeihung, wieviel Uhr ist es jetzt? ..."' Wenn es eine Karte der Zeit gäbe, wo bin ich auf der Karte der Zeit? Das ist für mich immer die Frage.[4]

Like the sailor, who attempts to plot the position of his ship at sea with the aid of a map and compass, it is her task as a writer to locate herself on a 'Karte der Zeit', to record her specific position in history. The image of the map lends a spatial dimension to this undertaking, revealing the passage of time to be linked to the experience of a particular place, and thus drawing a connection between chronography and topography, the recording of time and the description of place. Viewed in this light, the title of Liebmann's novel assumes a double-meaning, as the preposition 'in' comes to possess both spatial and temporal significance.[5] The question of what it means to be *in* Berlin refers not only to the city as a geographical location, but also to its historical identity; being in the city necessarily involves encountering it at a particular moment in time. The urban spaces which Liebmann depicts throughout her work can be read allegorically in this context, as figurations of the particular time and age which they evoke; not only do they embody different historical eras and conflicting ideological systems, but they also serve to reveal the influence of these on the identity of the human subject. Liebmann's fiction, along with its repeated references to her photographic work, can therefore be regarded as a means of mapping and remapping the historical and geographical terrain of the city; and her focus on displacement, on figures who do not belong on this map, raises implicit questions about the nature of habitation, about what it means to feel at home in a particular time and place.

In the same interview, Liebmann goes on to link her chronographical work with the process of learning to perceive the history which has been excluded from collective memory. In order to understand fully one's position in time, it is necessary to be aware of aspects of reality which normally remain hidden from view. As Liebmann explains:

> Die meisten Menschen sehen nicht, was sie sehen. Das habe ich ja auch in dem Buch *In Berlin* beschrieben. Ich habe alles vor Augen, und ich kann es nicht erkennen. Das ist [...] so ein Aufwachen, man muss nur sehen, was man sieht.[6]

The revelation which she describes is an overwhelmingly visual one; it is effected through the optical apparatus, and involves learning to see what is before one's very eyes. And yet, throughout Liebmann's work, the act of seeing is shown to possess a peculiarly tactile dimension. While the metaphorical sea which Liebmann attempts to negotiate might recall one of Deleuze and Guattari's 'smooth spaces', whose navigation demands the haptic perception of one's surroundings,[7] her fictional writing transfers this physical apprehension of the immediate environment onto the protagonist's experience of the city. In *In Berlin*, verbs such as 'fühlen', 'spüren', and 'festhalten' are frequently used in conjunction with references to the faculty of vision, thus lending the eye a tactile dimension. In a similar manner, the hand is often depicted as possessing a visual capacity, feeling its way through its surroundings and thereby enabling the subject to involve her body in the process of seeing. In addition, the hand and the eye are revealed to be a crucial part of the apparatus of representation; like the fingers of the mariner, which pin down ('feststellen') the position of the boat on the cartographic representation of the sea, so too are the hands of the writer-photographer bound up in the process of recording and representing the image seen by the eye.

As Laura Marks has argued, haptic perception offers a means of engaging with the world which differs from that of conventional optical visuality; rather than presupposing an onlooker who is distant and disengaged, 'haptic images invite the viewer to dissolve his or her subjectivity in the close and bodily contact with the image'.[8] In other words, they compel the viewer to identify with the image, abandoning his/her identity as a distinct individual and thereby calling into question the basic separation of self and other. For Liebmann, this form of haptic visuality enables her to bring about a personal engagement with the past like that described in *Stille Mitte von Berlin*. The ghostly, as that which is both seen and felt, is encountered directly, through the concerted action of hand and eye. Although the effects of phantom phenomena are essentially visual, they demand an alternative kind of seeing, one which draws on other senses and combines the optical with the tactile. Nevertheless, it will be argued here that such a partnership between hand and eye is inherently duplicitous. Through their position at the fluctuating margin between the self and the world, these organs of perception come to act as a passageway between the animate and the inanimate, as the eye is blinded and the hand deadened through their encounter with the ghostly. The protagonist acquires spectral characteristics through her engagement with supernatural phenomena. And as the boundaries of the subject begin to dissolve, so the possibility of autonomous action is called into question. Through her identification with the ghostly figures which she envisions, Liebmann's protagonist opens herself up to be governed by them; in learning 'zu sehen, was man sieht', in setting her eyes upon these phantoms, she comes to be touched, and ultimately possessed, by them.

Ekphrastic Images

In Berlin reflects on the nature of chronography through its thematization, both direct and indirect, of Liebmann's documentary volume, *Stille Mitte von Berlin*.[9] The protagonist is involved in revealing the hidden narratives of the past, delving into the repressed areas of her own family history, as well as investigating the way in which these intergenerational secrets are bound up with the wider history of Berlin. In particular, she engages in a historical project which directly recalls that undertaken by Liebmann: she attempts to uncover the pre-war history of Berlin-Mitte, drawing on a range of archival sources and interviews. Like Liebmann's own documentary work, this project is presented in a highly ambivalent light. While Liebmann abandoned her research because it became 'zu schwer' (*SM*, p. 9), in the novel this mental burden assumes a physical form, as the protagonist is literally encumbered by the weight of the paper stacked up underneath her desk (*IB*, p. 17). This physicality is revealed to be linked with the nature of the material itself, as Liebmann goes on to describe the contents of these sheets of paper: 'Es sind ganze Häuser im Grunde, auf Papier übertragen, die Einwohner von hundert Jahren, aus alten

Adressbüchern rausgesucht' (*IB*, p. 17). The pages are shown to bear the weight of the houses which form the centre of this historical project; even the very foundations of these buildings, their solid 'grounding', have been transferred onto the apparently fragile paper. It is against this 'ground', this architectural backdrop, that Liebmann's protagonist searches for the 'figures' of the former inhabitants of these buildings. By transferring these details onto paper, the protagonist seems to be lending her project a creative dimension; her writing seeks to stage a form of encounter with these absent figures, thus attempting to endow them with a form of textual life. And yet this animating gesture is countered by a realization that these people are all 'gestorben' (*IB*, p. 17), that nothing can restore the former inhabitants to life, no matter how many details she might collect about their lives. The promise of life offered by the address books is therefore elusive; their ability to detail not only the architectural layout of the city at any given time, but also the people who made these places their home, is called into question. As such, the volumes assume the function of a *Totenregister*; rather than enabling an encounter with the figures being sought, they merely serve as documents of their absence.[10]

Through the thematization of her documentary project, Liebmann raises questions about the mimetic potential of her novel and its ability to represent a material actuality which lies outside its bounds. On one level, her frequent references to this volume suggest an attempt to ground her narrative in the historical reality beyond the text. Allusions to photography, as a visual means of representation, occur both directly and indirectly throughout her novel. In particular, the narrative creates a series of ekphrastic descriptions of photographs, 'Bilder von Häusern, Toren und Einfahrten' (*IB*, p. 34), which resemble the images featured in *Stille Mitte von Berlin*. These representations of architectural details and thresholds serve to establish moments of passage between the fictional world of the protagonist and the historical reality beyond it, marking points of transition between the pages of the text and the spaces of the city. At times, they serve to confirm the memories of the protagonist and validate the historical details which she unearths, while at other points in the novel they reveal surprising details which prompt a reinterpretation of events. Through her creation of these textual images, Liebmann exploits the connection between the photograph and its referent, which, as Barthes suggests, is governed by a form of tactility, in an effort to root her artistic representation of the city in its material actuality. On another level, though, Liebmann complicates this relationship, revealing the link between text, photograph, and reality to be highly problematic. Her novel often refers to photographs without offering a clear description of what they portray, thus foreclosing the possibility of any direct relation to her documentary project. At other times, these descriptions lack the specificity needed to match the photographs precisely with those printed in *Stille Mitte von Berlin*. Occasionally, the very existence of these images is called into question, thus placing doubt on the reliability of the protagonist's memories and working to block the mimetic principle of the text. Not only are these textual references to photographs capable of becoming what Barthes would term a 'counter-memory',[11] standing in for the reality which they represent, they are also duplicitous in their failure to acknowledge the fundamental absence at their core.

Viewed in this light, Liebmann's novel seems to be centred on what W. J. T. Mitchell describes as the tension between 'ekphrastic hope' and 'ekphrastic fear'.[12] As 'the verbal representation of visual representation',[13] Mitchell argues, ekphrastic description seeks to incorporate the visual image, together with its utopian promise of creating a 'transparent window [...] onto reality',[14] into the linguistic form of the text. On the one hand, he suggests, the main aim of this technique is 'the overcoming of otherness';[15] the writer seeks to surmount the distinction between image and text by adopting a form of 'verbal "conjuring"', which invokes the image as a 'fictive, figural present' within the text.[16] Language is thereby put to the service of recreating a visual image in a textual form, and thus making something which is outside the text appear as though it belongs there. On the other hand, though, this process is perpetually undercut by a realization that 'the textual other' can 'never be [made] present', that it represents a 'potent absence' within the narrative, and that any form of presence given to the image is merely illusory.[17] Ekphrastic representation therefore serves to highlight a contradiction which is inherent to some degree in all linguistic representation; it seeks to endow language with an iconic status, so that it comes to resemble the artefacts which it describes, while also maintaining that this apparent capacity to evoke the image is actually no more than a 'deceitful illusion'.[18]

Such ambivalence is evident in Liebmann's description of a house on the Große Hamburger Straße which the protagonist recalls visiting as part of her research about the area. On one level, the reference can be read as an attempt to validate the protagonist's memory of the scene, lending a form of documentary authenticity to her narrative. The house itself is depicted as a ship, an image which recalls Liebmann's notion of the writer as a seafarer, whose task it is to plot the course of the vessel in space and time:

> Im Regen und Schnee ein weißes Schiff da vorn, Richtung Norden. Nicht mehr ausgekohlt innen und mit zerschlagener Eingangstür wie damals, wovon es ein Foto geben muß, von diesem verrußten, vollgekritzelten Treppenhaus, in dem sie umsonst auf alle Klingelknöpfe drücken. (*IB*, p. 50)

Liebmann's description of the geographical position of the house, situated to the north, is coupled with references to its historicity; the battered door and the sooty stairwell marred by graffiti serve as reminders of the testimony which the building has paid to the city's diverse past. The building's dilapidated condition resembles that of many of the houses pictured in *Stille Mitte von Berlin*, and this link seems to be strengthened, both by Liebmann's assertion that a picture of the building ought to exist somewhere, and by the form of the narrative, which seems to adopt a photographic quality: the absence of verbs in the first half of the description lends the scene a static character, recalling the atmosphere of arrest cultivated in her photographs, while the description of the protagonist pushing on the 'Klingelknöpfe' at the door of the house might resemble the photographer's action of manually operating the shutter of the camera. At the same time, however, the actual existence of this photograph is called into question through the modal construction 'geben muß', which casts doubt on the reliability of the protagonist's memory and thereby blocks the mimetic function of the narrative; just as the protagonist's attempts to gain entry to the house prove to be in vain and the door remains shut, so too is the passage between text and reality impeded. In this context, the photographic quality of Liebmann's narrative assumes a substitutive function, standing in for the missing photograph and thereby highlighting its non-existence.

Liebmann's allusions to photography in her fiction therefore serve as an attempt to lend presence to a reality which is characterized by absence. In this respect, it forms part of her continuing attempt to record narratives which have been excluded from conventional historiography, and, in doing so, to give a kind of voice to those figures which have been overwhelmingly silenced. Her technique of ekphrasis reverts in this context to its etymological meaning, functioning above all as a form of 'speaking out'; it signals an attempt to 'give voice to' the mute object which the fiction is representing.[19] Throughout the novel, Liebmann adopts a stream-of-consciousness style which enables the narrative to switch frequently between descriptive prose, reports of the protagonist's thoughts rendered in both the first and the third person, and a transcription of other voices, often belonging to the people whom the protagonist encounters on the streets of the city.[20] Because these shifts in perspective regularly occur in a single sentence, the different voices in the narrative tend to merge with one another, thus revealing the protagonist's own speech and thought patterns to be constructed from a collage of those belonging to other people. While the protagonist's sense of self is thereby revealed to be based on an encounter with alterity, more often than not these voices hinder rather than help her in her desire to engage with absent figures from the past. In fact, they frequently act on the side of this historical silencing, drowning out the less perceptible undertones which she tries to capture, and ultimately distracting her from her project. Her attempts to speak 'of' and 'for' the people whom history has ignored is always therefore threatened by voices which insist on speaking 'over' them.[21]

An example of this tension can be found towards the end of the novel, shortly after a description of the inhabitants of the Große Hamburger Straße who perished during the Third Reich. The narrator introduces an ironic reference to the way in which the protagonist has been influenced by the thoughts of other people:

> Wenn du das nicht tust, dann bist du ein Schwein, und wenn du jenes nicht tust, dann bist du doppelt ein Schwein, und weiter und weiter, duuu, duuu, Freundchen, wir, wir vor allem, dieses wir schon mal, wir durchschauen dich, [...], jaaa, das Gute und Richtige, das muß es sein, dann ist ja alles anders, denkt die Liebmann, dann habe ich mich abgequält wie eine Blöde für Gedanken aus Köpfen von anderen Leuten. (*IB*, p. 162)

The protagonist's interior monologue is flooded here by a stream of highly critical voices. Some seem to be connected to the people whom Liebmann interviews in *Stille Mitte von Berlin*; the prolonged vowel in the word 'duuu', for example, recalls the woman who over-pronounces this sound, particularly in the word 'Juden', but also in the street name 'Mulackstraße', as though expressing her feelings of disgust towards them (*SM*, pp. 20–22). Others echo the mélange of voices which Liebmann encounters in her 'Stammcafé': people who are so preoccupied with their lives in the present that they fail to pay any attention to what has happened in the past. Finally, the diminutive term 'Freundchen' might be linked with the protagonist's absent partner, whose voice is one she craves throughout the novel but which proves destructive, both to her sense of well-being and to her completion of the historical project. The rapid onslaught of these different voices, signalled by the short, breathless clauses and the transition to paratactic style, assumes an attritional function; it erodes the protagonist's self-confidence and undermines her ability to carry out her research effectively.

Through the changes in perspective marked by the alternation between 'du' and 'wir', the passage initially seems to present a distinction between the protagonist and these other voices, as she becomes the addressee of their speech. Such objectification is emphasized further by their claim that they can see right through her; although apparently disembodied, the voices possess the faculty of vision, and the protagonist comes under their scrutiny, being subjected to their mechanisms of surveillance and observation. At the same time, however, these disparate voices are intertwined with the protagonist's own thoughts, and they are rendered in her own idiom, so that they appear to have been spoken by one person. In employing the pronoun 'du', the protagonist appears to be addressing herself, as she often does throughout the novel; the clamour can therefore be read as part of her own internal thought process. Viewed in this context, the phrase 'die Liebmann', which marks a turn towards the third person, can be understood as signalling an attempt to gain control over these diverse voices by incorporating them within the written form of the narrative. And yet the colloquial tone of the phrase persists in alluding to the spoken word; the turn to the third person, to a narrative form, retains its connection with the vocal. The definite article here signals a form of objectification; despite her efforts to exercise her authority over them, the protagonist is objectified, reified, through her encounter with these ulterior voices. Her own writing assumes the qualities of the speech of the other, and yet the self-estrangement which this entails threatens the identity of the protagonist. The final statement in the first-person, with its defiant, albeit somewhat ironic tone, conveys a more forceful rejection of these contradictory voices; it suggests an attempt to assert the coherence of her own self and prevent it from disintegrating in this verbal cacophony.

'Lauter angehaltene Bilder'

In order to protect herself from this onrush of voices, Liebmann's protagonist comes to crave silence. Her retreat into a non-verbal realm is reflected typographically by the empty spaces which are increasingly used to separate the different sections of the narrative (*IB*, pp. 158–62). Silence becomes a means of staving off possession by these other voices, an attempt to maintain the integrity of her existence. However, the protagonist is also aware that such a retreat forecloses the very possibility of an encounter as medium or mediator with the spectral voices which her project seeks to enable. This ambivalence is expressed directly towards the end of the novel, as she describes how she has at times exploited her photographic project in order to cultivate silence: 'Still, denkt die Liebmann, Papier dazwischen. Solange das da ist, solange das alles so auf dem Papier steht, ist es da und auch nicht da, die Bomben, die Trümmer, die toten Juden, [...], nicht wirklich. Es ist aber wirklich passiert' (*IB*, p. 158). The paper is depicted here as a tangible barrier separating the protagonist from this vocal bombardment. Liebmann draws on the ambiguity of the adjective 'still', with its allusions to both silence, the arresting of sound, and stasis, the fixation of a body in time and space. Not only does the project foster a kind of wordlessness, it also serves to freeze past events and figures on the page, so that they are preserved both spatially and temporally. Their existence becomes characterized by a form of liminality, as they are neither fully present nor absent, and this in turn lends them an illusory quality. This is precisely where the protagonist's difficulty lies, since she feels compelled to insist on the reality of this history. The repetition of the adjective 'wirklich' echoes the phrase 'wirklich wissen', which Liebmann uses in *Stille Mitte von Berlin* to emphasize the personal connection needed when engaging with such a past (*SM*, p. 58). While the stillness created here serves to reassure the protagonist, it nevertheless prevents her from understanding this past as something which once really existed; it thwarts her efforts to relate to these absent figures as living individuals, consigning them instead to a permanent state of lifelessness.

Liebmann's novel at times seems to recreate the stasis associated with her photography by exploring the potential of narrative to arrest and frame the textual image. The text assumes a pictorial quality which is frequently depicted in terms of photography, with successive descriptions of the urban landscape taking on the character of stills created by a camera. The Oranienburger Straße, for example, is described as 'ein Bild im Regen' (*IB*, p. 44), while later in the novel the protagonist looks out of the window of an aeroplane, staring down at 'das Bild da unten' (*IB*, p. 94). At times, Liebmann's narrator finds herself able to control the zoom and focus of the image in the manner of a photographer (*IB*, p. 156), and this is in turn reflected in the form of the narrative; the short, fragmented clauses create an impressionistic image of the city, focusing on one small detail after another. By incorporating photographic techniques into her novel, Liebmann explores what Murray Krieger has described as the 'simultaneity, in the verbal figure, of fixity and flow'.[22] Challenging Lessing's conception of the distinction between temporal and spatial art forms, Krieger suggests that ekphrastic literature attempts to 'freeze itself into a spatial form' by incorporating aspects of visual art into the verbal sequence of its narrative.[23] While remaining dependent upon the temporal progression of language, such literature aspires to 'the spatiality of the pictorial instant';[24] it seeks to transcend the temporality of the literary medium by emulating the spatial stillness of the visual work of art. For Krieger, this stillness is desirable because it can be equated with a kind of permanence. The flow of time is disrupted by the frozen moment; narrative flux is transformed into the stasis of the visual arts. Because this stillness proves to be so enduring, the ekphrastic text offers a form of resistance to the impermanence and decay characteristic of all temporal objects. In Liebmann's novel, however, this creation of stasis is shown to rest on a darker principle: although the photographic quality of the narrative seems to offer protection against the passing of time, this can only be achieved by a form of mortification.[25] It is only by entering a death-like existence that characters can be preserved; they can only be shielded from their own transience if they are, paradoxically, exposed to it. In its reference to the camera's ability to confer a kind of immortality upon its subject, Liebmann's narrative simultaneously reveals photography's corresponding tendency to embalm human forms in a state of living death.

This double-bind is particularly apparent in Liebmann's descriptions of particular locations and architectural details in the city, which often evoke the photographic images in *Stille Mitte von Berlin*. The protagonist of the novel frequents a café on the Große Hamburger Straße, opposite the Jewish cemetery and the site of the former *jüdisches Altersheim*. The view from the window of this café directly recalls the photograph of this scene in Liebmann's documentary project, which features a stone memorial surrounded by blossoming plant life (*SM*, p. 77). When the image is evoked in *In Berlin*, the window functions as a framing device, like the aperture of a camera, and the protagonist's view of the scene is further defined by the leaves of the trees, whose vitality is shown to be excessive (*IB*, p. 166). The changes wrought by the passage of time are highlighted by Liebmann's description of the way in which the site has altered over the years. The sports hall which previously obscured the view of the cemetery has now been demolished (*IB*, p. 167),[26] and the stone memorial has been replaced by a group of 'Krüppelfiguren', a reference to a sculpture by the artist Will Lammert, which was erected on the site of the *Altersheim* in 1985 as a memorial to the victims of the deportations. On one level, Liebmann's description of these figures emphasizes their apparent resistance to temporality. The historical weight suggested by the bronze of the sculpture appears to be out of keeping with the modern neon lights which illuminate the rest of the street (*IB*, p. 39), and it lends the figures an appearance of solidity and permanence which the protagonist herself seem to lack. In particular, Liebmann focuses on the figures' lack of movement, describing them as 'alle still' (*IB*, p. 39), frozen to the spot.[27] Framed by the window of the cafe and by the leaves of the trees, they appear to be posing for a photograph; they seem to have been caught at a particular moment in time, a stilled image of something previously animate. While this stasis lends the figures their ability to transcend temporality, however, it also binds them in an inanimate state. The solidity of the bronze merely serves to highlight the absence of living bodies, and the street itself is described as being empty, despite the presence of these arrested forms (*IB*, p. 39). The ground which they inhabit is marked by a void; the architectural setting in which they belong has disappeared, and the figures themselves have a spectral existence, perpetually haunting the now vacant site of the building which once housed and imprisoned them.

While Liebmann seems at times to cultivate this photographic stillness, creating moments of fixture and slippage within the narrative, at other points in the novel she attempts to counter this mortal stasis by breathing life into the scenes which she depicts. Images of the city at different points in its history are often combined in a kaleidoscopic movement, linked by verbs such as 'wenden', 'drehen', 'kreisen', and 'herumfliegen', and the novel as a whole assumes a circular form, beginning and ending with images of the protagonist travelling from outside the city towards its centre. As Astrid Köhler notes, this circularity renders literal the metaphor of the 'Wende' and signals the distorted perception of space and time created by such an experience.[28] At the same time, the text's emphasis on rotation might also call to mind the movement of a film reel, animating stilled images by projecting them in quick succession. Indeed,

Liebmann often juxtaposes references to the photographic image with allusions to the cinematic apparatus. At one point, the protagonist retraces her steps after a journey into the West, and this act is likened to the process of rewinding a film and watching it backwards (*IB*, p. 90). Such allusions become particularly apparent in Liebmann's descriptions of the city's transport system, whose speed of movement is analogous with the dynamic procedure of the cinematic apparatus.[29] Thus Liebmann describes how the *S-Bahn* 'fährt schneller und quer über Brücken ins Bild' (*IB*, p. 135), and she adopts cinematic vocabulary in her portrayal of an approaching train, whose 'Bild [...] verwischt sich im Drecksturm' (*IB*, pp. 72–73). While the narrator adopts a reflective stance here, calmly watching and recording events as they unfold, elsewhere in the narrative she is shown to be 'mit im Bild',[30] participating in the frenzied motion of the city. Sitting inside a train, she watches as distorted, filmic images of the city are projected onto the screen-like windows of the carriage (*IB*, p. 103). And at times the narrator herself comes to resemble one of these spectral figures, a 'Geist, der um die Ecken düst' (*IB*, pp. 21–22); 'out of joint' with the reality in which she exists, she regards herself as a ghostly version of her past self, a phantom image of her corporeal existence which works to undo her material grounding in reality. The unusual use of the verb 'düsen' emphasizes the speed of her journeys around the city, linking this tempo with the motion captured by the cinematic medium. In adopting this multi-perspectival stance, Liebmann's narrative is able to alternate between creating detached, static images of the city and offering dynamic, subjective encounters with metropolitan life. It serves not only to record the day-to-day existence of Berlin, but also to create a ghostly impression of life, to respond to photographic stasis with the vivifying energy of its narrative impulse.

On one level, this mobile perspective enables the protagonist to relate more closely to the ghostly reality which she researches in her project, since aspects of the past seem to come alive in the present. And yet such animation is also revealed to be problematic, since the images risk either taking on a life of their own and escaping the control of the protagonist, or slipping back into the underlying stillness at the heart of filmic movement, thus revealing its apparent vivacity to be an illusion.[31] Towards the middle of the novel, Liebmann alludes to this fear in her description of the photographs taken by the protagonist's friend, who has recently died. She describes the way in which these images spill out into the room in remarkably similar terms to those evoking the pile of paper beneath the protagonist's own desk: 'Weiß dagegen, daß Freunde von ihm in seiner leeren Wohnung nach Fotos für eine Ausstellung suchten und ihnen lauter Bilder entgegenrutschten, als sie die Schränke öffneten [...], dieser Schreck' (*IB*, p. 34). The verb 'entgegenrutschen' lends the photographs a seemingly unstoppable momentum, which recalls the speed at which frames are projected in the cinema. Whereas Liebmann describes the material in *Stille Mitte von Berlin* as slipping away from her ('es ist mir entglitten', *SM*, p. 9), here the images are shown to move towards her characters, intruding into the domestic space of the apartment. While the exclamation 'dieser Schreck' is in part ironic, it nevertheless signals a certain sense of vulnerability on the part of the human beings; once these images have been unleashed, they cannot be restrained, and they threaten to overwhelm the individual, drowning him/her in this 'Flut von Papier' (*IB*, p.34).

This relentless stream of pictures is echoed later in the novel in a description of mental images which confront the protagonist: 'Jetzt steht die Liebmann [...] in ihrer alten Wohnung in Pankow, alleine, und wie ein Wasservorhang rauschen Bilder vor ihr runter, sie kann es nicht anhalten, aber es sind lauter angehaltene Bilder — Stopp und Stopp, alles stumm' (*IB*, p. 131). The earlier photographic images, 'lauter Bilder', seem to have been internalized by the protagonist, as her memories and historical knowledge are projected in her mind's eye. The flood of paper is transformed here into a 'Wasservorhang', which in turn echoes the description of the 'Eiserner Vorhang' at the opening of the novel (*IB*, p. 11);[32] the images are located at a boundary, between past and present, East and West, and yet this is nevertheless strangely intangible. Above all, Liebmann's emphasis on the animation of these images, and the silence associated with them, might recall the genre of 'Stummfilm'. The mute scenes resemble those to which she attempts to give voice in her narrative; here, though, the absence of words merely serves to highlight the artificial movement of the pictures, which have been animated mechanistically and therefore possess none of the vital qualities which signify human life. Liebmann's spectral protagonist has no control over these images, whose flow is apparently unstoppable, and she is shown to be entirely at their mercy. However, this apparent continuum is made up of stilled images, 'lauter angehaltene Bilder', which have been bound together to form a temporal sequence. When viewed in succession, these images appear to be connected to one another and to a wider whole, but they also contain moments of individual fixture which disrupt this flow, indicating the potential threat of seizure and arrest.

As Laura Mulvey argues, such points of stoppage can be enhancing, since they restore to film the 'privileged relation to time' which is characteristic of the photograph.[33] They enable an individual moment to be extracted from the continuity which the film fosters, and this isolation permits the image to be viewed in a new light.[34] At the same time, however, the possibility of stillness can also be threatening, since it 'marks a transition from the animate to the inanimate, from life to death'.[35] In particular, it risks overcoming and mortifying the spectator, whose efforts to 'possess' the film, to master it through a kind of fetishistic control, are countered by the possibility of being possessed by its latent stillness. In Liebmann's novel, the oscillation between cinematic and photographic narrative enables a reconsideration of conventional historical narratives. Unexpected connections between past and present are made through the author's choice of vocabulary. The café on the Große Hamburger Straße hosts discussions about 'Republikflucht' and the characters' dissatisfaction with the GDR of the 1980s, while the street becomes associated with departures, as people are granted passports and leave for the West (*IB*, p. 155). These become linked with the earlier deportations through the description of 'Gasautos', which 'holten die Leute ab' (*IB*, p. 155); while the reference here is enigmatic, hinting at the unspoken word 'Gaskammer', it is explained more fully in *Stille Mitte von Berlin*, where Liebmann describes the cars which would pull up before the *Altersheim*, collect the Jewish prisoners, and gas them by redirecting the exhaust fumes inside the vehicle (*SM*, p. 19). Such violence is also expressed through the lamps 'burning' in the windows of the café (*IB*, p. 33), which might recall the destruction of the November pogrom of 1933. Finally, the protagonist's description of herself as sitting 'festgehakt', 'wie ein Haken' (*IB*, p. 155), can be read as an allusion to the 'Hakenkreuz' (*IB*, p. 128), an interpretation which is strengthened by the next line of the novel: 'Café, Judenmord, Alt-Berlin' (*IB*, p. 155). The verb 'festgehakt' links with another thread of allusions to paralysis, seizure, and stasis which recur throughout the novel, particularly through the protagonist's repeated lament, 'ich kann nicht weitergehen'. The intrusion of the past into the present is shown to halt her, pinning her to the spot and preventing her from moving forward with her life. Although the protagonist has sought to enliven the figures and narratives which her documentary project attempts to record, in doing so, she risks becoming fixated, caught in a melancholic state of arrest.

'Glasige Augen'

Liebmann's thematization of the tension between the still image and the dynamic impulse of the narrative is developed further through a series of possible allusions to the tales of E. T. A. Hoffmann.[36] While Hoffmann's writing can at times be likened to a *camera obscura*, it also recalls the magic lantern, the precursor of the cinematic apparatus, in its ability to present 'a series of illuminations with a degree of overlay and continuity, but one equally prone to a sense of interruption and disjuncture'.[37] Like Liebmann's writing, Hoffmann's narratives work either to create stilled images, or to present the moving pictures of a 'magische Laterne' (H IV, 315),[38] which are projected in quick succession. His writing is driven by the Serapiontic desire to breathe life into the inert figures which he creates, to render them animate through his creative skill and endow them with a form of 'lebendige Bewegung' (H IV, 568). However, this act is always accompanied by the possibility of seizure; the life which the writer generates is shown to be deceptive, the figures which he creates are revealed to be automata, whose illusion of movement merely serves to reveal the fundamental stasis at their core. The writer risks becoming too absorbed in the apparent vivacity of his creation, being bewitched by it and therefore becoming indifferent to reality. Like Nathanael in *Der Sandmann*, who succumbs to delirium and death following his encounter with the animated puppet Olimpia, he faces the danger of being paralysed by the force of his imaginative vision. The writer's capacity to breathe life into his artistic creation is therefore founded on the possibility of his own mortification.[39]

In his *Nachtstück, Das öde Haus*, Hoffmann creates a vivid illustration of the dangers of Serapiontic excess, a scenario which takes place against the backdrop of Berlin's uncanny cityscape. The tale explores what Robert McFarland describes as 'the difficult process of mediation between the visible spaces and the invisible phenomena of the city'; it attempts to look beyond the visible surface of Berlin and probe the 'ephemeral, intangible, invisible forces that make up the unreal reality' beneath the discernible exterior of this urban space.[40] The protagonist, Theodor, finds himself repeatedly drawn to a forgotten house at the heart of the city, on Unter den Linden. The secrets which the building hides are intimated by its dilapidated state, its decrepit and 'farblose Mauern' (H III, 166), which contrasts with the other 'herrliche Prachtgebäude' on this boulevard (H III, 165). Through this contrast, Hoffmann highlights the building's concealment of a 'tiefe Wahrheit' (H III, 163), an invisible force which influences the phenomena of the visible world, and which can only be perceived by those who possess a sixth sense, a 'Sehergabe', providing insight into the invisible realm beyond the everyday (H III, 164). Theodor is identified as possessing such a gift, and his 'seltsame Blicke' (H III, 164) enable him to recognize peculiarities in the world around him and move beyond the boundaries of the visible world. However, his attempts to 'read' the significance of the 'ödes Haus', to piece together the meaning of the clues which it presents, are repeatedly frustrated. The windows of the house are all boarded-up, walled-in, or stuffed with paper, so that the inside remains hidden; the more the protagonist tries to gain a better view by moving closer to the building, the more his vision is obscured by passers-by, or by the closing of a curtain. These disruptions to the act of perception serve to render the building enigmatic. As a 'dunkele Stelle' in the topography of the city,[41] it resists interpretation, foreclosing any attempts to explain the truths which it contains.

Liebmann's novel recalls the setting of Hoffmann's tale through her focus on 'Randgebiete' which are paradoxically located at the heart of Berlin; like Theodor, her protagonist is shown to be 'in Berlin', yet simultaneously excluded from the city. Her reference to 'eine öde Straße' (*IB*, p. 113) and description of the crooked houses and 'dunkle', 'verschachtelte' buildings (*IB*, p. 106) evoke not only the dilapidated state of the houses in *Stille Mitte von Berlin*, but also the neglected building at the centre of Hoffmann's tale. Whereas for Liebmann these buildings bear testimony to the silenced history of the city, for Hoffmann's protagonist the mystery of the house is bound up with the enigmatic vision of a woman at one of the windows, which captures his imagination and arouses his desire. In both cases, these architectural structures point to the existence of a reality beyond that visible to the naked eye, and both protagonists employ optical instruments as a means of enhancing their perceptual ability and seeking to gain insight into this phenomenon. While 'die Liebmann' exploits the photographic medium in order to reveal that which was previously unseen, Theodor focuses his gaze upon the elusive figure at the window with the help of a pair of field glasses and a small pocket mirror. Although these optical instruments are intended to sharpen and clarify the viewed image, they actually serve as a means of obfuscating the boundary between the imaginative world of the protagonists and the reality outside; they endow the act of perception with a peculiarly subjective dimension. Like the field glasses and the mirror employed by Hoffmann's protagonist, which mediate between reality and the imagination, disclosing a fantastic realm beyond the visible reality of the everyday,[42] Liebmann's references to the photographic medium point towards an optical unconscious beneath the visible surface of the city. The camera depicts an objective reality by creating a historical record of something that once existed, yet it also cultivates a subjective response to this by drawing the observer's gaze towards particular details and thereby establishing a personal connection to these. It triggers the protagonist's own personal memories, linking her private past with the collective history of the city and revealing the way in which her subjective experience colours her understanding of her research.

Particularly striking in both texts is the way in which these optical devices mark points of transition between the animate and the inanimate. In *Das öde Haus*, the figure in the window initially appears to be lifeless; the narrator reports that her eyes '[hatten] etwas todstarres' (H III, 176), and her gaze is blank. And yet Theodor repeatedly insists on the figure's vitality: he believes he can see her hand and arm moving, and this apparent sign of life is apparently confirmed by her reflection in the pocket mirror (H III, 177). Through his imaginative capacity, the figure's lifeless eyes are transformed into shining 'Himmelsaugen' (H III, 178) which he reads as proof of her identity as a living being. As the figure in the window becomes increasingly animated, however, so does Hoffmann's protagonist find himself fixated, rooted to the spot. He is described as being 'festgebannt' (H III, 166), and he recalls how his first sight of the woman seemed to paralyse him: 'Mir war es, als lähme eine Art Starrsucht nicht sowohl mein ganzes Regen und Bewegen als vielmehr nur meinen Blick, den ich nun niemals würde abwenden können' (H III, 177). The 'Starrsucht' which overcomes Theodor recalls the description of the woman's eyes as 'todstarr', thus demonstrating a form of slippage between subject and object. The transition between movement and stillness is likened here to the passage between life and death; through his efforts to bring the woman to life, the protagonist assumes a spectral form, inhabiting the boundary between this world and the invisible realm beyond.

Hoffmann locates this movement between the animate and the inanimate in the eyes of his protagonist. It is primarily his gaze which is taken over by this sense of paralysis, a detail which is emphasized further by the text's references to his 'starre[s] Hineinblicken' (H III, 178), his 'wahnsinnige[s] Hineinstarren' (H III, 178), and its repetition of the adjective 'starr' in connection with references to his eyes. The deadening of the subject is felt most acutely through the fixation of his vision. As Anthony Vidler observes, the proliferation of references to the ocular in Hoffmann's work can be divided into three distinct categories.[43] First, there are the eyes of characters like the aptly named Klara in *Der Sandmann*, which 'see everything clearly as it is in the world'.[44] Second, there is the 'inner eye' of the artist, which projects its 'inner forces onto the outside world' and thereby creates a subjective engagement with reality.[45] While these eyes possess a visionary capacity, the ability to see beyond mere appearances, they often prove to be more vulnerable to impairment and disorder than the former, 'clear-sighted' eyes,[46] since they are easily deceived and deluded. Third, there are the 'mechanical copies',[47] which are either fashioned to resemble real eyes, as in the case of automata and glass eyes, or to supplement the faculty of vision, as in the case of eye glasses and binoculars. These replicas, Vidler suggests, can be viewed as 'doubles', as 'the products of art embellishing nature': in other words, they symbolize the mimetic power of art to reproduce reality.[48] And yet such imitation is revealed to be dangerous. While they trick the eye of the beholder by presenting an inanimate copy in place of the living one which they represent, they also have the power to 'reduce real eyes to dead ones',[49] fixing the gaze of the observer through their capacity for illusion and deception.

In Liebmann's novel, too, this danger is shown to be inherent in her portrayal of the eye as the prime site of spectral encounter. The text contains numerous allusions to the faculty of vision: the opening paragraph describes the protagonist opening her eyes (*IB*, p. 11), while the final pages are devoted to her predominantly visual impressions of the city (*IB*, pp. 167–70). Verbs such as 'sehen' and 'gucken' are found repeated throughout the novel, as are nouns such as 'Blick', and 'Auge'. Certain characters strive for precise vision, attempting to clear their eyes in order to see better (*IB*, p. 26), and yet their perception is at times revealed to be coloured or distorted by tricks of the light (*IB*, p. 57). Liebmann's protagonist is often shown to possess the kind of 'inner eye' which

Hoffmann associates with the creative artist; in this context her gaze is replaced by a more subjective 'Vorstellung' (*IB*, p. 150). The people whom she encounters on her travels through the city are, like Hoffmann's automata, characterized above all by their dead, lifeless eyes. Liebmann draws an analogy between the glass windows (*IB*, p. 22) of the buildings in her text, and the passers-by in the street, who are described metonymically as 'Glasaugen mit Sprung' (*IB*, p. 41); the cracked glass highlights the vulnerability of the visual apparatus and its propensity to be deformed by the sights which it encounters. In a similar vein, the novel creates a parallel between the 'blinde Fenster' (*IB*, p. 152) of a house on the corner of the Neueschönhauser Straße and the unseeing eyes of an elderly woman who lives in one such building (*IB*, p. 50). The vulnerability of the protagonist's own eyes is underlined by frequent references to 'erstarrte Augen', 'glasige Augen', 'ausgeschlagene Augen', and 'blinde Augen', which repeatedly point to the possibility that her perceptual apparatus will be damaged by the sights it encounters. Situated at the threshold between self and other, the inner and outer world, the eye is inherently flawed, constantly attended by its propensity to be impaired and blinded. And the animating gaze with which the writer breathes life into inanimate figures has the potential to turn back on her protagonist, rendering her correspondingly lifeless.

'Tote Hände'

The protagonist of *Das öde Haus*, in exercising his visionary powers, is forced to abandon the conventional techniques of rational observation and hypothesis, searching instead for a new way of engaging with the city. Rather than watching the urban scenes from a distance, shielded by a transparent window, he wanders through the streets, experiencing the city directly in the manner of a *flâneur*.[50] As Robert McFarland observes, Theodor's method of perception can be situated in the context of 'an abrupt shift in visual culture' which occurred during the first part of the nineteenth century. In a move away from established techniques of rational observation, this new visual culture emphasized the 'subjective, corporeal and ephemeral nature of vision'.[51] It challenged the Cartesian division of subject and object, since the viewer could no longer be regarded as a distinct entity, separate from the object under scrutiny.[52] Instead, he was obliged to adopt a more mobile perspective, participating physically in the scenes which he sought to observe and heightening his visual capabilities by involving other senses in the act of perceiving and representing reality. This move towards a more corporeal form of vision is signalled in Hoffmann's writing through the joint action of the eye and the hand. Acting together to create an altered way of engaging with the world, these organs work to increase the proximity between the subject and the other. And yet, just as the eye risks being blinded by the sights which it sees, so too is the hand in danger of being deadened or petrified through its contact with the world.

The duplicitous partnership of hand and eye is apparent in *Das öde Haus* through Hoffmann's manipulation of these organs as a driving force in the plot.[53] Theodor is drawn to the apparition in the window primarily by the glimpse he catches of her hand and arm (H III, 169), and by their tantalizing promise of a physical connection with the woman which they represent. Although he tries to gain a better view of the figure by moving closer to the building, his line of vision becomes increasingly interrupted and fragmented as he is jostled by the crowds on the pavement and caught up in their movement (H III, 176). Ultimately, his eye proves to be inadequate for the task of gaining access to this enigmatic being. As the protagonist then withdraws from the crowd, gazing into his pocket mirror and thereby attempting to obtain a better view of the mysterious woman, his faculty of vision assumes an increasingly tactile dimension. His gaze is shown to 'penetrate' the house (H III, 176); his eyes encounter the figure in the window and 'grasp' the image which confronts him. At the same time, however, the physical effects of his vision are inverted, as he finds himself gripped (H III, 178) by the same bodily condition as the figure in the window. When she appears pale and sickly, he experiences this corporeally, being struck down by 'ein körperliches Übelbefinden' (H III, 181). Often the woman's gaze has the same effect upon the protagonist as a physical encounter, as when the protagonist awakens from sleep, 'wie plötzlich durch äußere Berührung geweckt' (H III, 180). His dream-like encounters with the woman's eyes are experienced as a kind of manual contact, which is later rendered literal through his meeting with the figure of Angelika inside the house: 'Schon fühlt' ich mich von den Händen des Weibes berührt' (H III, 189). In looking at the image of the woman in the window, the protagonist feels himself to be touched by her hands. Rather than drawing him closer to the figure, though, this contact arouses a sense of terror and 'Befremdung' in Theodor, which manifests itself primarily in his eyes (H III, 191). Through this physical encounter with the woman in his vision, Hoffmann's protagonist is literally 'ent-setzt' (H III, 181), transported outside himself in such a manner that he is no longer fully in control of his thoughts and actions. His eyes prove to be instruments of deception, while his hands become double agents, caught in a conflict between voluntary and involuntary action.

For Liebmann, too, the experience of being in Berlin is shown to possess a corporeal dimension. The itinerant perspective created by the protagonist's journeys through the city is in part liberating, since it enables her to observe the urban landscape from different angles, crossing the border between East and West and personally experiencing the effects of these divisions on the human subject. At the same time, however, this mobility also poses restrictions, as the protagonist's perspective is limited by the physicality of her body and its existence in space. Descriptions of the city are repeatedly interrupted by disconnected thoughts and fragments of personal commentary, while the protagonist's movements are impeded by encounters with other people or by physical obstacles which hinder her progress. Rather than being detached from the city which she observes, she is shown to be 'ein Teil der Welt, ein Teil des Lebens' (*IB*, p. 161); the repetition of 'Teil' emphasizes not only her participation in the reality which she seeks to record, but also the incompleteness of her viewpoint, resulting from her inability to perceive the whole of Berlin at a single moment in time. The city is described as 'die Landschaft ihrer Gedanken' (*IB*, p. 156), an external projection of her inner thoughts, whose objective existence is inseparable from the protagonist's subjective perception of them. Above all, her visual perception of the city is inextricably linked with her corporeal experience of it. Despite the novel's numerous allusions to the faculty of vision, the protagonist often details phenomena which are experienced in a tactile manner as a kind of 'Berührung' (*IB*, p. 137) or 'Händedruck' (*IB*, p. 150). At times, she closes her eyes (*IB*, p. 135), thereby heightening the intensity of these non-visual impressions; at others, such tactile experiences seem to take over the power of sight, so that the eye assumes a haptic quality, casting its gaze over objects in order to obtain a palpable impression of them. The description of people's glassy eyes, for example, is linked with the verb 'spüren' (*IB*, p. 41); rather than seeing the city, these figures come to feel it, sensing with a kind of physical intuition the changes which have occurred in this urban space. This tactility is on one level compensatory, since it stands in for the flawed vision offered by the glazed eye, and yet it also has another function, serving to uncover aspects of reality which are not normally seen; it is therefore bound up with the uncanny task of revealing the invisible. However, this form of perception proves to be flawed, as its promise of a heightened apprehension of reality is undermined by the deadening or petrification of the touch; like the glassy eyes, whose vision is frozen, the motif of the dead hand can signal a distorted or blocked relation to reality.[54]

Significantly, many of Liebmann's references to hands and the sense of touch occur in conjunction with her allusions to photography. Rather than confirming the power of the photograph to evoke a material connection to the reality which they depict, these references reveal this link to be elusive. Towards the middle of the novel, the protagonist receives a bundle of photographs which were taken by the photographer some time before his death. She finds herself particularly attracted to an image of the photographer's fingers: 'Da sieht sie die Finger des Fotografen auf manchen Blättern, er hat die eigenen Finger mitfotografiert, beim Festhalten eines Adreßbuchs, schöne Finger, längst begraben' (*IB*, p. 51). The photographer here has fallen victim to the power of his camera to create a state of living death, becoming both the agent and the object of the photographic process. By inadvertently photographing his hands, he has left behind a posthumous trace of his presence, a reminder of his substantial, bodily existence. This presence is associated with the tactile; the repeated references to fingers, heightened by the alliterative repetition of 'Fotografen' and 'Festhalten', recall Barthes's suggestion that 'the Photographer's organ is not his eye [...] but his finger'.[55] The image serves as a reminder of the photographer's manual involvement in the process of representation, as his hands are not only featured holding the address book in the photograph, they also operate the trigger of the camera. His body comes to act as an interface between the viewer and the photographic image. It creates the impression of a material connection between the reality being photographed and the corporeal existence of the onlooker, and this connection is revealed to be both mechanical and organic, mediated by the technology of the camera and by the body of the photographer. However, this link is ultimately revealed to be founded on absence; in looking at his hands, the protagonist is unable to feel their touch. She can never recuperate the dead photographer, just as she is unable to bring to life the figures listed in the address book. The material trace of the photographer's existence is impalpable, resisting the protagonist's touch, while the illusory presence of his hand becomes a persistent ghostly remainder, recalling what Matthias Bickenbach describes as 'der Eingriff eines Gespenstes'.[56]

The inanimate state of the photographer's hand signals the gradual assimilation of his body into the photographic medium; the finger which operates the shutter of the camera becomes part of the mechanized production of the image, undergoing a kind of reification and calling into question its relation to the body to which it is prosthetically attached.[57] A similar depiction of the hand as a point of transition between the animate and the inanimate occurs in Liebmann's portrayal of the scene of writing and its association with the mechanical apparatus of the typewriter. Liebmann's descriptions of this device often reveal the sense of estrangement and loss of identity felt by its operator, recalling what Friedrich Kittler has identified as the fundamental disembodiment instigated by the typewriter. Handwriting, Kittler argues, conventionally testifies to the corporeal existence of its producer. The hand and the eye work together to guide the movement of the pen on the page, and this concerted action lends the written word a direct connection to the human body; it becomes an embodiment of the mental processes which the writer seeks to record. By contrast, the mechanism of the typewriter disrupts the physical link between the human body and the written word, thus causing the production of text to become disembodied. The physical action of typing relies on 'eine blinde und taktile Gewalt', which 'trennt die Kopplung von Hand, Auge, Letter', removing the hand's direct command over the marks inscribed on the paper.[58]

Through such automation, Kittler argues, the process of writing is liberated from the control of human consciousness; like the stills created by the camera, which capture otherwise indiscernible elements of the visual unconscious, the typewriter reveals points of slippage and difference in the written word which normally escape conscious perception.[59] This disclosure nevertheless occurs at a price, as the writing subject relinquishes control over the text on the page, becoming estranged from his/her body, which is partly incorporated into the machine of representation.

The experience of alienation at the scene of writing is particularly apparent towards the middle of Liebmann's novel, where the protagonist sees the dead hand of her father appear on the typewriter (*IB*, p. 109). The apparition marks a pivotal moment in the text, as the protagonist realizes that an engagement with the history of Berlin also involves facing up to her own family history; the encounter with her father's hand triggers a reflection on his experiences in the Third Reich and the early years of the GDR, which compels her to consider the personal implications of Germany's past and acknowledge the private questions raised by her historical project.[60] This act of unearthing personal memories from the unconscious is marked in the protagonist's visual field by a sudden move from darkness to light, which recalls the uncanny revelation at the heart of her historical project. At the same time, the supernatural encounter is also signalled by a disruption to the protagonist's sense of touch, as she describes the way in which the ghostly hand rests on top of her own: 'Eine Hand eben, liegt auf der Schreibmaschine, [...] bewegt sich, sie hebt sich und legt sich auf die andere Hand, die ist nicht betroffen, betroffen, wovon?' (*IB*, p. 130). This physical gesture might allude to the protagonist's desire to establish a direct connection with the past, one which will move her personally. And yet Liebmann renders this contact ambiguous through the phrase 'nicht betroffen, betroffen, wovon?'. Despite the tactility of this encounter with the ghostly hand, the protagonist experiences its touch as a kind of numbness. The negation of the adjective 'betroffen', with its implications of physical and emotional involvement, raises questions about the protagonist's capacity to feel moved by her knowledge of her family's past. Has she cut herself off from this history for so long that she is no longer capable of feeling a connection to it? Or is the assertion that she is not affected merely an attempt to protect herself by warding off the potentially negative effects of facing up to the past? On the other hand, the repetition of 'betroffen' might be read as a contradiction, a suggestion that the protagonist does actually feel the touch of this ghostly hand; viewed in this light, her encounter with the past assumes a palpable, corporeal dimension, and yet the origins of this tactile contact are unclear. The protagonist's confusion stems not only from the encounter itself, but also from her inability to detect where the ghostly hand emerges from and why it comes to affect her in such a way.

The ambiguity evoked by these questions also indicates an underlying doubt concerning the agency of the protagonist in relation to this ghostly hand. The movements of the hand, emphasized by the assonant repetition of 'hebt', 'bewegt', and 'legt', appear to be at once familiar and alien to the protagonist, and it becomes unclear who is governing this movement: the protagonist eventually realizes with some bewilderment that the ghostly hand on the typewriter is her own (*IB*, p. 109). Transfigured by the eerie light, her hand assumes an ethereal quality: it appears to be immaterial, and is therefore estranged from her physically. Signalling what Lucia Ruprecht terms 'the fault line between agency and impotence',[61] this slippage calls into question the ability of the protagonist to act as an autonomous being. From now on, she finds that whatever she does, she is accompanied by this dead hand (*IB*, p. 131), and when she attempts to write, it is unclear whose hand is actually controlling the production of the words on the page. Crucially, the protagonist's own arm acquires the spectral features of this 'tote Hand' (*IB*, p. 130), and this deadening is shown to alter her perception of events, both in the present and in the past; she is repulsed by the lifeless way in which her lover's arm hangs down from the sleeve of his coat (*IB*, p. 130) and disturbed by the realization that she can only recall the hand of her father, which she held so often as a child, as a dead hand (*IB*, p. 131). Such images project the features of the ghostly back onto the living, revealing the human subject to be always already marked by death, governed by an uneasy sense of lifelessness. This logic, operating both in and on the subject's perceptual apparatus, comes to control her relationship with the world, creating uncanny moments of slippage and disjuncture in her everyday experiences.

'Im Spiegel'

As points of contact between the self and the other, the hand and the eye often signal the sense of estrangement experienced by Liebmann's protagonist. In opening herself up to the ghostly other, she undergoes a metaphorical death which in turn renders her spectral. At times, Liebmann's depiction of this transition between self and other recalls the logic of the *Doppelgänger*. Following Jean Paul's description of doubles as 'Leute, die sich selber sehen',[62] she focuses on scenes where the subject becomes autoscopic or self-seeing, viewing herself as other, while at the same time being observed as an object by this other. Not only is she shown to *have* a spectral double, she also *is* one, since she unwittingly adopts the characteristic features of the other and appropriates them as her own. Her actions towards the other are often inverted and projected back onto herself, while her language is characterized by a kind of 'double talk', a series of linguistic doublings, parodies, and repetitions, which call into question her autonomy as a speaking subject.[63] In particular, her written efforts to engage with the inhabitants of the city are turned back on themselves, as the novel becomes increasingly preoccupied with the protagonist's own life story and her position 'in Berlin'. Through these doublings, Liebmann comments not only on the relationship between self and other and its influence on the development of human identity, but also on the partially flawed ability of the text to depict this connection.

In an interview conducted in 2005 by the journalist Eva Pfister, Liebmann made reference to her preoccupation with what some historians have termed 'counterfactual history' or '*uchronie*'.[64] Engaging with the past, she argues, involves paying attention to what might have happened had events been otherwise; similarly, any attempts to envisage the future involve a consideration of how things might be if events in the present were to unfold differently. She explains:

> Wir sind ja damit aufgewachsen, ohne zu wissen, dass es sich um Schweigen handelt. Wir dachten, die Welt besteht eben aus A, B, C, D, E und wussten nicht, dass da vielleicht A', B' und A'', B'' und sonst was alles hätte vorkommen können. Das muss man dann mit der Zeit entdecken, und dann die speziellen Leerstellen, die einen selbst betreffen.[65]

Viewed in this light, the doubling which occurs throughout *In Berlin* appears to be directly linked to Liebmann's project of revealing 'Leerstellen', those gaps and silences in our understanding of history, both personal and collective. For Liebmann, the task of relating to the past involves accepting that one's own life might have been different had one lived in a different historical, social, or geographical context. It entails acknowledging the possibility that one has a *Doppelgänger* in another historical or spatial realm, or rather, that one's own life is perhaps only the double of another. On one level, Liebmann's advocacy of the subject's identification with the other points to an alternative form of historical experience, founded on intuitive understanding and empathy. Such a connection would have the potential to overcome the 'Taubheit und Kälte' (*SM*, p. 18) of conventional historical thinking and counter the process of repression which excludes certain figures from collective memory. On another level, though, such empathy not only risks subjecting the individual to the painful experiences of the other, it also raises ethical questions about the appropriation and misappropriation of others' suffering.

An example of this doubling can be found towards the middle of *In Berlin*, where Liebmann describes an encounter between the protagonist and a woman in the West. While both figures had originally lived in Pankow and shared a desire to leave the GDR, they each met quite different fates: the protagonist succeeded in obtaining a visa which enabled her to travel back and forth between East and West, whereas the other woman was arrested and imprisoned, before finally being bought free by the Federal government (*IB*, p. 147). Liebmann emphasizes the similarities between these two women by presenting them as mirror images of one another:

> Diese Frau ist aus Pankow, will tauschen wie sie, und es geht nicht, seit ebenso langer Zeit, [...] und jetzt hat die Frau alles, was die Liebmann nicht hat, und was die Liebmann hat, das hat die nicht, und das ist nun die einzige, die mit ihr tauschen könnte, die steht mir gegenüber, das heißt was, wir sind jetzt wie Spiegel. (*IB*, p. 148)

The metaphorical doubling which occurs here is reflected on a formal level by the chiastic repetition of certain phrases, which serves to emphasize the interchangeable positions of these two women. While the verb 'tauschen' refers superficially to the characters' desire to swap their apartments, it also hints at a more fundamental exchange of identity, based on a loss of distinction between subject and other. As they stand opposite each other, the protagonist comes to see the woman as a mirror image of herself. She experiences the other's imprisonment as a form of psychological confinement, since, despite her freedom to travel, she feels herself to be restricted by the sense that she cannot go on (*IB*, p. 149). The mirror itself acts as a kind of prison, limiting the movement of the protagonist, who comes to feel that she is 'in dem Spiegel drin' (*IB*, p. 148), trapped inside it.[66] Above all, Liebmann signals a convergence of the two women's thoughts through the colloquial form of the narrative. The woman is apparently reified by the use of the pronoun 'die', and this is paralleled by the description of the protagonist as 'die Liebmann'. As the figures come to view themselves as other, the narrative perspective is progressively blurred, and it becomes increasingly unclear who is doubling whom.

In revealing the hypothetical potential of the protagonist's past, this specular relationship between the two women forms part of an attempt to engage productively with the alternatives and possibilities offered by historical experiences and thereby locate herself on the 'Karte der Zeit'. At the same time, however, they are shown to have a destabilizing effect on the protagonist's sense of self. The domestic space, the 'Wohnzimmer' in which these women meet, is described as 'unwohnlich', and when the protagonist returns to her own flat, she finds that this uninhabitable atmosphere has spread to her own room. Although she remarks that nothing has changed, that everything is 'wie immer' (*IB*, p. 152), she nevertheless feels that she cannot live here.[67] The room to which she returns is virtually empty; it contains 'nichts, was auf Leben hinweist' (*IB*, p. 152), nothing to keep her fixed in the present, and the protagonist feels uprooted, as though her very existence has been displaced. Her sense of dislocation is emphasized further through a subsequent reference to the image of the mirror. Liebmann writes: 'Es sieht aus, als ob niemand hier wohnt, denkt die Liebmann, im Spiegel, im Spiegel, wenn so etwas möglich wäre, sieht es aus, als ob jemand gestorben ist, grade gestorben, denkt, im Innersten ist es vielleicht schon passiert' (*IB*, p. 152–53). The vertiginous experience of the protagonist is underlined on a formal level by the textual doubling instigated by repetition of the phrase 'im Spiegel'. Liebmann transposes the traditional symbolism of the *Doppelgänger* as an omen of death onto a metaphorical level,[68] as the reflection of the self as other, together with the accompanying temporal and spatial dislocation, results in a deadening of the subject which occurs internally, 'im Innersten'. Due to the unusual use of the indicative mood after the conjunctive 'als ob', however, this internal death is shown to be a finality, irrecoverably negating the protagonist's sense of self.

For Liebmann's protagonist, this internal deadening is most often experienced when she travels across the border between the two halves of the city. The boundary itself is frequently signalled by the image of a mirror, with events in the East and the West unfolding as reflections of each other, and the act of crossing the border is shown to involve an encounter with another version of the self, one whose life has played out differently. At several points in the novel, Liebmann describes the way in which the protagonist, in transferring from one sector to another, has to walk down a corridor towards a large security mirror: 'Da geht die Liebmann mit Koffer und Plastiktüte diesen Gang lang im Dunkeln, einem Spiegelfenster entgegen, hinter dem welche sitzen, wahrscheinlich, in Uniformen, zugucken' (*IB*, p. 78). The threshold is marked by a 'Spiegelfenster', a window whose glass has become reflective, obscuring the passage of the gaze through it. The protagonist's own self-image seems to merge with the perspective of the security officials, thus depicting her observation of herself as a kind of surveillance. The point of entry into the new State is marked by an encounter with her estranged image, as she is made to walk towards the mirror, and her sense of foreboding is heightened by the symbolic darkness of the passageway.[69] Whereas the protagonist's daughter enjoys the experience of crossing the border, her ironic expression, 'ich lache mich tot' (*IB*, p. 79), is, for 'die Liebmann', transformed into a more negative awareness of her own mortality: 'Die Liebmann wird denken, ich auch, ich sterbe, es war niemand da' (*IB*, p. 79). The encounter with her specular double is marked by an absence, which, through the unexpected use of the past tense, is projected back onto her previous life, undermining any sense of vitality which she might once have possessed and rendering her existence spectral. Rather than opening up a productive realm of possibility, then, her journeys from one part of the city to another are characterized by a sense of unbeing, by a realization that her identity is scarred by the very life stories with which she seeks to engage.

— * —

Through her identification with other people's experiences, whether real or hypothetical, Liebmann's protagonist is struck by a feeling of numbness, a deadening of her senses which disrupts her ability to connect with the world. This lack of sensation might resonate with what Carolyn Dean terms 'the fragility of empathy'. Commenting on the 'compassion fatigue' evident in post-war culture, Dean argues that the 'recent history of genocide and totalitarianism' has led to a pervasive scepticism regarding conventional notions of empathy. Empathic identification is often considered to be 'theoretically ideal', since it offers a way of connecting with the suffering of humanity, and yet in reality it proves to be highly problematic. At best, expressions of empathy can appear to be 'insufficient or disingenuous';[70] at worst, they risk 'obliterating boundaries between self and other in order to take the victim's place'.[71] The power of the imagination to create an identification with the other becomes a tool with which to repress his/her difference; it signals a 'disguised form of [...] hegemony',[72] founded on the 'narcissistic blotting out of the other'.[73] Liebmann's novel initially appears to be illustrating this ethical problem of appropriating the experiences of the other in order to identify oneself as victim. However, in adopting the logic of the ghostly double, Liebmann counters the hegemony of the self which all too easily overshadows attempts at empathic identification. The protagonist learns to see with the eyes of the other and experiences the corporeality of her suffering on her own body.[74] And yet, rather than enacting an 'obliteration of Otherness',[75] she experiences this eradication projected back on herself, as an internal deadening. The empathic device by which the object of the imagination is absorbed and destroyed is inverted, as the protagonist herself comes to be possessed and potentially annihilated by the gaze of the other.

Notes to Chapter 4

1. See Gabriele Eckart, 'Ost-Frau liebt West-Mann: Zwei neue Romane von Irina Liebmann und Monika Maron', *Colloquia Germanica*, 30 (1997), 315–21; and Cornelia Geißler, 'Schwebezustand: Zu Irina Liebmanns Roman *In Berlin*', *Berliner Zeitung*, 4 June 1994. Lyn Marven views the text as an example of autobiographical fiction. See Marven, '"Die Landschaft ihrer Gedanken"', pp. 267–81.
2. I take the term from E. T. A. Hoffmann's *Serapionsbrüder* (H IV, 1115).
3. On the distinction between these modes of historical experience and their relation to the cinematic form, see Webber, *Berlin in the Twentieth Century*, pp. 152–53.
4. Liebmann in conversation with Smale, 21 July 2009. The quotation is taken from Ilja Ehrenburg, *Visum der Zeit* (1929), trans. by Hans Ruoff (Leipzig: Reclam, 1982), p. 13.
5. Lyn Marven overlooks this temporal dimension when she writes that '*In Berlin* is about "being in Berlin" — indeed, about "Irina Liebmann in Berlin"'. Marven, '"Die Landschaft ihrer Gedanken"', p. 267. Astrid Köhler raises this point indirectly when she asks, 'wie viel diese Berlins, die sie da sieht, überhaupt miteinander zu tun haben'. Köhler, *Brückenschläge*, p. 115.
6. Liebmann in conversation with Smale, 21 July 2009.
7. Gilles Deleuze and Félix Guattari, *A Thousand Plateaus: Capitalism and Schizophrenia*, trans. by Brian Massumi (Minneapolis: University of Minnesota Press, 1987), p. 474. See also Laura Marks, *Touch: Sensuous Theory and Multisensory Media* (Minneapolis: University of Minnesota Press, 2002), pp. 6–8.
8. Marks, *Touch*, p. 13.
9. Although the present book focuses on Liebmann's novels, she also refers to *Stille Mitte von Berlin* in two of the short stories in her collection *Mitten im Krieg* (Frankfurt a. M.:

Frankfurter Verlagsanstalt, 1989); in these, the protagonist's research is described using a montage of temporal layers, which illustrates the imaginative encounter with the past which such research demands, and also recalls the collapse of historical boundaries which occurs in her photographs.

10. Liebmann's fascination with the architectural documentation of human absence might recall Christian Boltanski's project, *The Missing House* (1990), on the Große Hamburger Straße, which calls to mind the predominantly Jewish inhabitants of a house that no longer exists by means of a series of placards positioned on the adjacent firewalls. See Webber, *Berlin in the Twentieth Century*, pp. 30–31; and Aleida Assmann, *Erinnerungsräume: Formen und Wandlungen des kulturellen Gedächtnisses* (Munich: Beck, 1999), pp. 375–77.
11. Barthes, p. 91.
12. William J. T. Mitchell, *Picture Theory: Essays on Verbal and Visual Representation* (Chicago: University of Chicago Press, 1994), p. 163.
13. Ibid., p. 152. See also James Heffernan, *The Museum of Words: The Poetics of Ekphrasis from Homer to Ashbery* (Chicago: University of Chicago Press, 1994), p. 3.
14. Mitchell, p. 156.
15. Ibid., p. 156.
16. Ibid., p. 158.
17. Ibid.
18. Ibid., p. 156.
19. Several theorists of ekphrasis have pursued this notion. Jean Hagstrum refers to the technique as 'that special quality of giving voice and language to the otherwise mute art object'. Jean Hagstrum, *The Sister Arts: The Tradition of Literary Pictorialism and English Poetry from Dryden to Gray* (Chicago: University of Chicago Press, 1958), p. 18. W. J. T. Mitchell suggests that it is one of 'the utopian aspirations of ekphrasis [...] that the mute image may be endowed with a voice'. Mitchell, p. 156. Similarly, James Heffernan argues that 'ekphrasis entails prosopopeia, or the rhetorical technique of envoicing a silent object'. Heffernan, p. 6.
20. Lyn Marven comments on these alterations in narrative perspective, suggesting that they present a deliberate reflection on the 'complications of autobiography', as well as capturing the internal and external sounds of the city and thereby representing on a formal level what Liebmann describes as 'die Landschaft ihrer Gedanken'. Marven, '"Die Landschaft ihrer Gedanken"', pp. 272–74.
21. The fact that Liebmann's protagonist never succeeds in giving voice to these spectral figures might suggest an acknowledgement of the much-discussed ethical impossibility of speaking on behalf of the dead. See Geoffrey Hartman, *The Longest Shadow: In the Aftermath of the Holocaust* (Bloomington: Indiana University Press, 1996), pp. 138–43; and Shoshana Felman and Dori Laub, *Testimony: Crises of Witnessing in Literature, Psychoanalysis and History* (New York: Routledge, 1992), pp. 80–86.
22. Murray Krieger, *Ekphrasis: The Illusion of the Natural Sign* (Baltimore: Johns Hopkins University Press, 1992), p. 11. See also Wendy Steiner's definition of ekphrasis as 'a literary topos in which poetry is to imitate the visual arts by stopping time, or more precisely, by referring to an action through a still moment that implies it'. Wendy Steiner, *The Colors of Rhetoric: Problems in the Relation between Modern Literature and Painting* (Chicago: University of Chicago Press, 1982), p. 41.
23. Krieger, p. 10.
24. Ibid., p. 45.
25. In this context, Liebmann seems to be drawing on one of the fundamental preoccupations of Romantic writers. See Frederick Burwick, 'Ekphrasis and the Mimetic Crisis of

Romanticism', in *Icons, Texts, Iconotexts: Essays on Ekphrasis and Intermediality*, European Cultures, 6, ed. by Peter Wagner (Berlin: de Gruyter, 1996), pp. 78–104 (pp. 78–81).

26. Liebmann further notes that these Jewish sites are now being guarded by policemen and security cameras (*IB*, p. 167), an observation which she also discusses in *Stille Mitte von Berlin* (*SM*, p. 60).
27. A similar image occurs in *Die freien Frauen*, where Liebmann describes the figures as 'zittrig' and 'klein' (*DfF*, p. 59). These adjectives lend the figures decidedly human qualities, as well as emphasizing their apparent vulnerability. At the same time, though, they create an impression of a tremulous movement, one which keeps the figures rooted to the spot.
28. Astrid Köhler, 'Whither? Away! Reflections on the Motifs of Travel and Identity in Recent East German Prose', in *German-Language Literature Today: International and Popular?*, ed. by Arthur Williams, Stuart Parkes, and Julian Preece (Oxford: Lang, 2000), pp. 207–20 (pp. 209–10).
29. On the relationship between cinema and trains, see Webber, *Berlin in the Twentieth Century*, pp. 156–67.
30. 'Irina Liebmann im Gespräch mit Hans Joachim Schröder', in Joachim Schröder, *Interviewliteratur zum Leben in der DDR: Zur literarischen, biographischen und sozialgeschichtlichen Bedeutung einer dokumentarischen Gattung*, Studien und Texte zur Sozialgeschichte der Literatur, 83 (Tübingen: Niemeyer, 2001), p. 244.
31. As Laura Mulvey writes, film is 'like the beautiful automaton', haunted by 'a residual trace of stillness'. Laura Mulvey, *Death 24x a Second: Stillness and the Moving Image* (London: Reaktion, 2006), p. 67.
32. The link is emphasized further by the repetition of 'Rausch' (*IB*, p. 11), and 'rauschen' (*IB*, p. 131).
33. Mulvey, p. 9.
34. Ibid., p. 13.
35. Ibid., p. 15.
36. Liebmann in conversation with Smale, 21 July 2009. Liebmann confirmed her interest in the writings of E. T. A. Hoffmann, although she did not directly state that *In Berlin* contains deliberate references to this author.
37. Webber, *The Doppelgänger*, p. 120.
38. For more detailed analyses of Hoffmann's references to the magic lantern, see Monica Schmitz-Emans, 'Die Laterna magica der Erzählung: Ein Bilderzeugungsverfahren als poetologische Metapher', *Globkult*, 7 November 2008; and Maik Müller, pp. 108–15.
39. As Claudia Lieb writes, 'Die Animation des künstlichen Gegenübers setzt die Mortifikation des Ichs voraus, was sich in den zahlreichen Erstarrungen des Helden zeigt, der mitunter "wie der Tod" persönlich erscheint'. Claudia Lieb, 'Und hinter tausend Gläsern keine Welt: Raum, Körper und Schrift in E. T. A. Hoffmanns *Das öde Haus*', *E. T. A. Hoffmann Jahrbuch*, 10 (2002), 58–75 (p. 67).
40. Robert McFarland, 'Reading "Das öde Haus": E. T. A. Hoffmann's Urban Hermeneutics', *Monatshefte*, 100 (2008), 489–503 (pp. 490–92).
41. Ibid., p. 498.
42. See Rupert Gaderer, *Poetik der Technik: Elektrizität und Optik bei E. T. A. Hoffmann*, Rombach-Wissenschaften/Edition Parabasen, 9 (Vienna: Rombach, 2009), p. 94.
43. Vidler, *The Architectural Uncanny*, pp. 33–35.
44. Ibid., p. 33.
45. Ibid.
46. Ibid., p. 33.
47. Ibid., p. 34.

48. Ibid.
49. Ibid., p. 34.
50. Walter Benjamin refers to 'Das öde Haus' in his description of the visual practice adopted by *flâneurs* like the narrator of Poe's 'The Man in the Crowd' and Theodor (WB, VII.1, 89).
51. McFarland, p. 495.
52. See also Jonathan Crary, *Techniques of the Observer: On Vision and Modernity in the Nineteenth Century* (Cambridge, MA: MIT Press, 1990), p. 98.
53. As Claudia Lieb notes, 'Es sind vor allem die toten Augen, die den Gang der Handlung bestimmen und zum Ziel- und Angriffspunkt der unterschiedlichsten Prinzipien werden'. Lieb, p. 68.
54. As Katherine Rowe writes,

> Dead hands challenge and complicate [the] 'common sense' logic of kinetic self-possession, both as a full account of bodily experience and as an ahistorical given. [...] They disrupt the familiar connections between cause and effect that permit us to attribute and interpret actions. And they stage sudden reversals of control [...] that direct us to the disabling, dependent, and self-alienating experiences of the acting self'.

> Katherine Rowe, *Dead Hands: Fictions of Agency, Renaissance to Modern* (Stanford, CA: Stanford University Press, 1999), p. xi.

55. Barthes, p. 15.
56. Matthias Bickenbach, 'Fotografierte Autorschaft: Die entzogene Hand', in *Manus Loquens: Medium der Geste — Gesten der Medien*, ed. by Matthias Bickenbach, Annina Klappert, and Hedwig Pompe, Mediologie, 7 (Cologne: DuMont, 2003), pp. 188–209 (p. 205).
57. This mechanization recalls Rowe's statement that 'dead hands come to resemble the accessories, tools, and marks they leave behind [...]. Wandering or ghostly, they symbolize the loss, theft, or withering of an individual's capacity to act with real political or personal effect. And their tenuous, prosthetic affiliation to the body raises questions about whether the powers they embody are in fact proper to any person'. Rowe, p. 4.
58. Friedrich Kittler, *Aufschreibesysteme: 1800/1900* (Munich: Fink, 1985), pp. 201–02. See also Sonja Neef, 'Die (rechte) Schrift und die (linke) Hand', *Kodikas/Ars Semiotica*, 25 (2002), 159–76, and Mark Seltzer, *Bodies and Machines* (New York: Routledge, 1992), p. 10.
59. Kittler, *Aufschreibesysteme*, p. 202.
60. The story which emerges bears much resemblance to the life of Liebmann's own father, Rudolf Herrnstadt, who was chief editor of the *Neues Deutschland* newspaper in the early GDR. Following accusations of responsibility for the Workers' Uprising of 17 June 1953, he lost his job and was expelled from the SED. Although much of Liebmann's writing circles around this trauma, it is only recently that she has felt able to address the event directly, in her biography of her father. See Irina Liebmann, *Wäre es schön? Es wäre schön! Mein Vater Rudolf Herrnstadt* (Berlin: Berlin Verlag, 2008).
61. Lucia Ruprecht, 'Ambivalent Agency: Gestural Performances of Hands in Weimar Dance and Film', *Seminar*, 46 (2010), 255–75 (p. 256).
62. Jean Paul, *Werke*, ed. by Norbert Miller, 6 vols (Munich: Hanser, 1970), III, 67.
63. See Webber, *The Doppelgänger*, p. 3, and Renate Lachmann, 'Der Doppelgänger als Simulakrum: Gogol, Dostoevskii, Nabokov', in Lachmann, *Gedächtnis und Literatur, Intertextualität in der russischen Moderne* (Frankfurt a. M.: Suhrkamp, 1990), pp. 463–89 (p. 465).

64. While the term occurs widely in historical discourse, the following are noteworthy for their consideration of its implications for narrative theory: Paul Alkon, 'Alternate History and Postmodern Temporality', in *Time, Literature and the Arts: Essays in Honor of Samuel L. Macey*, ed. by Thomas R. Cleary, ELS Monograph Series, 61 (Victoria: University of Victoria Press, 1994), pp. 65–85, and Jörg Helbig, *Der parahistorische Roman: Ein literaturhistorischer und gattungstypologischer Beitrag zur Allotopieforschung*, Berliner Beiträge zur Anglistik, 1 (Frankfurt a. M.: Lang, 1987).
65. Eva Pfister, 'Teuer erkaufte Freiheit: Irina Liebmann: *Die freien Frauen*', *Deutschlandfunk*, 4 January 2005, <http://www.dradio.de/dlf/sendungen/buechermarkt/337165/> (accessed 10 May 2010).
66. On the mirror image as a 'kind of captivity, antithetical to freedom', see Warner, pp. 169–72.
67. This recalls Andrew Webber's assertion that 'in the *Doppelgänger* scenario, the return home [often] involves dispossession [...], as the "unheimlich" is shown to be resident there'. Webber, *The Doppelgänger*, p. 45.
68. On this symbolism see Freud, 'Das Unheimliche', (SF 4, pp. 258–59), and Otto Rank, *Der Doppelgänger: Eine psychoanalytische Studie* (Leipzig: Internationaler Psychoanalytischer Verlag, 1925), pp. 95–117.
69. A similar blackout occurs on Liebmann's journey back to the East, where the shock of the border crossing, expressed by means of *nomen est omen* in the place name 'Invalidenstraße', is registered belatedly by the protagonist and the reader (*IB*, p. 130). For an analysis of border crossings in the novel and their relation to trauma, see Lyn Marven, 'Divided City, Divided Heaven? Berlin Border Crossings in Post-Wende Fiction', in *Berlin: Divided City, 1945–1989*, ed. by Philip Broadbent and Sabine Hake, Culture and Society in Germany, 6 (New York: Berghahn, 2010), pp. 184–93 (pp. 187–88).
70. Carolyn J. Dean, *The Fragility of Empathy after the Holocaust* (Ithaca: Cornell University Press, 2004), pp. 1–7.
71. Ibid., p. 9.
72. Ibid., p. 11.
73. Ibid., p. 13.
74. On the corporeal aspects of empathy, see Susan Leigh Foster, 'Kinaesthetic Empathies and the Politics of Compassion', in *Critical Theory and Performance*, ed. by Janelle G. Reinelt and Joseph R. Roach (Ann Arbor: University of Michigan Press, 2007), pp. 245–58.
75. Jonathan Boyarin, *Storm from Paradise: The Politics of Jewish Memory* (Minneapolis: University of Minnesota Press, 1992), p. 86.

CHAPTER 5

~

A Haunting Legacy: Irina Liebmann's *Die freien Frauen*

Irina Liebmann's most recent novel, *Die freien Frauen* (2004), initially appears to have little in common with her earlier fictional works. The conventional form of the text, with its clearly defined plot and omniscient, third-person narrator, marks a departure from the experimental prose of her previous writing, while its explicit emphasis on the fictional status of its action and characters implies a move away from the semi-autobiographical narrative of *In Berlin*. No longer are we presented with a fictional 'Liebmann', an imaginary alter ego of the author, whose dissatisfaction with the East led her to move to West Berlin with her daughter; instead, Elisabeth Schlosser, the protagonist of *Die freien Frauen*, is revealed to be living with her son in a flat in the district of Mitte, where she has remained since the days of the GDR. The narrative of this later novel takes place several years after the close of *In Berlin*, and the intervening years are shown to have altered the atmosphere of the city itself; the teeming plant-life and bustling public spaces described at the end of Liebmann's earlier text have been replaced by a bleak, wintry landscape with snow-covered streets and weary passers-by. In addition, the ramshackle *Mietshäuser* and dilapidated buildings which form the backdrop to the protagonist's identity crisis in *In Berlin* have been renovated and in part replaced by featureless *Neubau* constructions. Though apparently innovative, this act of urban regeneration is nevertheless founded upon a troubling erasure of historical traces, signalling a cultural amnesia characterized by what Astrid Köhler terms the 'Verschwinden [der] Geschichte in der neuen Gegenwart'.[1] The topography of Berlin, which was previously shown to contain secrets excluded from personal memory and historiographical discourses, is now at risk of losing its particular connection to the past, as the bulldozers and cranes threaten to reduce the city's historic buildings to dust.

Despite the overt differences between these two novels, however, Liebmann herself has insisted that they must be read in conjunction with one another:

'Beide Bücher, *In Berlin* und *Die freien Frauen*, gehören für meinen Begriff [...] zusammen'.[2] The plot of *Die freien Frauen* is haunted by unfinished business from Liebmann's earlier novel, with the protagonist's historical investigations marking a return to the 'ausstehende Arbeit an der Vergangenheit' which was left incomplete at the end of *In Berlin*.[3] The central characters of both novels frequent a cafe on the Große Hamburger Straße which overlooks the Jewish cemetery and the memorial to the victims of the deportations, and both become increasingly preoccupied with uncovering the collective memories and secrets concealed in this area of Berlin. At the same time, the protagonists share a traumatic family history which resists closure and resurfaces involuntarily in moments of disjuncture. They are each plagued by the absence of their Jewish grandparents, who disappeared without trace in Theresienstadt (*DfF*, p. 24). They both have fragmentary childhood memories of a father figure who was expelled from the Politbüro at the hands of Walter Ulbricht in the early years of the GDR. And they each have Russian heritage which has never been fully explained to them and has consequently been a source of puzzlement and embarrassment. The incomplete nature of these familial memories, the fact that they are interspersed with 'Erinnerungslücke[n]' (*DfF*, p. 146) and 'Leerstellen',[4] means that they cannot easily be assimilated into the protagonists' consciousness; they remain disavowed and are therefore compelled to return repeatedly, tormenting the living and serving to undermine their efforts to weave together a coherent fiction of identity.[5]

In both texts, the task of engaging with repressed memories and silenced histories is cast in a highly ambivalent light. Like the protagonist of *In Berlin*, Elisabeth Schlosser is a writer and dramatist whose efforts to express her thoughts on paper are at times hindered by the weight of the subject matter which she seeks to address. Her assertion, 'ich kann's nicht ertragen' (*DfF*, p. 64), suggests that she feels encumbered by the historical knowledge which she unearths; like the heaviness of the piles of papers described in *In Berlin*, the protagonist's investigations into the past are portrayed as a physical burden which she at times feels unable to bear. Both figures share a sense of being held up by obstacles ('gehindert' — *DfF*, p. 70), a feeling of psychological 'Stillstand' (*DfF*, p. 195), which results in a form of physical paralysis ('[sie] rührte sich nicht von der Stelle' — *DfF*, p. 141). Indeed, the narrator's assertion in *Die freien Frauen* that Elisabeth Schlosser 'glaubte, nicht mehr weitergehen zu können' (*DfF*, p. 139) can be read as a direct echo of the protagonist's repeated lament, 'Ich kann nicht weitergehen' (*IB*, p. 149), in *In Berlin*. In their efforts to bring the past to life, both figures risk becoming frozen, fixated in a melancholic state of arrest which threatens to impede their ability to move forward with their lives. And yet Elisabeth Schlosser proves to be less susceptible to the paralysing consequences of her attachment to the past than the protagonist of *In Berlin*.

While 'Die Liebmann' ultimately flees to the West in an attempt to escape the psychological after-effects of her family's history,[6] Elisabeth Schlosser is determined to confront this legacy. Assuming the role of a detective (*DfF*, p. 138), she pieces together clues and snippets of information in an effort to uncover the details of her father's past. In doing so, she attempts to free herself from the grasp of this traumatic inheritance, taking leave of the phantoms which haunt her and seeking to become one of the 'freie Frauen' to which the title of the novel alludes.

The previous chapter argued that Liebmann's first novel sought to create living images, enlivening inanimate memories through the dynamic momentum of the narrative and thereby creating the uncanny semblance of life. Her efforts to animate the past, to bring it to life in the present, can be viewed as a continuation of the desire expressed in *Stille Mitte von Berlin* to develop a personal connection to historical events and thereby resist the emotional detachment which forecloses the work of mourning.[7] This chapter examines Liebmann's preoccupation with family history in *Die freien Frauen* in the light of her desire to delve beneath official narratives and cultivate a private, subjective understanding of the past. More specifically, it argues that the protagonist's determination to engage with the phantoms transmitted by her father's silences marks a realization that she can only begin to comprehend the wider history of the twentieth century by approaching it through the personal medium of a family narrative. Referring to her own decision to publish a biography of her father, Rudolf Herrnstadt, in 2008, Liebmann has described the way in which her efforts to come to terms with the 'Schicksal des 20. Jahrhunderts' have become increasingly intertwined with her need to face up to 'sein Schicksal', the fate of her father.[8] Similarly, the protagonist of *Die freien Frauen* is only able to engage emotionally with the history of Berlin by coming to understand her family's place in it. Liebmann's emphasis on a subjective means of engaging with the past does not seek to lay claim to what has been termed 'the authority of experience',[9] the problematic notion that personal experience has more validity with regard to historical investigation than documentary and archival material. Rather, it suggests a desire to cultivate an active relationship with the past founded on the mediation between individual and collective experience; in approaching the history of the twentieth century through the lens of her family's experience, the protagonist of *Die freien Frauen* is able to develop her connection to it and maintain 'diese Vorstellung, das alles könnte einmal belebt gewesen sein' (*SM*, p. 11).

Familial Haunting

Throughout *Die freien Frauen*, the protagonist is haunted by a family history which is characterized by gaps of memory and silences (*DfF*, p. 27). Towards the opening of the novel, she identifies her main concern as being 'Familie und noch etwas anderes, wofür es gar keine Worte gibt' (*DfF*, p. 8), thus introducing a connection between her family's experiences and the aura of unspeakability which surrounds them. The protagonist is struck by a realization that certain historical events cannot be relayed in words, that their destructive consequences undermine or forestall the expressive capability of language. Moreover, the negative effects of this unnarrated family history are shown to be passed on from one generation to the next. The protagonist's elderly father evades her attempts to question him about his past, replying with the enigmatic half-words 'Ach', 'Nöo', and 'Äh' (*DfF*, pp. 19–21), linguistic fragments which hint at the disjointed 'scars of memory' buried inside his psyche.[10] Inheriting her father's silence, acutely aware of the gaps in his narrative yet unsure of the history to which they refer, the protagonist finds herself similarly impeded in her ability to speak about the past; at the outset, her family history is shown to be something which she cannot narrate ('wovon zu reden mir [...] nicht möglich war' — *DfF*, p. 8), and later in the novel she realizes that, despite her research, she is also compelled to remain silent about her discoveries ('ich habe ebenso geschwiegen' — *DfF*, p. 128). This inability to communicate is in turn passed on to the protagonist's son; unable or unwilling to speak to his mother, he remains a melancholic figure, who sits at the kitchen table, silently pushing crumbs around his plate and persistently refusing to eat.[11]

To some extent, Liebmann's depiction of the intergenerational transmission of this absence resonates with the pattern of haunting outlined by Nicholas Abraham in his 'Notes on the Phantom'. For Abraham, the experience of trauma, or the failure to mourn for a lost love object, can cause a 'gap' or hole in the psyche of an individual, which is transmitted to future generations through the genealogical inheritance of the unconscious.[12] This gap is concealed by a 'phantom', sustained by 'secreted words',[13] which functions like a 'foreign body',[14] like 'a stranger within the subject's own mental topography'.[15] Rather than being shaped and controlled by events in his/her own past, the individual is shown to be governed by traces of a history which (s)he did not experience directly. In other words, the phantom is radically heterogeneous to the subject, and yet its existence within the individual's psyche means that it comes to be perceived as an integral part of his/her identity. In Liebmann's novel, it is this legacy of an unmastered past that fuels the protagonist's existential unease. Her inheritance of her father's gaps and silences is shown to have been internalized and incorporated into her sense of self, and this involuntary appropriation of his experiences is in turn shown to govern her behaviour. Thus, as well as commenting on her inner sense of emptiness, the protagonist insists that the different paths and routes taken in her life always lead her to the same 'lang gezogene[r] leere[r] Fleck' (*DfF*, p. 11). And her existence in the city is marked by a compulsion to visit and revisit urban spaces which are described as 'leer' (*DfF*, p. 87), 'entleert' (*DfF*, p. 111), and 'menschenleer' (*DfF*, p. 83). Her obsessive attachment to these vacant sites can be read both as an expression of the protagonist's disturbed mental state and as an involuntary attempt to 'stage' her father's silences.[16] Through her restless existence, the protagonist becomes the performative agent of her father's past, acting out the gaps in his narrative and, in doing so, revealing herself to be beholden to their 'phantom effect[s]'.[17]

One such 'phantom effect' can be seen in the protagonist's response to her father's body language. As Abraham argues, the phantom operates primarily through language, working to undermine the communicative power of particular linguistic expressions and manifesting itself in empty speech and hollow words. More specifically, it signals the fact that certain words and phrases relating to the concealed historical event have been evacuated of their emotional content, because such emotions were so overwhelmingly negative. As a result, traces of this repressed sentiment, removed from speech, become visible in the corporeal signals of the individual.[18] Through physical gestures and less overt somatic expressions, the individual passes on signs of his/her unassimilated traumatic experience to his/her offspring, who becomes the unwitting recipient of this fragmented history. In Liebmann's novel, the father's silences are accompanied by a range of physical signals — a raised left eyebrow (*DfF*, p. 19), a shocked frown (*DfF*, p. 20) and half-closed eyes (*DfF*, p. 21) — which allude to the emotional power of his unspoken memories. Indeed, the narrator comments on the way in which these gestures appear to replace his words, at times assuming a theatrical dimension which appears to be at odds with his refusal to speak: 'Über diese Jahre sprach er niemals, tat nur so, als ob er in die kochende Schüssel der Weltgeschichte geblickt hatte und zum Schweigen verurteilt worden war' (*DfF*, p. 27). The phrase 'so tun, als ob' might seem to call into question the veracity of the father's behaviour, implying that his silence is merely a theatrical pretence and lending his gestures the quality of empty rhetoric. And yet the subsequent use of the indicative undermines this doubt; it suggests that his inability to speak is actually an involuntary response to his past and that his body language serves to express the disjuncture between the intensity of his experience and this failure to convey it in words.

This body language is in turn registered and assimilated — often involuntarily — by the protagonist herself. She becomes adept at reading the corporeal signals of her father (*DfF*, p. 19), aware that they refer to a 'geheime[r] Teil seines Lebens' (*DfF*, p. 27), and she senses that these physical gestures serve in part to compensate for his inability to speak about his experiences (*DfF*, p. 127). At the same time, she is shown to adopt his posture and facial expressions, reflecting them in her own; she shakes her head (*DfF*, p. 210) in the same manner as him, and her hands begin to tremble like his (*DfF*, p. 122). This range of corporeal signals is, in turn, passed on to the protagonist's son, whose gaunt, emaciated body seems to exemplify the existential emptiness which he has inherited. Towards the beginning of the novel, Elisabeth Schlosser passes on a message to her son by means of knocking or tapping on his shoulder (*DfF*, p. 37), and this gesture is later echoed in a more violent manner when he strikes his mother in response to her attempt to lay her hand on him (*DfF*, pp. 198–99). His shaking limbs (*DfF*, p. 200) recall the trembling hand of the protagonist, and the narrator also observes that his gesticulations are similar to those made previously by his father (*DfF*, p. 200). Above all, the son's physical appearance is shown to resemble that of his grandfather; while the old man is described as a 'Gespenst' (*DfF*, p. 182), the protagonist's son is portrayed as a ghost-like figure ('ein Gespenst auf der Bank' — *DfF*, p. 199), whose movements are ethereal, even 'geisterhaft' (*DfF*, p. 200). In their unwitting adoption of aspects of her father's behaviour, both the protagonist and her son are reacting to the legacy of the traumatic history which the elderly man experienced. They each internalize his body language, which functions as an 'innere Bewegung' (*DfF*, p. 49), an inner repertoire of gestures and expressions which is mobilized as a protective mechanism whenever they feel that the coherence of their identity is challenged. Whereas for the protagonist's father these corporeal signals serve to express an emotion relating to an event which has been removed from his speech, for Elisabeth Schlosser and her son these bear little relation to their own experience; instead, they act as a kind of mask, serving to cover over the gaps in their family history and compensating for the sense of emptiness which they have inherited.

As a result of this 'phantomatic haunting',[19] the protagonist, and her son are shown to be influenced by a heterogeneous presence which they have internalized and made their own. For each of them, this ambiguous relationship with their family history results in a profound sense of self-alienation, a feeling of being distanced from themselves. While at times they are unable to recognize the alterity within them, at other points in the novel these characters prove to be tormented by a realization that their lives are not their own. When the son accuses his mother of being 'die Falsche' (*DfF*, p. 55), he seems to be confirming her own sense that she is not who she ought to be, that she is both the wrong daughter and the wrong mother (*DfF*, p. 55). Her thoughts are characterized by the prevalence of the adjective 'falsch' — 'irgendwas war falsch' (*DfF*, p. 16), 'es waren die falschen' (*DfF*, p. 16), 'ich wäre die Falsche' (*DfF*, p. 55), '[es schien] ihr falsch' (*DfF*, p. 140) — and her existence in the city is marked by a feeling of being 'fehl am Platze' (*DfF*, p. 70). Her experience of psychic displacement is reflected spatially in the recurrent motif of her 'verlorene Wohnung' (*DfF*, p. 160), which is in danger of being removed from her possession and torn apart (*DfF*, p. 168); she becomes an alien figure in the city ('fremd' — *DfF*, p. 72), estranged from the time and place in which she resides and trying desperately to maintain a grasp on the uncontrollable events of her own life (*DfF*, p. 11). And as the protagonist becomes aware of the otherness within herself, she is increasingly unable to record her experiences in the first person; her episodic letters recounting her innermost reflections are abandoned (*DfF*, p. 193), and the narrator adopts the free indirect style, recording the exact idiom of her thoughts and feelings in the third person. Although less overt than the alternation between first- and third-person narrative in *In Berlin*, the technique nevertheless serves a similar purpose, highlighting the protagonist's self-alienation and cultivating a sense that she is observing herself from a position of alterity.

'Eine Verwechslung im Grunde'

Towards the outset of *Die freien Frauen*, the protagonist highlights her conviction that she has been the victim of a historical error, of what she describes as 'eine Verwechslung im Grunde, im Grunde der Seele natürlich, im tiefsten Grunde' (*DfF*, p. 17). The repetition of the phrase 'im Grunde', which recalls Liebmann's preoccupation with rootedness and grounding in *In Berlin* and Wolf's attempts to reveal what lies beneath the surface of the city, serves here to emphasize the double-ground at the base of the protagonist's existence. Convinced that she ought to have been named Olga (*DfF*, p. 10) and aware that she has been leading a life that is not her own, the protagonist embarks upon a quest to find the reason ('Grund' — *DfF*, p. 170) behind her sense of psychic displacement.[20] This quest leads her into the landscape of her father's past; here, the protagonist seeks to retrace his steps, visiting the places which were significant to him and in doing so attempting to uncover the experiences which he had there. Her return to the ground of his earlier life marks an attempt to bring to life the figures which once inhabited it, to reanimate the people who previously lived there. What concerns the protagonist, however, is not so much the objective history of these places, but rather her personal connection to them; she explores the way in which they constitute the foundation of her own existence and uses them as the basis for a journey inside herself, an attempt to discover what lies at the base of her identity ('was liegt dort noch auf dem Grund meiner Seele' — *DfF*, p. 114). Apparently promising the key to understanding her own existence, these real locations become the setting for a highly subjective psychological drama which takes place above all in the mind of the protagonist.[21]

Throughout the narrative of *Die freien Frauen*, Liebmann reveals the way in which this 'Verwechslung im Grunde' is enacted through various encounters with places and objects relating to the protagonist's family history. As Elisabeth Schlosser begins to uncover material about her father's past, for example, she becomes aware of his pre-war relationship with Gerda Bruhn, a member of the Main Intelligence Directorate of the Soviet Union (GRU) who worked for the underground resistance in the Third Reich until her execution at Plötzensee in 1942.[22] Because this liaison belongs to the untold era of her father's life (*DfF*, p. 107), the protagonist initially becomes aware of its existence in a surprisingly impersonal manner, stumbling upon a reference to Gerda Bruhn in a book about famous spies (*DfF*, p. 107). In reporting this discovery, the protagonist adopts a dry, matter-of-fact tone, with short, simple sentences conveying her lack of emotional connection to the subject matter which has been revealed. It is only when she discovers a photograph of this figure that the protagonist begins to develop a personal bond with her. In looking at the image, Elisabeth Schlosser is drawn to Gerda's 'aufgerissene Augen' (*DfF*, p. 137), which appear to light up ('leuchtend' — *DfF*, p. 137) and fix the onlooker's gaze.[23] Just as references to the eye were used in *In Berlin* to highlight a passage from the animate to the inanimate, so too does the image mark a moment of transition for the protagonist of *Die freien Frauen*. While her gaze seems to enliven the picture of Gerda Bruhn, apparently drawing her out of the picture, Elisabeth Schlosser's eyes are in turn shown to be fixated ('[sie] konnte sich nicht losreißen' — *DfF*, p. 137) and deadened by this encounter. Liebmann creates a striking contrast between the shining eyes of the dead woman and the lifeless, 'trübe Augen' (*DfF*, p. 137) of the protagonist, thus signalling the latter's inner mortification.

This moment of transmission between the animate and the inanimate serves to highlight the protagonist's identification with the dead figure of Gerda Bruhn. Blurring the distinction between the two people, between the living and the dead, the protagonist is shown to incorporate aspects of Gerda Bruhn's life into her own: 'Da konnte man hingehen. Man konnte sehen, was diese Gerda gesehen hatte. Man konnte etwas Wahres sich aneignen aus ihrem Leben, etwas ganz Unberührtes' (*DfF*, p. 137). Elisabeth Schlosser comes to regard herself as Gerda's successor, following in her footsteps and viewing the world through her eyes. She adopts the perspective of this dead figure, regarding her experiences as her own and preserving her existence within herself. In particular, she believes that she has been conditioned to identify with Gerda through her father's behaviour towards her: 'Er hat mit ihr gesprochen wie damals mit dieser Gerda, und sie hatte es angenommen. | Die Rolle, sie hat nicht gepasst' (*DfF*, p. 117). Unable to speak of his relationship with Gerda and her subsequent death, the protagonist's father has projected onto her his disavowed feelings and unwittingly compelled her to act as a kind of replacement for his deceased lover, thus forcing her to play a role which was not her own.[24] The protagonist becomes increasingly aware of the fact that her father's language, which never quite seemed to fit the situation in which it was used, was actually intended for Gerda's ears (*DfF*, p. 116). And she realizes that she has become a kind of messenger ('Botin' — *DdF*, p. 180), assuming the position of Gerda Bruhn in order to perpetuate her father's fantasies and fuel his unconscious desire to maintain his attachment to this dead woman. The effort of adopting this role is shown to have a lasting influence on the protagonist's psyche, undermining her ability to assert the independence of her identity and distorting her perception of her life (*DfF*, p. 117).[25]

Despite her discovery of her father's relationship with Gerda Bruhn, however, the protagonist remains sceptical about its potential to elucidate her experience of an internal 'Verwechslung'. She briefly considers the possibility that she is a reincarnation of this earlier woman (*DfF*, p. 110), yet such a model does not fit with the chronology of their respective lives, as Elisabeth Schlosser had already been born when Gerda was executed (*DfF*, pp. 110–11). This explanation, Liebmann suggests, is not only too simple to be plausible (*DfF*, p. 117), but it also fails to match the complexity of the protagonist's experience ('Es passt ungefähr, aber genau passt es nicht' — *DfF*, p. 111). In particular, the notion that Elisabeth is in some respects a replacement for Gerda fails to provide a credible reason for her conviction that she ought to have been called Olga (*DfF*, p. 10). Following her dissatisfaction with these explanations, the protagonist begins to explore alternative possibilities in her imagination. Convinced that Olga did once exist ('Es hat diese Olga gegeben' — *DfF*, p. 144), she comes to view her as an elder sister (*DfF*, p. 145), who was conceived as a result of the relationship between her father and Gerda, but who, unlike her, was never given the chance to live (*DfF*, p. 144). This child becomes a kind of personal ghost, haunting the protagonist and sustained by her own and by her family's silence:

> Elisabeth Schlosser spürte es daran, dass sie nicht wagte von dem zu reden, was vor ihrer eigenen Geburt sich abgespielt hatte, eben dieser älteren Schwester Olga, die sie hätte haben können und die sie von Anfang an auf dem Buckel trug. (*DfF*, pp. 157–58)

The events which played out ('abgespielt') before the protagonist's birth are shown to be connected to the 'Drama' (*DfF*, p. 115) of her own life; rather than acting her own part, the protagonist is burdened with playing the role of Olga, whose own drama was never allowed to take place.

Viewed in this context, then, Liebmann's protagonist can be read as a kind of 'replacement child',[26] understood in psychoanalytic terms as 'a child born to parents who have had a child die and then conceive the second child in order to fill the void left by the loss of the first'.[27] Supposedly standing in for the loss of an elder sibling, replacement children are the product of a failed work of mourning, of what might be termed a 'manic defense against death'.[28] Because the parents are unable to come to terms with the death of their child, their unconscious fantasies try to undo this event by projecting onto the living offspring the characteristics of their deceased sibling. The replacement child is therefore compelled to lead a life which is not his/her own, taking on a substitutive role and thus never being able to assert his/her own identity. Moreover, as Gabriele Schwab points out, the concept of the replacement child is closely linked to the pattern of inherited trauma signalled by the phantom.[29] She explains: 'Replacement children are subjected to the no-place and no-time, "the nothing" of trauma. Replacement children often literally know *nothing* about the child they are supposed to replace'.[30] The living child 'inherits the legacy of the sibling's traumatic death and failed mourning',[31] being plagued by the silences and gaps in his/her parents' discourse and, above all, being haunted by the ghost of the dead child, which exists in 'a "no-place"' and 'never acquires a real presence'.[32] Conceived in order to 'fill an emptiness, a nothing',[33] replacement children often function as a kind of 'living corpse',[34] incorporating features of the dead child into their own identity and in doing so acting out the spectral existence of their elder sibling.[35] And yet any efforts to exorcise the ghost of the dead sibling are ethically problematic, since they involve committing a kind of double murder, killing the child once again and in doing so repeating the violence to which (s)he was initially subjected.[36]

In Liebmann's novel, this understanding of the protagonist as a replacement child is underlined by her description of herself as a 'Stellvertreterin [...] für eine gewisse Olga, die nicht hatte leben dürfen' (*DfF*, p. 180). Aware of the disappearance of her sister (*DfF*, p. 144), and conscious that she is living the future that her sibling never had (*DfF*, p. 144), Elisabeth Schlosser attempts to keep this dead figure alive inside her. Her dulled eyes and lifeless countenance now come to signal the protagonist's attachment to her lost sibling, highlighting the fact that her efforts to animate her absent sister come at the price of her own internal mortification, and she comes to lead a spectral existence, inhabiting the boundary between life and death. At the same time, however, the narrative stresses the impossibility of laying this deceased figure to rest, since her ghostly existence within the protagonist poses a challenge to the dynamic of repression and silencing which characterizes her family history and prevents her from disappearing altogether. The protagonist's sibling is thus depicted as one of many victims of violence whose deaths have been covered over: 'Wo sind sie alle hin, die nicht in Frieden Verstorbenen, die Ermordeten und die Erschlagenen, von denen man uns so viele verschwiegen hat? Glauben Sie, die verschwinden so einfach?' (*DfF*, p. 144). Rather than disappearing, these figures live on as ghosts among the living, thus resisting the very logic of repression which created them in the first place: 'Ganz und gar mächtig und endlos klingt es nun, [...], wie der Sturm, der solche Ermordeten treibt, solche Geister, so klingt es. | Mir klingt es so, [...] und ich glaube, es treibt sie in unsere Nähe, natürlich, sie wollen zu uns' (*DfF*, p. 145). Inhabiting a silence, an emptiness, these ghosts exist in order to draw attention to that gap, thus ensuring that they are not forgotten. Their spectral presence becomes a kind of strength (*DfF*, p. 144), a signal of their unwillingness to be consigned once again to death.

Uchronian Narratives

As the narrative of *Die freien Frauen* develops, Liebmann's protagonist increasingly begins to identify with Olga, her elder sister. Towards the middle of the novel, for example, she reflects on what might have happened, had she been conceived in Olga's stead:

> Es gehe ihr nicht um die Juden, aber was sie erzählen wolle, das hänge nun einmal mit denen zusammen, es gehöre dazu, wäre sie sonst im Ausland geboren, sie selber? Denn hier in Berlin wäre sie nie geboren, oder dann gleich auch getötet worden, so sei es nun mal, und wie sie es sagte, bereute sie es sofort, denn nun hatte sie das Gefühl, dass auch ihre eigene Geschichte niemals hätte geschehen dürfen, oder wenigstens niemals erzählt. (*DfF*, p. 158)

The use of the pronoun 'sie' in this passage is ambiguous, apparently referring both to Elisabeth Schlosser and to her elder sister; such slippage blurs the distinction between the two figures, thus signalling the protagonist's identification with Olga and marking her development of a personal, empathic connection to her sister's past founded on subjective perception and 'Gefühl'. Although she realizes that the fate of her sister is inseparable from the collective experience of Berlin's Jews, the protagonist is concerned primarily with the private implications of this figure's existence. The fragmentary style of the passage, with its short, breathless clauses and internal contradictions, conveys the emotional disturbance wrought by this consideration of Olga's history; in placing herself in her sister's position, the protagonist is brought face to face with the prospect of her own death. Her efforts to imagine what life was like for her sibling lead her to consider the possibility that her own life might not have existed, and that her story might never have been told. Above all, they compel her to confront the existential void in her which has been created by her sister's absence.

Liebmann's narrative at this point shifts into the subjunctive mood, thus indicating the protagonist's reflection on what *might have* happened had events progressed differently. This apparently minor grammatical alteration signals the novel's increasing preoccupation with counterfactual fantasies offering alternatives to the established versions of historical events. More specifically, it points to the text's status as an *uchronie*, a term coined by the nineteenth-century French writer Charles Renouvier to describe any narrative that represents 'l'histoire, non telle qu'elle fut, mais telle qu'elle aurait pu être'.[37] Deriving from the Greek *uchronos* ('no-time'), the term *uchronie* transposes the spatial model of utopian thinking onto a temporal framework, referring to an imagined time running counter to the actual course of history.[38] Like the utopia, which is 'simultaneously constituted by a movement of affirmation and denial', defined as 'a place which is a non-place',[39] the *uchronie* lends a figurative existence to a historical time which never actually came into being. Such narratives are founded upon the notion that any given historical situation contains a multitude of unrealized possibilities and options, whose latent potential has never been explored. By presenting literary accounts of these unfulfilled opportunities, uchronian narratives seek to recuperate some of these losses, rewriting past events in order to bring to light the wasted chances which they contained. Whereas utopian literature employs depictions of alternative places in order to highlight the possibility of change in the future, uchronian texts serve to alter our understanding of the present. By holding up a contrasting model to the established historical narratives, they reveal current events to be contingent and therefore open to modification.[40] Such texts thereby possess what Karen Hellekson describes as a means of 'reconfiguring historical time'.[41] They undo the tendency of historiography to '*make the past remote* from the present',[42] seeking instead to bring the lost opportunities and possibilities of the past to life and in doing so working to 'transform [...] the world and our understanding of reality'.[43]

Liebmann's novel adopts the logic of the *uchronie* in order to resist the dynamic of silencing and repression which characterizes the protagonist's relation to her family history. The protagonist tries to keep the secret relationship between her father and Gerda alive in her mind's eye, and, through the workings of her imagination, she attempts to give their unborn daughter an existence which she never really had. Wondering what would have happened had Gerda survived, she asks whether they would have ever met one another (*DfF*, p. 114). These counterfactual fantasies signal an attempt to undo the chronology of historical time by drawing together both real and imagined, hypothetical events in the present. Events in her everyday life are interrupted by the protagonist's fantasies about her family's past, and she comes to believe that her father and Gerda are regulars at the cafe which she visits (*DfF*, p. 187). The presence of these ghostly figures, whose appearance here is intertwined with a series of references to the Holocaust and its haunting legacy (*DfF*, p. 159),[44] renders her locality 'unheimlich' (*DfF*, p. 173); the cafe itself is described as 'nicht geheuer' (*DfF*, p. 159), 'als ob es hier spuke' (*DfF*, p. 159), while its proprietor jokes about having her own 'Gruselkeller' (*DfF*, p. 172). This interweaving of different temporal realms plunges the protagonist into what she describes as a questionable timeframe: 'Ich befand mich in fragwürdigen Zeiten, in Zeiten, die ich mir gar nicht erklären kann, nur eben das eine weiß ich: Die Gegenwart war es nicht' (*DfF*, p. 128). She comes to exist in a liminal realm between past and present, fiction and reality. This alternative time period is described in negative terms as a kind of 'Nicht-Zeit'; aware that she is not living in the present, the protagonist comes to believe that she has fallen into a 'tiefes Loch' (*DfF*, p. 128), a void outside the bounds of historical time. Paradoxically, however, this uchronian realm proves to be a positive dimension, becoming more convincing to the protagonist than her actual reality and rendering the absent historical figures of her family's past more present (*DfF*, p. 186) than the real people in her life. In opening up a realm beyond the chronology of historical time, it offers the protagonist a means of countering the amnesiac existence of her parents, who 'lebten ganz in der Gegenwart' (*DfF*, p. 128); it enables her to attend to the ghosts of her family's past by refiguring the events of their lives and thereby endowing them with a fictive presence in her imagination.

As Elisabeth Wesseling notes, uchronian narratives are 'situated in a twilight zone between historiography and fiction', since they reshape and embellish the established versions of historical events with inventive reflections on what might have happened had they taken an alternative path.[45] Whereas the actual course of history is rendered illusory by this technique of fictionalization, the counterfactual account is by contrast depicted as real and credible.[46] This blurring of the distinction between history and fiction can be found to operate on two distinct levels in Liebmann's novel. First, the text repeatedly calls into question the possibility of establishing whether or not the historical details uncovered by the protagonist are based in reality. Each time she comes close to discovering a crucial fact or piece of evidence which would confirm her suspicions, she finds that this is either missing, or that another event occurs which prevents her from gaining access to it (*DfF*, p. 171; p. 180). And the protagonist expresses her doubt over the likelihood of being able to succeed in her task of exposing her family's past: 'Sie würde es nicht mehr erfahren, ob diese Geschichte wahr war oder ob sie nur reingefallen war auf Spinnerei. Spinnerei anderer Leute und ihre eigene auch' (*DfF*, p. 179–80). The narrator's use of the free indirect style here casts further doubt on the credibility of Elisabeth Schlosser's discovery, since its rendering of her internal thoughts in the third person highlights the subjective and potentially unreliable nature of the narrative itself; it reveals that her apparently factual account of the past might in fact be the fantasy of another. And yet the protagonist deliberately exploits this slippage between fact and fiction by transforming the historical material which she unearths into the plot for a film: 'Es gelang ihr, diese Geschichte von Liebe und Tod in Kattowitz und Berlin als eine *story* zu sehen, eine *story* eben. | Je mehr Szenen Elisabeth Schlosser sich ausdachte für ihre Figuren, umso leichter wurde ihr, denn das war ja nicht wirklich Vergangenheit, sondern *fiction*, ein Spiel eben, ein elegantes' (*DfF*, p. 135). Punning on the double meaning of 'Geschichte' as both history and fiction, the protagonist develops an alternative means of engaging with her family's past. Through her imagination, she is able to adopt a more playful approach to this historical subject matter, using it as the impetus for her own creative reflection and thereby cultivating a living connection to the absent figures which haunt her.

The protagonist's explanation of her fictionalization of historical experience can also, as Lyn Marven notes, be read as a comment on Liebmann's novel as a whole.[47] The narrative of *Die freien Frauen* combines references to her documentary project, *Stille Mitte von Berlin*, and to her biography of her father, *Wäre es schön? Es wäre schön*, with overt allusions to other fictional works, and this technique serves Liebmann's attempt to expand and embellish the historical framework of her factual texts through the creative form of the novel. In particular, a significant part of the narrative is structured around letters written by the protagonist to the central character of Jiří Kratochvil's novel, *Unsterbliche Geschichte oder Das Leben der Sonja Trotzkij-Sammler oder Karneval*.[48] Kratochvil's work is, like that of Liebmann, concerned primarily with challenging the boundary between historiography and fiction. The novel narrates the history of the twentieth century from the perspective of the centenarian Sonja Trotzkij-Sammler, whose personal life is shown to have been deeply influenced by the political events of Europe's recent past. Rather than offering a conventional account of this history, however, Kratochvil adopts elements of the fantastic, presenting an array of unexpected figures such as ghosts, clones, doubles, talking animals, and characters which repeatedly defy death and return to life in different forms. Such figures serve to challenge conventional understanding of the past, undermining the reader's perception of cause and effect and offering alternative — often comic — interpretations of why historical events progressed in the way they did. Taking as a starting point the protagonist's programmatic assertion that 'alle Geschichten sind wahr',[49] Kratochvil's novel repeatedly adopts fictional techniques in order to reveal previously unnoticed aspects of historical experience. Rather than undermining the novel's rootedness in material reality, they serve to emphasize its ambition to shed new light on the past and uncover the unrealized opportunities and possibilities inherent in it.

Viewed in this context, Liebmann's references to Kratochvil's work can be read as part of her exploration of the 'spielerische[s] Verhältnis von Geschichte und Fiktion'.[50] On a thematic level, Liebmann's protagonist is drawn to Sonja Trotzkij-Sammler because she regards her as 'eine Frau, der die Toten und die Lebenden gleich gegenwärtig waren' (*DfF*, p. 179); like Elisabeth Schlosser, this woman is haunted by ghostly apparitions which interrupt the present and seem to be as real as the living people surrounding her. The affinity between the two figures is developed further by the fact that Liebmann's protagonist begins to identify with the central character of Kratochvil's novel. She remarks that upon reading Sonja's narrative she felt as though she was being presented with an account of her own life (*DfF*, p. 9), and she imagines herself as one of the figures in Kratochvil's text by developing a particularly personal connection to the bland picture on the front cover: 'Und jetzt, Sonja, muss ich Ihnen etwas Wichtiges sagen: Dieser Mann auf dem Umschlag von Ihrem Buch könnte mein Vater sein, damals, im Jahr '45, mit Hut und im Mantel' (*DfF*, p. 15). If this man were her father, she continues, then the child in the pram pushed by him would have to be — or have been — either her or Olga (*DfF*, p. 17). The protagonist's description of the photograph and her identification with the figures in it might initially suggest an attempt to ground her fantasy about Olga's existence in the reality implied by the documentary power of the camera. However, this apparent proof is undermined by the fact that the photograph appears on the front of a fictional text about someone else; its real referent remains unknown, thus blocking the protagonist's efforts to validate the content of her imagination. Liebmann adds another level to this intertextual web by creating a further allusion to her biography of her own father, where she describes him as a man 'im hellen Trenchcoat' wearing a hat;[51] the man on the front cover of Kratochvil's novel might, in this context, also be Liebmann's father. By linking the three texts in such a way through the photographic image, Liebmann repeatedly establishes and then undermines the connection of her fiction to historical reality. Calling into question the possibility of ever uncovering the details which she hopes to unearth, she transforms this doubt into a creative exercise, using alternative narratives as a means of highlighting and sustaining the gaps in her factual knowledge.

Other Spaces

In her efforts to engage with the phantoms of her family's past, the protagonist of *Die freien Frauen* undertakes a journey to Kattowice and Gliwice, formerly Kattowitz and Gleiwitz, the places of her father's youth.[52] The trip marks a development in the protagonist's relation to the past, triggering her emotional connection with the story of Gerda and her father and enabling her to start unravelling the mystery surrounding the existence of Olga. At the same time, it signals the beginning of a passage into an other space, an alternative geographical realm whose existence has the potential to alter her understanding of the city in which she lives. Poland is cut off from Berlin by a closed border (*DfF*, p. 77), and the protagonist's journey there is characterized by a feeling of being separated from all that is familiar: the train travels past 'unbewohnte Gebäude', ominous 'dunkle Brücken', and unrecognizable steel constructions which all instil in her an overwhelming sense of fear (*DfF*, p. 77). The names of the cities are all disconcertingly strange, and yet their similarity to their previous German titles makes them recognizable and therefore uncannily familiar: 'Wrocław, Opole, Gliwice. — Breslau, Oppeln, Gleiwitz' (*DfF*, p. 78). And, despite their strangeness, Kattowitz and Gleiwitz contain various characteristics which link them with the protagonist's life in Germany; not only do the buildings in these Polish towns recall the houses in her locality in Mitte, so too is their transport system likened to the Berlin *S-Bahn* (*DfF*, p. 86). Viewed in this context, Liebmann seems to be projecting her preoccupation with uchronian narratives onto the spatial organization of the novel, revealing the topography of these Polish towns to be a space of alternatives, a realm of lost potential inhabited by ghostly presences and uncanny figures.

Liebmann's depiction of Poland as an other space seems to resonate with Foucault's description of the heterotopia as a 'counter-site [...], a kind of effectively enacted utopia in which the real sites, all the other real sites that can be found within the culture, are simultaneously represented, contested and inverted'.[53] Whereas for Foucault, the utopia is an imaginary place which does not exist in reality, the heterotopia can be found in a real location; and yet its position of otherness means that it is always simultaneously 'outside of all places'.[54] The heterotopia therefore works to call into question the boundaries between inside and outside, reality and the imagination. It challenges conventional spatial order by 'juxtaposing in a single real place several spaces, several sites that are in themselves incompatible',[55] rendering familiar locations strange and thereby revealing aspects of reality which have not previously been observed. Above all, the heterotopia is also heterochronic in inclination. It has the potential to signal 'a sort of absolute break with [...] traditional time';[56] through its reconfiguration of spatial relations, it brings about an altered relation to time, revealing a breach in the experience of temporal reality as a chronological progression. The fact that Liebmann's protagonist comes to regard Poland as 'irgendwo anders' (*DfF*, p. 70) can thus be read on both a temporal and spatial level; the country's alterity is revealed through its geographical distance from Berlin and through the changed connection to time which the protagonist experiences when she is there. And this alterity serves a transformative purpose, bringing Elisabeth Schlosser into contact with unexpected events and thus causing her to regard the locations of her everyday life in a new light.

On one level, the protagonist's journey into this alternative space prompts her to reflect on the former GDR and the private significance of its disappearance. Her train journey reminds her of a previous trip to Poland when it still belonged to the Eastern Bloc, and she remarks that it is 'alles wie früher' (*DfF*, p. 77). A few lines later, she develops this observation further, suggesting that the country's resemblance to the former GDR is the source of her sense of anxiety:

'Früher hatte es im Osten genauso ausgesehen entlang von Bahngleisen, das war es vielleicht, was ihr Angst machte' (*DfF*, p. 77). While the border itself used to be open to citizens of the GDR, now it is closely guarded by soldiers, thus leading the protagonist to experience an 'Anmutung von Knast' (*DfF*, p. 77); the train compartment becomes a kind of prison, one of Foucault's models of heteropic institutions, and the sense of confinement which it prompts reminds Elisabeth Schlosser of her restricted existence in East Berlin. Later in the novel, the protagonist once again reflects on her perception of the similarities between present-day Poland and the former GDR, observing, 'dass das Ganze dem Osten, wie er damals gewesen war, immer noch ähnlich sah, dem ganzen, versunkenen Land' (*DfF*, p. 113). The geographical landscape of this other place, characterized by dilapidated buildings and marked by a sense of 'Verwahrlosung' (*DfF*, p. 106), lends a visible presence to her memories of East Germany, endowing her internal recollections with a concrete, external form and juxtaposing this with her experience of present-day Berlin (*DfF*, p. 81). By bringing to light what she has lost, the Polish landscape enables the protagonist to acknowledge her need to mourn:

> Da konnte ich es zum ersten Mal in meinem Herzen spüren, dass es weg ist und wie es gewesen war. Ich, die es immer gehasst hatte, fühlte einen Schmerz [...]. Mein Leben lang bin ich auf so was gelaufen, auf Straßen und Trottoiren, wie sie in Katowice noch still und jeder verschieden und geflickt so daliegen. (*DfF*, p. 113–14)

The uneven ground on which the protagonist walks introduces a form of involuntary corporeal memory in the Proustian style; her experience of wandering through the streets of present-day Kattowitz transports her back into the geography of her childhood, thus prompting her to reflect on the pain caused by its loss and recognize the extent to which the disappearance of the GDR has contributed to her current identity crisis.

On another level, Liebmann's depiction of Kattowitz and Gleiwitz as heterotopic spaces resonates with her portrayal of East Berlin in the photographs of *Stille Mitte von Berlin*. The Polish towns are characterized by the same sense of desolation and stasis, with empty streets ('leer' — *DfF*, p. 87) and rundown buildings ('grindig, kapputt, abgefleddert' — *DfF*, p. 105) signalling their neglected existence. And the protagonist is acutely aware of entering a space in which time has stopped ('stehen geblieben' — *DfF*, p. 83), in which the urban landscape seems to belong to a past era ('aus einer vergangenen Zeit' — *DfF*, p. 83). Like the area of Mitte, Kattowitz is also built around a set of heterotopic institutional spaces — a cemetery, which exists behind a symbolic wall (*DfF*, p. 85), a former school (*DfF*, p. 89), and an empty site where there used to be a synagogue (*DfF*, p. 89) — whose existence signals an alterity at the centre of the urban landscape. Like the images in Liebmann's documentary volume, these places are marked by absence, being described as 'menschenleer' (*DfF*, p. 83), 'verlassen' (*DfF*, p. 86), and 'still' (*DfF*, p. 87). Just as Liebmann herself becomes preoccupied with thresholds, points of entry and exit into buildings, in her photographic project, so too does the protagonist of *Die freien Frauen* take pictures of doors, windows, and gateways (*DfF*, p. 88) in an effort to document the existence of the people who once inhabited these places. And, while Liebmann's project on Mitte keeps returning her to the 'jüdische Schicksale' which haunt the region, here the protagonist's project keeps drawing her back to sites of violence and points of departure, to the station from which trains used to leave for Auschwitz (*DfF*, p. 83). While the history of Berlin is apparently reflected in the landscape of this Polish town, however, the protagonist repeatedly comes across points of discrepancy which undermine the parallel; such moments reveal her assumptions about the history of Kattowitz to be unfounded, thus calling into question the validity of her 'Nachforschungen' (*DfF*, p. 151).

Liebmann's depiction of Poland therefore seems to be based on a similar temporal logic to the photographs found in her documentary volume. The topography of Kattowitz draws together different temporal layers in the present, thus resonating with what Foucault saw as the ability of the heterotopia to present 'slices in time'.[57] Mirroring the history of Berlin, the town alludes at once to its pre-war past, its existence under a Communist regime, and its regeneration in the new millennium, where it becomes 'ein Kattowitz voller Baustellen, Neubauten, Zäune' (*DfF*, p. 206). At the same time, this other space becomes the setting for the drama of the protagonist's and her son's family history, the 'Ort seiner Urgroßeltern, der Vorfahren und des Großvaters auch' (*DfF*, p. 209). It comes to stand at the boundary between reality and fantasy, providing a space for the protagonist's archival research into the past but also acting as the setting for her fictional account of this history. Its connection to 'vergangene Zeiten' (*DfF*, p. 87) transports the protagonist into an imaginative world where the ghostly figures of her family history seem to live on in the lives of fictional characters which she creates (*DfF*, p. 134). The town thereby assumes a psychotopographical dimension, with its narrow, interconnected streets and twisting paths (*DfF*, p. 103) coming to resemble the 'Bündel von Wegen' (*DfF*, p. 11) that constitutes the protagonist's own life. At once shaping and shaped by the internal fantasies of this figure, the urban landscape of Kattowitz becomes an alternative space in which the haunting legacy of her father's past can be addressed and embraced.

'Eine unsterbliche Geschichte'

At the end of *Die freien Frauen*, Elisabeth Schlosser returns to the heterotopic space of Kattowitz in a final attempt to come to terms with her family history and rescue her lost connection to her son. While some critics have viewed the protagonist's journey as an effort to draw together the various strands of her historical investigations and thereby obtain closure on her family history,[58] Liebmann undermines this clear outcome by casting the trip to Poland in an ambiguous light. More specifically, the final pages of the novel are structured around a series of oppositions — between continuity and rupture, life and death, appearance and disappearance — which resist resolution and highlight the potentially unending quality of the narrative (*DfF*, p. 212). Kattowitz itself is shown to have altered considerably since the protagonist's previous visit, with the appearance of new buildings and Western products signalling a break with the town's recent past (*DfF*, p. 204). Despite this apparent juncture, however, the urban landscape still bears some traces of the past; whereas the topography of Kattowitz was previously marked by its connection to the town's pre-war history, this time it is also shadowed by the unrelenting spectre of Communist rule. Not only do its buildings bear some resemblance to the Soviet architecture of Moscow (*DfF*, p. 206), the protagonist is also stopped in her tracks by a towering monument (*DfF*, p. 205), whose enormity is reminiscent of the exaggerated scale of Socialist design. On her wanderings through the streets, Elisabeth Schlosser is repeatedly confronted with reminders of 'Revolution' (*DfF*, p. 205), particularly in the form of the retro 'Steppjacken' (*DfF*, p. 205) worn by the town's inhabitants. While the newly renovated Café Europa also seems to have turned its back on its history, it, too, remains bound to the continuing legacy of Communism; the proprietor's red dress assumes a particular symbolic significance (*DfF*, p. 209), and the title of the cafe links it with the vision of Europe reflected in Marx's dictum, 'Ein Gespenst geht um in Europa'. Viewed in this context, the building assumes an allegorical quality, signalling the way in which post-Communist ghosts are at large in the new Europe.

Throughout the protagonist's final journey, Kattowitz is depicted as an ambiguous historical space, a chronotope in which the boundaries between past and present, reality and imagination are repeatedly called into question. The town is shrouded in a veil of fog which creates a sense of 'Desorientierung' (*DfF*, p. 205), and the protagonist finds herself in danger of losing her way, of relinquishing her fixed location in time and space. This sense of dislocation is emphasized further by her fear that the ground beneath her feet will subside at any moment (*DfF*, p. 206); her perception of this Polish town as resting on precarious foundations highlights its unstable spatial and temporal organization. Like Berlin, a city which is famously built on sand,[59] and whose foundations are revealed in the novel to be profoundly unstable (*DfF*, p. 190), Kattowitz exists in a constant state of flux, marked by its transience and shadowed by the omnipresent danger of collapse. Its shifting ground means that the past and the present are alternately buried and brought to the surface in a manner which disrupts the chronology of historical events. The protagonist comes to view the landscape as a kind of palimpsest, in which different temporal layers are projected simultaneously onto the present; the anticipatory vision of the future manifest in the topography of Kattowitz becomes intertwined with the hazy after-image of the town's past (*DfF*, p. 206). The protagonist's inability to separate these images from one another (*DfF*, p. 206) is at once disorientating and potentially liberating; it calls into question the stability of her identity in the present, yet also frees her from existing historical models, enabling her to regard the past in a new light.

It is against this backdrop, in the evacuated time-space of the Café Europa, that the protagonist's son comes back to life. His renewed vitality is signalled by the 'riesige[r] Teller' of fish and potatoes which he consumes (*DfF*, p. 210), and by the ease with which he devours this meal; his earlier ethereal existence, marked by his lack of appetite and rejection of physical sustenance, has been replaced by signs of corporeal vigour, while his previous sense of dislocation has been transformed into an impression of being fully at ease in his surroundings. Above all, the son's return to life is signalled by the rediscovery of his ability to speak; once a silent figure, an embodiment of the gaps in his family history, he is now highly communicative, engaged in a seemingly unstoppable flow of conversation (*DfF*, p. 211). Although these signs of life appear to mark a positive development in the plot, signalling the possible reconciliation of mother and son, Liebmann undermines their optimistic potential by repeatedly stressing the incredible nature of the son's transformation: 'Würde das Ganze als Traum sich erweisen, ein Traumbild, ein Wahnbild, ein Wunsch bloß?' (*DfF*, p. 211). While the protagonist's experience of Kattowitz is characterized by her inability to distinguish between past and present, reality and fantasy, so too is her perception of her son shaped by the visions and imaginary scenarios which she has created in her mind's eye. His lively form is capable of freezing at any moment (*DfF*, p. 211), of slipping back into a melancholic state of arrest. And his vitality is shown to be disconcerting, like the animated form of the undead, whose uncanny semblance of life is merely an illusion. Accompanied by the waitress, whose name transforms her into a ghostly *revenant* of Olga (*DfF*, p. 211), the son assumes a role in the protagonist's fantastic rewriting of her family history; he plays a part in acting out the 'Geschichte von Liebe und Tod' (*DfF*, p. 135) which takes place in the other space of Kattowitz.

Rather than lending closure to the novel, the uncanny animation of the protagonist's son merely serves to highlight its open-endedness. Like Jiří Kratochvil's 'unsterbliche Geschichte', the story of Elisabeth Schlosser's family history is one which 'niemals ein Ende nehme' (*DfF*, p. 172), and which is compelled to repeat itself 'für immer' (*DfF*, p. 64). The final sentence of the text, 'es schneite' (*DfF*, p. 212), refers back to the opening of the novel ('es schneit [...] und wird weiterschneien' — *DfF*, p. 7), and this repetition lends the narrative a circular structure which highlights its enduring relation to the past.[60] The closing image, which depicts the protagonist standing in the 'Grünanlage' opposite the Café Europa (*DfF*, p. 212),[61] surrounded by the endlessly falling snowflakes, recalls an earlier passage in the novel, where she walks past a snow-covered statue of Chamisso in a park in Berlin (*DfF*, p. 18). Adopting a similar pose to this figure, Elisabeth Schlosser is cast as an after-image of this exemplary Romantic writer, whose task is to create a living relationship to the past through her art. The snow which surrounds her can be regarded as a motif of obliteration, signalling the blanking out of traumatic memories and the mechanism of forgetting which the protagonist constantly tries to resist. Through its ability to dissolve the landscape of the city and obscure the protagonist's faculty of vision (*DfF*, p. 17), it alludes to the mechanism of repression which works to conceal aspects of the past and prevent unwanted memories from coming to light. At the same time, however, the image of the unending snow is also linked with the protagonist's creative project, functioning as a kind of blank page or empty screen for the casting of written figures into space and onto ground.[62] Like the empty manuscript on which the protagonist writes, the snow becomes a tool in her literary endeavour, providing her with a means of realizing her internal fantasies. Above all, the snowflakes at the end of the novel create an imaginary 'Raum' (*DfF*, p. 211), a potentially free time-space, into which the protagonist can continue to project alternative images and uchronian narratives. This evacuated space, unclaimed and unoccupied, paradoxically threatens and sustains her relationship with the past; it creates a semblance of life for the phantoms which haunt her, yet also calls into question the very possibility of such an existence.

Notes to Chapter 5

1. Köhler, *Brückenschläge*, p. 128.
2. Liebmann in conversation with Smale, 21 July 2009.
3. Köhler, *Brückenschläge*, p. 124. Lyn Marven makes a similar point, arguing that the creation of 'a web of intertextual links amongst and between Liebmann's works' implies a degree of continuity in the historical investigation which they invoke. See Marven, '"Die Landschaft ihrer Gedanken"', pp. 279–81.
4. Irina Liebmann in conversation with Pfister, 'Teuer erkaufte Freiheit'.
5. As Ariane Eichenberg points out, the heirs of traumatic memories are placed in a unique situation: because they lack personal experience, their access to the past is always mediated. At the same time, however, the traumatic nature of this past means that it can also resurface unexpectedly: 'Und doch kann es sein, dass Vergangenes plötzlich mit aller Unmittelbarkeit vortritt'. Ariane Eichenberg, *Familie, Ich, Nation:*

Narrative Analysen zeitgenössischer Generationsromane (Göttingen: Vandenhoeck & Ruprecht, 2009), p. 153.
6. See Köhler, *Brückenschläge*, p. 125.
7. Liebmann's emphasis on the emotional disavowal of historical experience recalls Eric Santner's suggestion that a rational knowledge of historical facts is not necessarily accompanied by an emotional or experiential connection to them. Eric Santner, 'History beyond the Pleasure Principle', in *Probing the Limits of Representation: Nazism and the Final Solution*, ed. by Saul Friedlander (Cambridge, MA: Harvard University Press, 1992), pp. 143–54 (p. 150). See also Schwab, pp. 11–13.
8. Irina Liebmann in conversation with Philipp Krohn, 'Jetzt ist die Zeit gekommen zu differenzieren', *Deutschland Radio Kultur*, 15 March 2008. A transcript of the interview is available at <http://www.dradio.de/dlf/sendungen/interview_dlf/754727/> (accessed 11 April 2011).
9. For a detailed critique of the concept, see Joan Scott, 'The Evidence of Experience', *Critical Inquiry*, 17 (1991), 773–97.
10. As Gabriele Schwab writes, 'victims of trauma live with the scars of memory so to speak — gaps, amnesia, distortion, revision, or even fugue states or intrusive flashbacks'. Schwab, p. 14.
11. Astrid Köhler views this pattern of familial inheritance slightly differently, arguing that the protagonist's son represents 'der unglückliche Schatten ihres Vaters'; for Köhler, the son possesses a knowledge about the past which ought to belong to his grandfather. See Köhler, *Brückenschläge*, p. 124.
12. Abraham, 'Notes on the Phantom', p. 171.
13. Ibid., p. 175.
14. Ibid., p. 174.
15. Ibid., p. 173.
16. Ibid., p. 176.
17. Ibid.
18. Gabriele Schwab suggests that 'second-generation children' inherit or 'absorb' the 'optical unconscious' of their parents: 'Without being fully aware of it, they become skilled readers of the optical unconscious revealed in their parents' body language'. Schwab, p. 14.
19. Abraham, p. 166.
20. Liebmann herself describes this quest as 'eine sehr unlogische, ganz realistische Spurensuche', thus recalling the 'Spurensuche' in the title of *Stille Mitte von Berlin*. She continues:

    Dieses Unlogische immer, erstens mal, sie weiß nicht weiter, da macht sie eine Hypnose, wie soll ihr das nun helfen? Und dass sie dann das, was sie in der Hypnose sieht, so ernst nimmt, dass sie dann wieder dort hinfährt, das ist das Unlogische, das Fantastische. Die Orte, die sie dann trifft, sind real.

    See Liebmann in conversation with Pfister, 'Teuer erkaufte Freiheit'.
21. In this respect, the novel can be read as a substitute for the dramas which the protagonist tries but fails to write. See Köhler, *Brückenschläge* , p. 126; and Marven, '"Die Landschaft ihrer Gedanken"', p. 281.
22. The fictional character seems to be based on the historical figure of Ilse Stöbe, whose relationship with Liebmann's own father is detailed in the latter's biography, *Wäre es schön? Es wäre schön. Mein Vater Rudolf Herrnstadt*. The identification between these two figures is strengthened by the fact that Stöbe provided the inspiration for the central character of Theodor Wolff's novel, *Die Schwimmerin* (Zurich: Oprecht,

1937), which, like Liebmann's fictional text, renames the historical figure 'Gerda'. For information about the relationship between Herrnstadt and Stöbe, see Ulrich Sahm, 'Ilse Stöbe', in *Die Rote Kapelle im Widerstand gegen den Nationalsozialismus*, ed. by Hans Coppi, Jürgen Danyel, and Johannes Tuchel (Berlin: Gedenkstätte Deutscher Widerstand, 1994), pp. 262–76 (p. 264); Helmut Müller-Enbergs, *Der Fall Rudolf Herrnstadt: Tauwetterpolitik vor dem 17. Juni* (Berlin: LinksDruck, 1991), p. 34; and Rudolf Herrnstadt, *Das Herrnstadt-Dokument: Das Politbüro der SED und die Geschichte des 17. Juni 1953*, ed. by Nadja Stulz-Herrnstadt (Reinbek bei Hamburg: Rowohlt, 1991), p. 46.

23. In *Wäre es schön?*, Liebmann is also struck by the shining quality of Ilse Stöbe's eyes: 'Was man heute noch sehen kann, sind Fotos: eine lachende, junge Frau. Auf einigen Bildern sind es die Augen, die auffallen, weil sie von innen zu leuchten scheinen' (p. 62).
24. As Astrid Köhler writes, 'Demnach wäre sie [...] "nicht die Richtige" gewesen, aber den Ansprüchen an die richtige ausgesetzt'. Köhler, *Brückenschläge*, p. 126.
25. 'So einfach sollte etwas sein, was ihr das ganze Leben verdreht hat [...]?' (*DfF*, p. 117). Liebmann's use of the verb 'verdrehen' to highlight the disruptive influence of this role reversal recalls the imagery of turning and spinning which recurs throughout *In Berlin*. The link implies a further correlation between the two novels.
26. Astrid Köhler notes in passing that Elisabeth Schlosser is an 'Ersatztochter' (Köhler, *Brückenschläge*, p. 126), but she does not develop the implications of this observation.
27. Leon Anisfeld and Arnold Richards, 'The Replacement Child: Variations on a Theme in Individual and Collective History and Psychoanalysis', *Psychoanalytic Study of the Child*, 55 (2000), 301–18 (p. 303).
28. Schwab, p. 124.
29. Ibid., p. 143.
30. Ibid., p. 123.
31. Ibid.
32. Ibid.
33. Ibid.
34. Ibid., p. 87.
35. On the connection between Replacement Child Syndrome and the psychoanalytic notion of incorporation, see Schwab, pp. 55–56; and Nick Totton, *Psychoanalysis and the Paranormal: Lands of Darkness* (London: Karnac, 2003), pp. 162–63.
36. Serge Leclaire, drawing on his experiences of analysing an adult patient with Replacement Child Syndrome, explains this killing as follows:

    If he wishes to live, he must [...] once more kill his brother, thereby wreaking havoc with his mother's dream, doing in the immortal child of her desire: he must kill the very representative he has himself enshrined as the core, however foreign, of his own being.

    Serge Leclaire, *A Child is Being Killed: On Primary Narcissism and the Death Drive*, trans. by Marie Claude Hays (Stanford: University of Stanford Press, 1998), p. 11.
37. Charles Renouvier, *Uchronie (l'utopie dans l'histoire): Esquisse historique apocryphe du développement de la civilisation européenne tel qu'il n'a pas été, tel qu'il aurait pu être* (Paris: Bureau de la critique philosophique, 1876), p. ii. Various terms for this type of narrative have been used in literary criticism, including *'uchronie'*, 'counterfactual narrative', 'parahistory', 'virtual history', 'alternate history', and 'subjunctive history'. For a detailed discussion of the relative merits of each of these terms, see Christoph Rodiek, *Erfundene Vergangenheit: Kontrafaktische Geschichtsdarstellung (Uchronie) in der Literatur*, Analecta romanica, 57 (Frankfurt a. M.: Klostermann, 1997), pp. 25–31.

38. On the relation between the utopia and the *uchronie*, see Richard Saint-Gelais, 'Impossible Times: Some Temporal Labyrinths in Science Fiction', in *Worlds Enough and Time: Explorations of Time in Science Fiction and Fantasy*, ed. by Gary Westfahl, George Slusser, and David Leiby, Contributions to the Study of Science Fiction and Fantasy, 101 (Westport: Greenwood, 2002), pp. 25–36 (pp. 28–29).
39. Fatima Vieira, 'The Concept of Utopia', in *The Cambridge Companion to Utopian Literature*, ed. by Gregory Claeys (Cambridge: Cambridge University Press, 2010), pp. 3–27 (p. 4).
40. As Christoph Rodiek explains: 'Ein bestimmter Abschnitt der Vergangenheit [...] wird neu erzählt bzw. umgeschrieben, und zwar dergestalt, daß die tatsächliche Ereigniskette noch als Kontrastfolie durchscheint'. Rodiek, p. 10.
41. Karen Hellekson, *The Alternate History: Refiguring Historical Time* (Kent, OH: Kent State University Press, 2001), p. 1.
42. Ibid., p. 20.
43. Ibid., p. 4.
44. Recalling Liebmann's initial statement in *Stille Mitte von Berlin*, which she subsequently modifies, the narrator insists here that 'Es ging hier um keinen Fall um die Juden [...], es ging um was anderes' (*DfF*, p. 159).
45. Elisabeth Wesseling, 'Historical Fiction: Utopia in History', in *International Postmodernism: Theory and Literary Practice*, ed. by Hans Bertens, Comparative History of Literatures in European Languages, 11 (Amsterdam: Benjamins, 1997), pp. 203–12 (p. 204).
46. As Christoph Rodiek writes: 'Die Wirklichkeit [...] wird irrealisiert, während der kontrafaktische Geschichtsverlauf die Bestimmtheit des Realen annimmt'. Rodiek, p. 26.
47. See Marven, '"Die Landschaft ihrer Gedanken"', p. 281.
48. Kratochvil's novel was originally published in Czech under the title *Nesmrtelný příběh aneb život Soni Trocké-Sammlerové čili román karneval* (Brno: Atlantis, 1997). I refer here to the German edition of the text. Jiři Kratochvil, *Unsterbliche Geschichte oder Das Leben der Sonja Trotzkij-Sammler oder Karneval*, trans. by Kathrin Liedtke and Milka Vagadayová (Zurich: Ammann, 2000).
49. Ibid., p. 139. Liebmann has made a similar assertion, suggesting that all her creative work, regardless of the genre, is concerned with truth: 'Es geht um Wahrheit und gar nichts anderes'. Liebmann in conversation with Smale, 21 July 2009.
50. Köhler, *Brückenschläge*, p. 125.
51. Liebmann, *Wäre es schön?*, p. 7.
52. As Yvonne Gebauer notes in her review of *Die freien Frauen*: 'Die Autorin schickt sie nach Polen, nach Kattowitz und Gleiwitz und tief in die Vergangenheit, in ein fast märchenhaftes Grenzland zwischen Erfindung, Spinnerei und längst verjährter, unscharfer Erinnerung'. Yvonne Gebauer, 'Schnee über Berlin: Irina Liebmanns Roman *Die freien Frauen*', *Süddeutsche Zeitung*, 10 November 2004.
53. Michel Foucault, 'Of Other Spaces', *Diacritics*, 16 (1986), 22–27 (p. 24).
54. Ibid., p. 24.
55. Ibid.
56. Ibid.
57. Ibid., p. 26.
58. Köhler, *Brückenschläge*, p. 129.
59. On the symbolism of sand in literature relating to Berlin, see Ulrich Giersch, 'Berliner Sand: Materie, Medium und Metapher einer Stadt', in *Mythos Berlin: Zur Wahrnehmungsgeschichte einer industriellen Metropole*, ed. by Eberhard Knödler-Bunte (Berlin: Ästhetik und Kommunikation, 1987), pp. 71–78.

60. Iris Radisch reads the snow, by way of an intertextual reference to Wolf's *Nachdenken über Christa T.*, as an emblem of melancholia. Iris Radisch, 'Die Schneekönigin', *Die Zeit*, Literatur, 7 October 2004.
61. This space is the vacant site once occupied by the town's synagogue, which corresponds with the position occupied by the figures from the Holocaust memorial opposite the Berlin café on the Große Hamburger Straße. The connection thus resituates the protagonist's family history in the context of the wider German past.
62. The connection between snow and the written word is evident from the outset of the novel, where the narrator links the phrases 'es schneit [...] und es wird weiterschneien' and 'sie schreibt und wird weiterschreiben' (*DfF*, p. 7). Elsewhere in the novel, she describes the snow, using vocabulary which recalls the production of text; the flakes create 'Punkte' and 'Pünktchen' (*DfF*, p. 212), for example, which interrupt the 'Zeilen' (*DfF*, p. 7) formed by the city's streets. In another passage, the snow intermingles with the father's memories of his work as a journalist, slipping 'in die Texte' which appear in his mind's eye (*DfF*, p. 60). These texts appear to the father as if on screens, recalling the narrator's earlier assertion that 'es schneite wie im Kino' (*DfF*, p. 59) and introducing an intermedial element to the link between snow and creative activity.

CONCLUSION

Berlin is a notoriously haunted city. Inhabited by the historical phantoms that Brian Ladd describes in his *Ghosts of Berlin*, its public and private spaces have been conceptualized as the setting for uncanny encounters with the legacy of Germany's past.[1] As well as hosting personal ghosts which attend individual identity and are bound to particular sites in the city, the landscape of Berlin is also shadowed by the more general spectres of various political and cultural projects that it has staged. Through its analysis of five works by Christa Wolf and Irina Liebmann, this book has shown how Berlin is depicted in these texts as a haunting ground, a city whose uncanny topography bears visible remainders of its history. This urban territory, whose thresholds and boundary spaces provide a material reminder of the country's political division, forms the *Schauplatz* for these writers' exploration of the ghostly legacy of the Third Reich and the GDR. As a city which 'bear[s] the shadow of historical melancholy' and 'feel[s] the potential for uncanny returns',[2] Berlin is particularly suited to hosting these acts of *revenance* and ghostly repetition. Although the texts occasionally focus on other places, alternative towns with contrasting histories, these are invariably evoked in order to cast a certain light on Berlin as the eerie capital of what has been termed the 'Phantomrepublik'.[3] In depicting this city as a Gothic time-space, at once central and peripheral, 'out of joint' with its place in history, these writers raise questions about habitation and belonging, asking what it means to be at home in Berlin, and, in particular, in post-*Wende* Berlin.

As both a real space and a form of psychotopography, a city which reflects and shapes individual and collective fantasies of identity, Berlin has played host to numerous debates about the continuing legacy of various political and cultural movements which have made their mark on the city. In its examination of works by Wolf and Liebmann, this book has shown how two such 'afterlives' have come to haunt the post-*Wende* period. Through their retrospective engagement with the lost hopes and ideals of Socialist thinking, these authors endow the GDR and its unique form of literature with a spectral existence which allows it to live on in an altered form beyond its apparent demise. While this persistent attachment to the lost State might indicate a forward-looking attempt to reanimate past utopias and transport certain aspects of Socialist thinking into the ideological framework of the Federal Republic, it also betrays a melancholic refusal to accept the loss of the GDR, an inability to relinquish any emotional connection to it and to learn to live on without its presence. The spectre of Marx is shown to live on in these texts, emerging through direct references to the infamous 'Gespenst' which 'geht um in Europa' (*IB*, p. 27) and through more veiled allusions to particular features of Communist ideology. As a lasting reminder of the buried hopes and desires of these authors, it shadows their efforts to assert their role in the new Federal Republic. At the same time, the book has suggested that the writing of Wolf and Liebmann is haunted by the ghost of Romanticism, a cultural *revenant* marking the return of a tradition which was largely suppressed in the GDR. Drawing on a repertoire of imagery from the writings of Romantic writers such as E. T. A. Hoffmann and Adelbert von Chamisso, these authors rekindle the 'chronic dualism' of Romantic irony, affirming a vision of creative vitality while also undermining it through their peculiar attachment to images of death and mortality and to uncanny second selves.

The ghost therefore emerges in these texts as a highly contradictory figure, at once facilitating and undermining the writers' engagement with the hidden histories beneath the visible surfaces of the city. Invoked as the object of investigation, as the purveyor of a repressed past whose unfinished business needs to be addressed, the figure also appears as an unwilled side-effect of the act of revelation itself. Making its shadowy presence felt when a particular light has been shed on the past, it signals a troubling disturbance in the process of historical investigation, challenging the concept of 'Wahrheit' which these authors pursue and calling into question their efforts to uncover what lies at the base of past events. Through its ability to cross boundaries and defy established limits, the ghost opens up a realm in which the relations between past and present can be assessed and renegotiated. It enables new connections to be made between historical events and existing circumstances, thus creating an active, dynamic relation towards the past, which prevents it from being reified and regarded as an inanimate object. This productive potential is, however, shadowed by a more ominous prospect: through the challenge it poses to temporal boundaries, the ghost is able to interrupt the present, destabilizing the individual's position in time and working to undo her sense of historical grounding. No longer contained by the fixity of established borders, it takes on a life of its own, resisting efforts to control it and subjecting the writer to its unpredictable effects. She becomes both subject and object, invoking the ghost as part of her literary engagement with the past, yet also laying herself bare to its potentially destructive actions.

The first two chapters of the book have shown how this ambivalence is played out in the writing of Christa Wolf. The imagery of haunting was revealed here to be both a conscious response to the legacy of Romanticism, and the fantastic writing of E. T. A. Hoffmann in particular, and an involuntary phenomenon which shadows the author's utopian project without her knowledge. As a predominantly visual occurrence, the ghost emerges here in the figure of the 'Phantombild', the retinal trace of an image which lingers in the mind's eye following the disappearance of the original visual object. Operating by the logic of *Nachträglichkeit*, this scopic after-image signals the belated registering to consciousness of a past event, a moment of insight or recognition that occurs in the wake of what has already happened. At the same time, however, it highlights the way in which the consequences of bygone occurrences can persist in the visual field, rendering the subject's perceptual apparatus uncanny and distorting her perception of present reality. In Wolf's case, it was argued, this haunting effect is bound up with the legacy of surveillance and her former complicity with the Stasi. Signalling a slippage between subject and object, it reveals the way in which the surveillance apparatus of the State becomes incorporated into the visual mechanism of her protagonist, so that she comes to view herself and the world with its eyes. Despite Wolf's own assertion, 'Mit dem Apparat habe ich nichts zu tun' (CW XII, 453), the book has shown how the central characters of her texts are depicted as parts in a larger apparatus, whose ghostly effects blur the distinction between self and other, subject and State. Through their engagement with the phantom effects of surveillance, these works cast doubt on the autonomy of the individual's actions, revealing the subject to be a double agent who acts on behalf of the uncanny figures which haunt her.

A comparable preoccupation with technological apparatus and its role in the creation of ghostly images has been identified in the writing of Irina Liebmann. This author is less concerned with outlining the ghostly consequences of surveillance than with exploring the role of fiction and other forms of artistic representation in her creative engagement with the history of Berlin. Her documentary project exploits the capacity of the photographic medium to create images of living death, stilling isolated moments and freezing them in the 'stasis of an *arrest*'.[4] The photographic image, with its attachment to forms of still or deadened life, is used here as a means of evoking absences and signalling the invisible histories which are missing from the everyday existence of the city. Frequent references to these ghostly images are made in Liebmann's fictional texts, which seek to animate the frozen scenes of her photographs through the dynamic principle of her narrative and thereby endow them with a semblance of life. The evacuated streets of her photographs are shown to come alive through a series of encounters with the ghostly figures of the city's past, bringing about a living encounter with Berlin's history. Though motivated by an ethical desire to redeem the victims of Germany's violent past, this apparent animation is nevertheless shadowed by its propensity to slip back into a state of arrest. The impression of life created by the writer proves to be illusory, an uncanny copy which betrays a fundamental absence at its core. The texts' references to various mechanical devices involved in the mediation of these uncanny figures — in particular the camera and the typewriter — serve to highlight the way in which the spectral condition is, in fact, created by the apparatus of representation, whose tendency to blur the distinction between human and machine produces artificial ghosts in the machines of artistic invention.

The ghost, as both a historical figure and the product of creative endeavour, calls into question the distinction between fact and fiction, 'Geschichte' and 'Geschichten'. Through their allusions to the Hoffmannesque predicament of the artist, who becomes so absorbed in the apparent vivacity of his creation that he loses touch with the real world, both Wolf and Liebmann raise questions about the mimetic potential of literature and the role of art as an uncanny double of life. The phantom imaging of the relationship between literature and reality reflects upon the repressive effects of the doctrinaire realism that governed the cultural system of the GDR. Yet this self-conscious reflection on the nature of their creative projects also assumes an ethical dimension which links their writing with contemporary debates about the function of art in a post-Holocaust age. Through their adoption of a hybrid genre which blends elements of fiction and historiography, Wolf and Liebmann blur the boundary between fantasy and reality, using their art as a means of creating an imaginary life for the dead. The ghost appears in this context as a figure of alternatives, whose presence in the texts opens up a counterfactual space, an uchronian realm in which the lost possibilities and opportunities of the past can be recovered and explored. At the same time, however, it reveals the potential for the present and the future to be scarred by similar losses and traumatic experiences. Pointing towards both the past and the anterior future, the 'what-will-have-been', of the city, the ghost offers an ambivalent view of historical progress, revealing any implicit possibility of redemption to be overshadowed by uncanny acts of *revenance* and return.

Notes to the Conclusion

1. See Ladd, pp. 1–5; and Webber, *Berlin in the Twentieth Century*, p. 40.
2. Webber, *Berlin in the Twentieth Century*, p. 299.
3. Fritz Göttler, 'Leben jenseits der Brücke: Bilder aus der Phantomrepublik — Christian Petzolds "Gespenster" kommt in die Kinos', *Süddeutsche Zeitung*, 14 September 2005.
4. Barthes, p. 91.

BIBLIOGRAPHY

~

ABRAHAM, NICHOLAS, 'Notes on the Phantom' (1975), in *The Shell and the Kernel*, ed. by Abraham and Torok, pp. 171–76
ABRAHAM, NICHOLAS, and MARIA TOROK, *The Shell and the Kernel: Renewals of Psychoanalysis*, trans. by Nicholas Rand (Chicago: University of Chicago Press, 1994)
ALKON, PAUL, 'Alternate History and Postmodern Temporality', in *Time, Literature and the Arts*, ed. by Cleary, pp. 65–85
ANISFELD, LEON, and ARNOLD RICHARDS, 'The Replacement Child: Variations on a Theme in Individual and Collective History and Psychoanalysis', *Psychoanalytic Study of the Child*, 55 (2000), 301–18
ANZ, THOMAS, ed., *'Es geht nicht um Christa Wolf': Der Literaturstreit im vereinigten Deutschland* (Munich: Spangenberg, 1991)
ARNOLD, HEINZ LUDWIG, and FRAUKE MEYER-GOSAU, eds, *Die Abwicklung der DDR* (Göttingen: Göttinger Sudelblätter, 1992)
ARNOLD-DE SIMINE, SILKE, ed., *Memory Traces: 1989 and the Question of German Cultural Identity*, Cultural History and Literary Imagination, 5 (Berne: Lang, 2005)
ASSMANN, ALEIDA, *Erinnerungsräume: Formen und Wandlungen des kulturellen Gedächtnisses* (Munich: Beck, 1999)
ATGET, EUGÈNE, *Lichtbilder: Photographe de Paris*, ed. by Camille Recht (Paris: Jonquières, 1930)
BAAB, PATRICK, 'Die Mitwelt hat Anspruch auf Auskunft: Konzeptuelle Wandlung der Rezeption des "negativen" romantischen Erbes in der DDR am Beispiel von Christa Wolf', *die horen*, 29 (1984), 49–61
BACH, JONATHAN, 'Vanishing Acts and Virtual Reconstructions: Technologies of Memory and the Afterlife of the GDR', in *Memory Traces*, ed. by Arnold-de Simine, pp. 261–80
BACHMANN, INGEBORG, *Werke*, ed. by Christine Koschel, Inge von Weidenbaum, and Clemens Münster, 4 vols (Munich: Piper, 1978)
BALFOUR, ALAN, *Berlin* (London: Academy Editions, 1995)
BARTHES, ROLAND, *Camera Lucida: Reflections on Photography*, trans. by Richard Howard (London: Jonathan Cape, 1982)
BASSLER, MORITZ, BETTINA GRUBER, and MARTINA WAGNER-EGELHAAF, 'Einleitung', in *Gespenster: Erscheinungen, Medien, Theorien*, ed. by Baßler, Gruber, and Wagner-Egelhaaf, pp. 9–24
——, eds, *Gespenster: Erscheinungen, Medien, Theorien* (Würzburg: Königshausen & Neumann, 2005)
BECKER, JUREK, 'Die Wiedervereinigung der deutschen Literatur', *The German Quarterly*, 63 (1990), 359–66
BENJAMIN, WALTER, *Gesammelte Schriften*, ed. by Rolf Tiedemann and Hermann Schweppenhäuser, 7 vols (Frankfurt a. M.: Suhrkamp, 1991)

BENNETT, TONY, *Pasts beyond Memory: Evolution, Museums, Colonialism* (London: Routledge, 2004)

BERGMANN, CHRISTIAN, *Die Sprache der Stasi: Ein Beitrag zur Sprachkritik* (Göttingen: Vandenhoeck & Ruprecht, 1999)

BERTENS, HANS, ed., *International Postmodernism: Theory and Literary Practice*, Comparative History of Literatures in European Languages, 11 (Amsterdam: Benjamins, 1997)

BEYER, MARCEL, *Spione: Roman* (Cologne: DuMont, 2000)

BEYER, MARTIN, *Das System der Verkennung: Christa Wolfs Arbeit am Medea-Mythos*, Epistemata, 590 (Würzburg: Königshausen & Neumann, 2007)

BICKENBACH, MATTHIAS, 'Fotografierte Autorschaft: Die entzogene Hand', in *Manus Loquens: Medium der Geste — Gesten der Medien*, ed. by Matthias Bickenbach, Annina Klappert, and Hedwig Pompe, Mediologie, 7 (Cologne: DuMont, 2003), pp. 188–209

BICKENBACH, MATTHIAS, ANNINA KLAPPERT, and HEDWIG POMPE, eds, *Manus Loquens: Medium der Geste — Gesten der Medien*, Mediologie, 7 (Cologne: DuMont, 2003)

BLOCH, ERNST, *Das Prinzip Hoffnung*, 3 vols (Berlin: Aufbau, 1959)

—— *Verfremdungen*, 2 vols (Frankfurt a. M.: Suhrkamp, 1962)

BOA, ELIZABETH, 'Christa Wolf: Kindheitsmuster', in *Landmarks in the German Novel 2*, ed. by Hutchinson and Minden, pp. 77–92

BOA, ELIZABETH, and JANET WHARTON, eds, *Women and the* Wende: *Social Effects and Cultural Reflections of the German Unification Process*, German Monitor, 31 (Amsterdam: Rodopi, 1994)

BORMANN, ALEXANDER VON, ed., *Wissen aus Erfahrungen: Werkbegriff und Interpretation heute: Festschrift für Herman Meyer zum 65. Geburtstag* (Tübingen: Niemeyer, 1976)

BÖRTHIG, PETER, *Christa Wolf: Eine Biografie in Bildern und Texten* (Munich: Luchterhand, 2004)

BOYARIN, Jonathan, *Storm from Paradise: The Politics of Jewish Memory* (Minneapolis: University of Minnesota Press, 1992)

BROADBENT, PHILIP, and SABINE HAKE, eds, *Berlin: Divided City, 1945–1989*, Culture and Society in Germany, 6 (New York: Berghahn, 2010)

BROCKMANN, STEPHEN, 'Literature and Convergence: The Early 1980s', in *Beyond 1989*, ed. by Bullivant, pp. 49–67

—— 'Preservation and Change in Christa Wolf's *Was bleibt*', *The German Quarterly*, 67 (1994), 73–85

BRONFEN, ELISABETH, *The Knotted Subject: Hysteria and its Discontents* (Princeton: Princeton University Press, 1998)

BRÜNS, ELKE, '*Leibhaftig*: Christa Wolfs Gang ins Totenreich', in *Literatur im Krebsgang*, ed. by de Winde and Gilleir, pp. 145–58

BRUYN, GÜNTER DE, ed., *E. T. A. Hoffmann: Gespenster in der Friedrichstadt. Berlinische Geschichten* (Berlin: Der Morgen, 1986)

BUCH, ROBERT, and JOHANNES TÜRK, eds, *Figures and Figurations of the (Un-)Dead*, Special Issue of *Germanic Review*, 82 (2007)

BULLIVANT, KEITH, ed., *Beyond 1989: Re-Reading German Literary History since 1945*, Modern German Studies, 3 (Providence: Berghahn, 1997)

BURWICK, FREDERICK, 'Ekphrasis and the Mimetic Crisis of Romanticism', in *Icons, Texts, Iconotexts*, ed. by Wagner, pp. 78–104
BUSE, PETER, and ANDREW STOTT, 'Introduction: A Future for Haunting', in Buse and Stott (eds), *Ghosts*, pp. 1–20.
—— (eds), *Ghosts: Deconstruction, Psychoanalysis, History* (Basingstoke: Macmillan, 1999)
CASPARI, MARTINA, 'Im Kern die Krisis: Schuld, Trauer und Neuanfang in Christa Wolfs Erzählung *Leibhaftig*', *Weimarer Beiträge*, 49 (2003), 135–38
CASTEIN, HANNE, and ALEXANDER STILLMARK, eds, *Deutsche Romantik und das 20. Jahrhundert* (Stuttgart: Heinz, 1986)
CASTLE, TERRY, *The Female Thermometer: Eighteenth-Century Culture and the Invention of the Uncanny* (New York: Oxford University Press, 1995)
CASTRICANO, JODEY, *Cryptomimesis: The Gothic and Jacques Derrida's Ghost-Writing* (Montreal: McGill-Queen's University Press, 2001)
CATLING, JO, ed., *A History of Women's Writing in Germany, Austria and Switzerland* (Cambridge: Cambridge University Press, 2000)
CLAEYS, GREGORY, ed., *The Cambridge Companion to Utopian Literature* (Cambridge: Cambridge University Press, 2010)
CLARKE, DAVID, and RENATE RECHTIEN, eds, *The Politics of Place in Post-War Germany: Essays in Literary Criticism* (Lewiston, NY: Edwin Mellen, 2009)
CLEARY, THOMAS R., ed., *Time, Literature and the Arts: Essays in Honor of Samuel L. Macey*, ELS Monograph Series, 61 (Victoria: University of Victoria Press, 1994)
COLTON, CHRISTOPHER, '*Was bleibt*: Eine neue Sprache?', in *Christa Wolf in Perspective*, ed. by Wallace, pp. 207–26
COOKE, PAUL, '"GDR Literature" in the Berlin Republic', in *Contemporary German Fiction* ed. by Taberner, pp. 56–71
COOKE, PAUL, and ANDREW PLOWMAN, eds, *German Writers and the Politics of Culture: Dealing with the Stasi* (Basingstoke: Palgrave Macmillan, 2003)
COPPI, HANS, JÜRGEN DANYEL, and JOHANNES TUCHEL, eds, *Die Rote Kapelle im Widerstand gegen den Nationalsozialismus* (Berlin: Gedenkstätte Deutscher Widerstand, 1994)
COSENTINO, CHRISTINE, '"Aus Teufels Küche": Gedanken zur Teufelsfigur in der Literatur nach 2000: Christoph Heins *Willenbrock*, Christa Wolfs *Leibhaftig* und Monika Marons *Endmoränen*', *Germanic Notes and Reviews*, 35 (2004), 121–27
COSTABILE-HEMING, CAROL, 'Illness as Metaphor: Christa Wolf, the GDR, and Beyond', *Symposium*, 64 (2010), 202–19
COTTINGHAM, JOHN, ed., *The Cambridge Companion to Descartes* (Cambridge: Cambridge University Press, 1992)
CRARY, JONATHAN, *Techniques of the Observer: On Vision and Modernity in the Nineteenth Century* (Cambridge, MA: MIT Press, 1990)
DAVIS, COLIN, *Haunted Subjects: Deconstruction, Psychoanalysis and the Return of the Dead* (Basingstoke: Palgrave Macmillan, 2007)
—— 'Hauntology, Spectres and Phantoms', *French Studies*, 59 (2005), 373–79
DEAN, CAROLYN J., *The Fragility of Empathy after the Holocaust* (Ithaca: Cornell University Press, 2004)
DEHIO, GEORG, *Handbuch der deutschen Kunstdenkmäler: Berlin*, 2nd edn, rev. by Michael Bollé (Munich: Deutscher Kunstverlag, 2000)

DEIRITZ, KARL, and HANNES KRAUSS, eds, *Der deutsch-deutsche Literaturstreit oder 'Freunde, es spricht sich schlecht mit gebundener Zunge': Analysen und Materialien* (Hamburg: Luchterhand, 1991)
DELEUZE, GILLES, and FÉLIX GUATTARI, *A Thousand Plateaus: Capitalism and Schizophrenia*, trans. by Brian Massumi (Minneapolis: University of Minnesota Press, 1987)
DEMPS, LAURENZ, *Die Oranienburger Straße: Von der kurfürstlichen Meierei zum modernen Stadtraum* (Berlin: Parthas, 1998)
DERRIDA, JACQUES, *Béliers: Le dialogue ininterrompu: entre deux infinis, le poème* (Paris: Éditions Galilée, 2003)
—— *Specters of Marx: The State of Debt, the Work of Mourning and the New International*, trans. by Peggy Kamuf (London: Routledge, 1994)
DERRIDA, JACQUES, and BERNARD STIEGLER, *Echographies of Television: Filmed Interviews*, trans. by Jennifer Bajorek (Cambridge: Polity Press, 2002)
DUECK, CHERYL, *Rifts in Time and in the Self: The Female Subject in Two Generations of East German Women Writers*, Amsterdamer Publikationen zur Sprache und Literatur, 154 (Amsterdam: Rodopi, 2004)
Diagnostic and Statistical Manual of Mental Disorders, 4th edn (Washington, DC: American Psychiatric Association, 1994)
ECKART, GABRIELE, 'Ost-Frau liebt West-Mann: Zwei neue Romane von Irina Liebmann und Monika Maron', *Colloquia Germanica*, 30 (1997), 315–21
EHRENBURG, ILJA, *Visum der Zeit* (1929), trans. by Hans Ruoff (Leipzig: Reclam, 1982)
EICHENBERG, ARIANE, *Familie, Ich, Nation: Narrative Analysen zeitgenössischer Generationsromane* (Göttingen: Vandenhoeck & Ruprecht, 2009)
ENG, DAVID, and DAVID KAZANJIAN, *Loss: The Politics of Mourning* (Berkeley: University of California Press, 2003)
ERLL, ASTRID, and ANN RIGNEY, eds, *Mediation, Remediation, and the Dynamics of Cultural Memory*, Media and Cultural Memory, 10 (Berlin: de Gruyter, 2009)
FARRELL, JOHN, *Freud's Paranoid Quest: Psychoanalysis and Modern Suspicion* (New York: New York University Press, 1996)
FEHERVARY, HELEN, and BERND FISCHER, eds, *Kulturpolitik und Politik der Kultur: Festschrift für Alexander Stephan*, German Life and Civilization, 47 (Oxford: Lang, 2007)
FELMAN, SHOSHANA, and DORI LAUB, *Testimony: Crises of Witnessing in Literature, Psychoanalysis and History* (New York: Routledge, 1992)
FEYERABEND, WOLFGANG, *Durch das Scheunenviertel und die Spandauer Vorstadt: Vom versunkenen zum wiedererfundenen Stadtteil* (Berlin: Haude & Spener, 2004)
FOSTER, SUSAN LEIGH, 'Kinaesthetic Empathies and the Politics of Compassion', in *Critical Theory and Performance*, ed. by Reinelt and Roach, pp. 245–58
FOUCAULT, MICHEL, 'Of Other Spaces', *Diacritics*, 16 (1986), 22–27
FREUD, SIGMUND, *Studienausgabe*, ed by Alexander Mitscherlich, Angela Richards, and James Strachey, 11 vols (Frankfurt a. M.: Fischer, 1969–75)
FRIEDLANDER, SAUL, ed., *Probing the Limits of Representation: Nazism and the Final Solution* (Cambridge, MA: Harvard University Press, 1992)
FRIES, MARILYN SIBLEY, ed., *Responses to Christa Wolf* (Detroit: Wayne State University Press, 1989)
—— 'When the Mirror is Broken, What Remains? Christa Wolf's *Was bleibt*', *GDR Bulletin*, 17 (1991), 11–15

FUCHS, ANNE, *Phantoms of War in Contemporary German Literature, Films and Discourse: The Politics of Memory* (Basingstoke: Palgrave Macmillan, 2008)
FUCHS, ANNE, KATHLEEN JAMES-CHAKRABORTY, and LINDA SHORTT, eds, *Debating German Cultural Identity since 1989* (Rochester, NY: Camden House, 2011)
FÜHMANN, FRANZ, *Fräulein Veronika Paulmann aus der Pirnaer Vorstadt oder Etwas über das Schauerliche bei ETA Hoffmann* (Rostock: Hinstorff, 1979)
FULBROOK, MARY, *Anatomy of a Dictatorship: Inside the GDR 1949-1989* (Oxford: Oxford University Press, 1995)
—— *A History of Germany 1918-2008: The Divided Nation*, 3rd edn (Malden, MA: Wiley-Blackwell, 2009)
GADERER, RUPERT, *Poetik der Technik: Elektrizität und Optik bei E. T. A. Hoffmann*, Rombach-Wissenschaften/Edition Parabasen, 9 (Vienna: Rombach, 2009)
GALVAN, JILL, *The Sympathetic Medium: Feminine Channeling, the Occult and Communication Technologies, 1859-1919* (Ithaca, NY: Cornell University Press, 2010)
GASKILL, HOWARD, KARIN MCPHERSON, and ANDREW BARKER, eds, *Neue Ansichten: The Reception of Romanticism in the Literature of the GDR*, GDR Monitor Special Series, 6 (Amsterdam: Rodopi, 1990)
GEBAUER, YVONNE, 'Schnee über Berlin: Irina Liebmanns Roman *Die freien Frauen*', *Süddeutsche Zeitung*, 10 November 2004
GEISSLER, CORNELIA, 'Schwebezustand: Zu Irina Liebmanns Roman *In Berlin*', *Berliner Zeitung*, 4 June 1994
GERSTENBERGER, KATHARINA, *Writing the New Berlin: The German Capital in Post-Wall Literature* (Rochester, NY: Camden House, 2008)
GIERSCH, ULRICH, 'Berliner Sand: Materie, Medium und Metapher einer Stadt', in *Mythos Berlin*, ed. by Knödler-Bunte, pp. 71-78
GLAESER, ANDREAS, 'Monolithic Intentionality, Belonging, and the Production of State Paranoia: A View through the Stasi onto the Late GDR', in *Off Stage/On Display*, ed. by Shryock, pp. 244-78
GOETHE, JOHANN WOLFGANG, *Werke*, ed. by Erich Trunz, 14 vols (Munich: Beck, 1981)
GOODBODY, AXEL, and DENNIS TATE, eds, *Geist und Macht: Writers and the State of the GDR*, German Monitor, 29 (Amsterdam: Rodopi, 1992)
GÖTTLER, FRITZ, 'Leben jenseits der Brücke: Bilder aus der Phantomrepublik — Christian Petzolds "Gespenster" kommt in die Kinos', *Süddeutsche Zeitung*, 14 September 2005
GRAVES, PETER, 'Christa Wolf in the 1990s', in *Legacies and Identity*, ed. by Kane, pp. 167-80
—— 'The Treachery of St. Joan: Christa Wolf and the Stasi', in *Christa Wolf in Perspective*, ed. by Wallace, pp. 1-12
GREINER, ULRICH, 'Mangel an Feingefühl', *Die Zeit*, 1 June 1990
GUERIN, FRANCES, *A Culture of Light: Cinema and Technology in 1920s Germany* (Minneapolis: University of Minnesota Press, 2005)
HAGSTRUM, JEAN, *The Sister Arts: The Tradition of Literary Pictorialism and English Poetry from Dryden to Gray* (Chicago: University of Chicago Press, 1958)
HALLAM, ELIZABETH, JENNIFER HOCKNEY, and GLENNYS HOWARTH, *Beyond the Body: Death and Social Identity* (London: Routledge, 1999)

HARDY, BEVERLEY, 'Romanticism and Realism: Christa Wolf's "Unter den Linden": The Appropriation of a Hoffmannesque Reality', in *Neue Ansichten*, ed. by Gaskill, McPherson, and Barker, pp. 73–84

HARTMAN, GEOFFREY, *The Longest Shadow: In the Aftermath of the Holocaust* (Bloomington: Indiana University Press, 1996)

HARVEY, JOHN, *Photography and Spirit* (London: Reaktion Books, 2007)

HEFFERNAN, JAMES, *The Museum of Words: The Poetics of Ekphrasis from Homer to Ashbery* (Chicago: University of Chicago Press, 1994)

HELBIG, JÖRG, *Der parahistorische Roman: Ein literaturhistorischer und gattungstypologischer Beitrag zur Allotopieforschung*, Berliner Beiträge zur Anglistik, 1 (Frankfurt a. M.: Lang, 1987)

HELL, JULIA, 'Loyal Dissidents and Stasi Poets: Sascha Anderson, Christa Wolf, and the Incomplete Project of GDR Research', *German Politics and Society*, 20 (2002), 82–118

HELL, JULIA, and ANDREAS SCHÖNLE, eds, *Ruins of Modernity* (Durham, NC: Duke University Press, 2010)

HELLEKSON, KAREN, *The Alternate History: Refiguring Historical Time* (Kent, OH: Kent State University Press, 2001)

HERMANN, JUDITH, *Nichts als Gespenster: Erzählungen* (Frankfurt a. M.: Fischer, 2003)

HERRNSTADT, RUDOLF, *Das Herrnstadt-Dokument: Das Politbüro der SED und die Geschichte des 17. Juni 1953*, ed. by Nadja Stulz-Herrnstadt (Reinbek bei Hamburg: Rowohlt, 1991)

HERZINGER, RICHARD, 'Vom Nutzen und Nachteil der DDR-Literatur', in *Die Abwicklung der DDR*, ed. by Arnold and Meyer-Gosau, pp. 76–81

HEUKENKAMP, URSULA, 'Diskurse über den Irrationalismus in der SBZ/DDR zwischen 1945 und 1960', in *Neue Ansichten*, ed. by Gaskill, McPherson, and Barker, pp. 98–113

HIRSCH, MARIANNE, *Family Frames: Photography, Narrative and Postmemory* (Cambridge, MA: Harvard University Press, 1997)

—— 'Surviving Images: Holocaust Photographs and the Work of Postmemory', in *Visual Culture and the Holocaust*, ed. by Zelizer, pp. 215–46

HOFFMANN, E. T. A., *Sämtliche Werke*, ed. by Wulf Segebrecht and Hartmut Steinecke, 6 vols (Frankfurt a. M.: Deutscher Klassiker, 1985–2004)

HOHBEIN-DEEGEN, MONIKA, *Reisen zum Ich: Ostdeutsche Identitätssuche in Texten der neunziger Jahre*, East German Studies, 17 (Berne: Lang, 2010)

HOLBECHE, YVONNE, *Optical Motifs in the Works of E. T. A. Hoffmann*, Göppinger Arbeiten zur Germanistik, 141 (Göppingen: Kümmerle, 1975)

HÖLDERLIN, FRIEDRICH, *Sämtliche Werke und Briefe*, ed. by Jochen Schmidt, 3 vols (Frankfurt a. M.: Deutscher Klassiker, 1992)

HORSTKOTTE, SILKE, 'Die Geister von Auschwitz: Fotografie und spektrale Erinnerung in Stephan Wackwitz' *Ein unsichtbares Land* und *Neue Menschen*', in *Literatur im Krebsgang*, ed. by de Winde and Gilleir, pp. 273–98

HURLEY, KELLY, *The Gothic Body: Sexuality, Materialism, and Degeneration at the fin de siècle*, Cambridge Studies in Nineteenth-Century Literature and Culture, 8 (Cambridge: Cambridge University Press, 1996)

HUTCHINSON, PETER, and MICHAEL MINDEN, eds, *Landmarks in the German Novel 2*, British and Irish Studies in German Language and Literature, 47 (Oxford: Lang, 2010)
HUYSSEN, ANDREAS, 'The Voids of Berlin', *Critical Inquiry*, 24 (1997), 57–81
JENNINGS, MICHAEL, *Dialectical Images: Walter Benjamin's Theory of Literary Criticism* (Ithaca, NY: Cornell University Press, 1987)
JONES, SUSANNE LENNÉ, 'What's in a Frame? Photography, Memory, and History in Contemporary German Literature' (unpublished doctoral dissertation: University of Cincinnati, 2005; abstract in *Dissertation Abstracts International*, 66 (2006), 4035–36)
KAMMERTÖNS, HANNS-BRUNO, and STEPHAN LEBERT, 'Bei mir dauert alles sehr lange', *Die Zeit*, 29 September 2005, pp. 17–20
KANE, MARTIN, ed., *Legacies and Identity: East and West German Literary Responses to Unification*, British and Irish Studies in German Language and Literature, 31 (Oxford: Lang, 2002)
KAUFMANN, HANS, *Versuch über das Erbe* (Leipzig: Reclam, 1980)
KITTLER, FRIEDRICH, *Aufschreibesysteme: 1800/1900* (Munich: Fink, 1985)
—— *Grammophon Film Typewriter* (Berlin: Brinkmann & Bose, 1986)
KLINGER, JUDITH, and GERHARD WOLF, eds, *Gedächtnis und kultureller Wandel: Erinnerndes Schreiben — Perspektiven und Kontroversen* (Tübingen: Niemeyer, 2009)
KNÖDLER-BUNTE, EBERHARD, ed., *Mythos Berlin: Zur Wahrnehmungsgeschichte einer industriellen Metropole* (Berlin: Ästhetik und Kommunikation, 1987)
KOELB, CLAYTON, and ERIC DOWNING, eds, *German Literature of the Nineteenth Century: 1832–1899*, Camden House History of German Literature, 9 (Rochester, NY: Camden House, 2007)
KÖHLER, ASTRID, 'Begegnungen unter den Linden: Der etwa tausendste Versuch zum Thema Christa Wolf und die Romantik', *Weimarer Beiträge*, 52 (2006), 587–601
—— *Brückenschläge: DDR-Autoren vor und nach der Wiedervereinigung* (Göttingen: Vandenhoek & Ruprecht, 2007)
—— 'Whither? Away! Reflections on the Motifs of Travel and Identity in Recent East German Prose', in *German-Language Literature Today*, ed. by Williams, Parkes, and Preece, pp. 207–20
KONZETT, MATTHIAS, 'Christa Wolf's *Was bleibt*: The Literary Utopia and its Remaining Significance', *Monatshefte*, 85 (1993), 438–52
KOSKINAS, NIKOLAOS-IOANNIS, *'Fremd bin ich eingezogen, fremd ziehe ich wieder aus': Von Kassandra, über Medea, zu Ariadne: Manifestationen der Psyche im spätesten Werk Christa Wolfs* (Würzburg: Königshausen & Neumann, 2008)
KRATOCHVIL, JIŘÍ, *Unsterbliche Geschichte oder Das Leben der Sonja Trotzkij-Sammler oder Karneval*, trans. by Kathrin Liedtke and Milka Vagadayová (Zurich: Ammann, 2000)
KRAUSS, HANNES, 'Was ist geblieben? Rückblicke auf einen (Literatur-)Streit', in *Kulturpolitik und Politik der Kultur*, ed. by Fehervary and Fischer, pp. 263–76
KRAUSS, ROLF, *Beyond Light and Shadow: The Role of Photography in Some Paradoxical Phenomena: A Historical Survey* (Munich: Nazraeli, 1995)

KRIEGER, MURRAY, *Ekphrasis: The Illusion of the Natural Sign* (Baltimore: Johns Hopkins University Press, 1992)
KROHN, PHILIPP, 'Jetzt ist die Zeit gekommen zu differenzieren', *Deutschland Radio Kultur*, 15 March 2008. A transcript of the interview is available at <http://www.dradio.de/dlf/sendungen/interview_dlf/754727/> (accessed 11 April 2011)
KUHN, ANNA, *Christa Wolf's Utopian Vision: From Marxism to Feminism* (Cambridge: Cambridge University Press, 1988)
—— '"Eine Königin köpfen ist effektiver als einen König köpfen": The Gender Politics of the Christa Wolf Controversy', in *Women and the Wende*, ed. by Boa and Wharton, pp. 200–15
—— '"Zweige vom selben Stamm"? Christa Wolf's *Was bleibt*, *Kein Ort. Nirgends* and *Sommerstück*', in *Christa Wolf in Perspective*, ed. by Wallace, pp. 187–225
LACHMANN, RENATE, *Gedächtnis und Literatur, Intertextualität in der russischen Moderne* (Frankfurt a. M.: Suhrkamp, 1990)
LADD, BRIAN, *The Ghosts of Berlin: Confronting German History in the Urban Landscape* (Chicago: University of Chicago Press, 1997)
LANGNER, BEATRIX, 'Gespenster am Krankenbett. *Leibhaftig*: Christa Wolf lässt die Vergangenheit aufleben', *Neue Zürcher Zeitung*, 23 February 2002
LECLAIRE, SERGE, *A Child is Being Killed: On Primary Narcissism and the Death Drive*, trans. by Marie Claude Hays (Stanford: University of Stanford Press, 1998)
LEDANFF, SUSANNE, *Hauptstadtphantasien: Berliner Stadtlektüren in der Gegenwartsliteratur 1989–2008* (Bielefeld: Aisthesis, 2009)
LEEDER, KAREN, 'Dances of Death: A Last Literature from the GDR', in *Twenty Years On*, ed. by Rechtien and Tate, pp. 187–202
—— '"Nachleben": Volker Braun and the Death and Afterlife of the GDR', *German Life and Letters*, 63 (2010), 265–79
LEHMANN, JOACHIM, *Die blinde Wissenschaft: Realismus und Realität in der Literaturtheorie der DDR* (Würzburg: Königshausen & Neumann, 1995)
LIEB, CLAUDIA, 'Und hinter tausend Gläsern keine Welt: Raum, Körper und Schrift in E. T. A. Hoffmanns *Das öde Haus*', *E. T. A. Hoffmann Jahrbuch*, 10 (2002), 58–75
LIEBMANN, IRINA, *Die freien Frauen: Roman* (Berlin: Berlin, 2004)
—— *In Berlin: Roman* (Cologne: Kiepenheuer & Witsch, 1994)
—— *Mitten im Krieg* (Frankfurt a. M.: Frankfurter Verlagsanstalt, 1989)
—— *Stille Mitte von Berlin: Eine fotografische Spurensuche rund um den Hackeschen Markt* (Berlin: Berlin, 2009)
—— *Wäre es schön? Es wäre schön! Mein Vater Rudolf Herrnstadt* (Berlin: Berlin, 2008)
LOVE, MYRA, *Christa Wolf: Literature and the Conscience of History*, East German Studies, 6 (New York: Lang, 1991)
LUKÁCS, GEORG, *Kurze Skizze einer Geschichte der neueren deutschen Literatur* (Darmstadt: Luchterhand, 1975)
MAGENAU, JÖRG, *Christa Wolf: Eine Biographie* (Berlin: Kindler, 2002)
MANGER, PHILIP, 'Auf der Suche nach dem ungelebten Leben: Christa Wolf — *Unter den Linden*', in *Wissen aus Erfahrungen*, ed. by Bormann, pp. 903–16
MARKS, LAURA, *Touch: Sensuous Theory and Multisensory Media* (Minneapolis: University of Minnesota Press, 2002)

MARVEN, LYN, '"Die Landschaft ihrer Gedanken": Autobiography and Intertextuality in Irina Liebmann's Berlin Texts', in *New German Literature*, ed. by Preece, Finlay, and Owen, pp. 267–82
—— 'Divided City, Divided Heaven? Berlin Border Crossings in Post-*Wende* Fiction', in *Berlin, Divided City*, ed. by Broadbent and Hake, pp. 184–93
—— '"Souvenirs de Berlin-Est": History, Photos, and Form in Texts by Daniela Dahn, Irina Liebmann, and Sophie Calle', *Seminar*, 43 (2007), 220–33
MCDONAGH, JOSEPHINE, 'Writings on the Mind: Thomas De Quincey and the Importance of the Palimpsest in Nineteenth-Century Writing', *Prose Studies*, 10 (1987), 207–24
MCFARLAND, ROBERT, 'Reading "Das öde Haus": E. T. A. Hoffmann's Urban Hermeneutics', *Monatshefte*, 100 (2008), 489–503
MCGRATH, JOHN, *Loving Big Brother: Performance, Privacy and Surveillance Space* (London: Routledge, 2004)
MATHY, JEAN-PHILIPPE, *Melancholy Politics: Loss, Mourning, and Memory in Late Modern France* (University Park, PA: Pennsylvania University Press, 2011)
MATTSON, MICHELLE, *Mapping Morality in Postwar German Women's Fiction: Christa Wolf, Ingeborg Drewitz, and Grete Weil* (Rochester, NY: Camden House, 2010)
MICHAELIS, ROLF, 'Krankengeschichten. Heilgeschichten. Wenn der (Staats-)Körper leidet: Christa Wolfs Erzählung *Leibhaftig*', *Die Zeit*, 28 February 2002
MITCHELL, WILLIAM J. T., *Picture Theory: Essays on Verbal and Visual Representation* (Chicago: University of Chicago Press, 1994)
MÜLLER, HEINER, *Germania 3: Gespenster am toten Mann* (Cologne: Kiepenhauer & Witsch, 1996)
MÜLLER, MAIK, 'Phantasmagoria und bewaffnete Blicke: Zur Funktion optischer Apparate in E. T. A. Hoffmanns *Meister Floh*', *E. T. A. Hoffmann Jahrbuch*, 11 (2003), 104–21
MÜLLER-ENBERGS, HELMUT, *Der Fall Rudolf Herrnstadt: Tauwetterpolitik vor dem 17. Juni* (Berlin: LinksDruck, 1991)
MÜLLER-FUNK, WOLFGANG, *Die Farbe Blau: Untersuchungen zur Epistemologie des Romantischen* (Vienna: Turia & Kant, 2000)
MULVEY, LAURA, *Death 24x a Second: Stillness and the Moving Image* (London: Reaktion, 2006)
NEEF, SONJA, 'Die (rechte) Schrift und die (linke) Hand', *Kodika/Ars Semiotica*, 25 (2002), 159–76
OWEN, RUTH J., *The Poet's Role: Lyric Responses to German Unification by Poets from the GDR*, Amsterdamer Publikationen zur Sprache und Literatur, 147 (Amsterdam: Rodopi, 2001)
PAUL, GEORGINA, 'Text and Context: *Was bleibt* 1979–1989', in *Geist und Macht*, ed. by Goodbody and Tate, pp. 117–28
PAUL, JEAN, *Werke*, ed. by Norbert Miller, 6 vols (Munich: Hanser, 1970)
PAUL, WILLIAM, 'Uncanny Theatre: The Twin Inheritances of the Movies', *Paradoxa*, 3 (1997), 322–23
PEUCKER, BRIGITTE, 'Dream, Fairy Tale, and the Literary Subtext of "Unter den Linden"', in *Responses to Christa Wolf*, ed. by Fries, pp. 303–11

PFISTER, EVA, 'Teuer erkaufte Freiheit: Irina Liebmann: *Die freien Frauen*', *Deutschlandfunk*, 4 January 2005, <http://www.dradio.de/dlf/sendungen/buechermarkt/337165/> (accessed 10 May 2010)
PHILIPSEN, BART, 'Literatur und Spektralität: Zur Einführung', in *Literatur im Krebsgang*, ed. by de Winde and Gilleir, pp. 13–22
PREECE, JULIAN, FRANK FINLAY, and RUTH J. OWEN, eds, *New German Literature: Life-Writing and Dialogue with the Arts*, Leeds–Swansea Colloquia on Contemporary German Literature, 1 (Oxford: Lang, 2007)
RADISCH, IRIS, 'Die Schneekönigin', *Die Zeit*, Literatur (October 2004)
RAND, NICHOLAS, 'Introduction: Renewals of Psychoanalysis', in Abraham and Torok, *The Shell and the Kernel*, pp. 1–22
RANK, OTTO, *Der Doppelgänger: Eine psychoanalytische Studie* (Leipzig: Internationaler Psychoanalytischer Verlag, 1925)
RASHKIN, ESTHER, *Unspeakable Secrets and the Psychoanalysis of Culture* (Albany, NY: State University of New York Press, 2008)
RECHTIEN, RENATE, 'From a Topography of Hope to a Nightmarish "Non-Place": Chronotopes in Christa Wolf's "June Afternoon", "Unter den Linden" and *What Remains*', in *The Politics of Place in Post-War Germany*, ed. by Clarke and Rechtien, pp. 261–84
RECHTIEN, RENATE, and DENNIS TATE, eds, *Twenty Years On: Competing Memories of the GDR in Postunification German Culture* (Rochester, NY: Camden House, 2011)
REINELT, JANELLE G., and JOSEPH R. ROACH, eds, *Critical Theory and Performance* (Ann Arbor: University of Michigan Press, 2007)
RENOUVIER, CHARLES, *Uchronie (l'utopie dans l'histoire): Esquisse historique apocryphe du développement de la civilisation européenne tel qu'il n'a pas été, tel qu'il aurait pu être* (Paris: Bureau de la critique philosophique, 1876)
RESINA, JOAN RAMON, and DIETER INGENSCHAY, eds, *After-Images of the City* (Ithaca, NY: Cornell University Press, 2003)
RODIEK, CHRISTOPH, *Erfundene Vergangenheit: Kontrafaktische Geschichtsdarstellung (Uchronie) in der Literatur*, Analecta romanica, 57 (Frankfurt a. M.: Klostermann, 1997)
ROWE, KATHERINE, *Dead Hands: Fictions of Agency, Renaissance to Modern* (Stanford, CA: Stanford University Press, 1999)
ROYLE, NICHOLAS, *The Uncanny: An Introduction* (Manchester: Manchester University Press, 2003)
RUGG, LINDA, *Picturing Ourselves: Photography and Autobiography* (Chicago: University of Chicago Press, 1997)
RUGOFF, RALPH, 'More than Meets the Eye', in *The Scene of the Crime*, ed. by Rugoff, pp. 59–108
RUGOFF, RALPH, ed., *The Scene of the Crime* (Cambridge, MA: The Museum in association with MIT, 1997)
RUPRECHT, LUCIA, 'Ambivalent Agency: Gestural Performances of Hands in Weimar Dance and Film', *Seminar*, 46 (2010), 255–75
SAHM, ULRICH, 'Ilse Stöbe', in *Die Rote Kapelle im Widerstand gegen den Nationalsozialismus*, ed. by Coppi, Danyel, and Tuchel, pp. 262–76
SAINT-GELAIS, RICHARD, 'Impossible Times: Some Temporal Labyrinths in

Science Fiction', in *Worlds Enough and Time*, ed. by Westfahl, Slusser, and Leiby, pp. 25–36

SALZANI, CARLO, 'The City as Crime Scene: Walter Benjamin and the Traces of the Detective', *New German Critique*, 34 (2007), 165–88

SANTNER, ERIC, 'History beyond the Pleasure Principle', in *Probing the Limits of Representation*, ed. by Friedlander, pp. 143–54

SCHENK, KLAUS, 'Erinnerndes Schreiben: Zur Autobiographik der siebziger Jahren und ihren didaktischen Konsequenzen', in *Gedächtnis und kultureller Wandel*, ed. by Klinger and Wolf, pp. 19–32

SCHMIDT, RICARDA, 'GDR Women Writers: Ways of Writing for, within and against Socialism', in *A History of Women's Writing in Germany, Austria and Switzerland*, ed. by Catling, pp. 190–99

—— 'Religiöse Metaphorik im Werk Christa Wolfs', in *Christa Wolf in Perspective*, ed. by Wallace, pp. 73–106

SCHMITZ-EMANS, MONICA, 'Die Laterna magica der Erzählung: Ein Bilderzeugungsverfahren als poetologische Metapher', *Globkult*, 7 November 2008

SCHRÖDER, JOACHIM, *Interviewliteratur zum Leben in der DDR: Zur literarischen, biographischen und sozial-geschichtlichen Bedeutung einer dokumentarischen Gattung*, Studien und Texte zur Sozialgeschichte der Literatur, 83 (Tübingen: Niemeyer, 2001)

SCHWAB, GABRIELE, *Haunting Legacies: Violent Histories and Transgenerational Trauma* (New York: Columbia University Press, 2010)

SCHWENGER, PETER, *Fantasm and Fiction: On Textual Envisioning* (Stanford, CA: Stanford University Press, 1999)

SCONCE, JEFFREY, *Haunted Media: Electronic Presence from Telegraphy to Television* (Durham, NC: Duke University Press, 2000)

SCOTT, JOAN, 'The Evidence of Experience', *Critical Inquiry*, 17 (1991), 773–97

SCRIBNER, CHARITY, *Requiem for Communism* (Cambridge, MA: MIT Press, 2003)

—— 'Von *Leibhaftig* aus zurückblicken: Verleugnung als Trope in Christa Wolfs Schreiben', *Weimarer Beiträge*, 50 (2004), 212–26

SEGHERS, ANNA, *Sonderbare Begegnungen* (Berlin: Aufbau, 1973)

SEIBT, GUSTAV, 'Wer mit dem Meißel schreibt, hat keine Handschrift: Ein neuer Anfang lyrischen Sprechens im Ausgang einer Epoche. Aus Anlaß eines Gedichts von Heiner Müller', *Frankfurter Allgemeine Zeitung*, 1 June 1993

SELTZER, MARK, *Bodies and Machines* (New York: Routledge, 1992)

SHRYOCK, ANDREW, ed., *Off Stage/On Display: Intimacy and Ethnography in the Age of Public Culture* (Stanford, CA: Stanford University Press, 2004)

SONTAG, SUSAN, *On Photography* (London: Picador, 1977)

STEINER, WENDY, *The Colors of Rhetoric: Problems in the Relation between Modern Literature and Painting* (Chicago: University of Chicago Press, 1982)

STIFFLER, MURIEL, *The German Ghost Story as Genre* (New York: Lang, 1993)

SWANSON, DAVID W., PHILIP J. BOHNERT, and JACKSON A. SMITH, *The Paranoid* (Boston: Little, Brown & Co., 1970)

TABERNER, STUART, ed., *Contemporary German Fiction: Writing in the Berlin Republic* (Rochester, NY: Camden House, 2005)

TANNER, LAURA E., *Lost Bodies: Inhabiting the Borders of Life and Death* (Ithaca: Cornell University Press, 2006)

TATE, DENNIS, *Franz Fühmann, Innovation and Authenticity: A Study of his Prose-Writing*, Amsterdamer Publikationen zur Sprache und Literatur, 117 (Amsterdam: Rodopi, 1995)

—— *Shifting Perspectives: East German Autobiographical Narratives before and after the End of the GDR* (Rochester, NY: Camden House, 2007)

THOMPSON, PETER, '"Die unheimliche Heimat": The GDR and the Dialectics of the Home', *Oxford German Studies*, 38 (2009), 278–87

TIEDEMANN, ROLF, *Dialektik im Stillstand: Versuche zum Spätwerk Walter Benjamins* (Frankfurt a. M.: Suhrkamp, 1983)

TOTTON, NICK, *Psychoanalysis and the Paranormal: Lands of Darkness* (London: Karnac, 2003)

TROTTER, DAVID, *Paranoid Modernism: Literary Experiment, Psychosis and the Professionalisation of English Society* (Oxford: Oxford University Press, 2001)

VIDLER, ANTHONY, 'Air War and Architecture', in *Ruins of Modernity*, ed. by Hell and Schönle, pp. 29–41

—— *The Architectural Uncanny: Essays in the Modern Unhomely* (Cambridge, MA: MIT Press, 1992)

—— 'The Exhaustion of Space at the Scene of the Crime', in *The Scene of the Crime*, ed. by Rugoff, pp. 131–42

VIEIRA, FATIMA, 'The Concept of Utopia', in *The Cambridge Companion to Utopian Literature*, ed. by Claeys, pp. 3–27

WACKWITZ, STEPHAN, *Ein unsichtbares Land: Familienroman* (Frankfurt a. M.: Fischer, 2003)

—— *Neue Menschen: Bildungsroman* (Frankfurt a. M.: Fischer, 2005)

WAGNER, PETER, ed., *Icons, Texts, Iconotexts: Essays on Ekphrasis and Intermediality*, European Cultures, 6 (Berlin: de Gruyter, 1996)

WALLACE, IAN, ed., *Christa Wolf in Perspective*, German Monitor, 30 (Rodopi: Amsterdam, 1994)

WALTHER, JOACHIM, *Sicherungsbereich Literatur: Schriftsteller und Staatssicherheit in der Deutschen Demokratischen Republik*, Analysen und Dokumente, 6 (Berlin: Links, 1996)

WARNER, MARIA, *Phantasmagoria: Spirit Visions, Metaphors, and Media into the Twenty-First Century* (Oxford: Oxford University Press, 2006)

WEBBER, ANDREW J., 'The Afterlife of Romanticism', in *German Literature of the Nineteenth Century*, ed. by Koelb and Downing, pp. 23–43

—— *Berlin in the Twentieth Century: A Cultural Topography* (Cambridge: Cambridge University Press, 2008)

—— *The Doppelgänger: Double Visions in German Literature* (Oxford: Clarendon, 1999)

—— 'Topographical Turns: Casting Berlin in Contemporary Film', in *Debating German Cultural Identity 1989 to the Present*, ed. by Fuchs, James-Chakraborty, and Shortt, pp. 67–81

WEIGEL, SIGRID, *Body- and Image-Space: Re-reading Walter Benjamin*, trans. by Georgina Paul (London: Routledge, 1996)

—— *Genea-Logik: Generation, Tradition und Evolution zwischen Kultur- und Naturwissenschaften* (Paderborn: Fink, 2006)

—— *Literatur als Voraussetzung der Kulturgeschichte: Schauplätze von Shakespeare bis Benjamin* (Munich: Fink, 2004)

WERNER, HANS-GEORG, *E. T. A. Hoffmann, Darstellung und Deutung der Wirklichkeit im dichterischen Werk*, Beiträge zur deutschen Klassik, 13 (Berlin: Aufbau, 1971)

—— 'Romantische Traditionen in epischen Werken der neueren DDR Literatur', *Zeitschrift für Germanistik*, 4 (1980), 398–416

—— '*Unter den Linden*: Three Improbable Stories', in *Responses to Christa Wolf*, ed. by Fries, pp. 279–302

WESSELING, ELISABETH, 'Historical Fiction: Utopia in History', in *International Postmodernism*, ed. by Bertens, pp. 201–12

WESTFAHL, GARY, GEORGE SLUSSER, and DAVID LEIBY, eds, *Worlds Enough and Time: Explorations of Time in Science Fiction and Fantasy*, Contributions to the Study of Science Fiction and Fantasy, 101 (Westport: Greenwood, 2002)

WILDNER, SIEGRUN, *Experimentum mundi: Utopie als ästhetisches Prinzip: Zur Funktion utopischer Entwürfe in Irmtraud Morgners Romanwerk* (St Ingbert: Röhrig, 2000)

WILKE, SABINE, *Ausgraben und Erinnern: Zur Funktion von Geschichte, Subjekt und geschlechtlicher Identität in den Texten Christa Wolfs*, Epistemata, 110 (Würzburg: Königshausen & Neumann, 1993)

WILLIAMS, ARTHUR, STUART PARKES, and JULIAN PREECE, *German-Language Literature Today: International and Popular?* (Oxford: Lang, 2000)

WILPERT, GERO VON, *Die deutsche Gespenstergeschichte: Motiv, Form, Entwicklung* (Stuttgart: Kröner, 1994)

WINDE, ARNE DE, and ANKE GILLEIR, eds, *Literatur im Krebsgang: Totenbeschwörung und* memoria *in der deutschsprachigen Literatur nach 1989*, Amsterdamer Beiträge zur neueren Germanistik, 64 (Amsterdam: Rodopi, 2008)

WOLF, CHRISTA, *Leibhaftig: Erzählung* (Munich: Luchterhand, 2002)

—— *Ein Tag im Jahr* (Munich: Luchterhand, 2003)

—— *Werke*, ed. by Sonja Hilzinger, 12 vols (Munich: Luchterhand, 1999–2001)

WOLFF, THEODOR, *Die Schwimmerin* (Zurich: Oprecht, 1937)

WOLFREYS, JULIAN, *Victorian Hauntings: Spectrality, Gothic, the Uncanny and Literature* (Basingstoke: Palgrave, 2002)

WOLLEN, PETER, 'Vectors of Melancholy', in *The Scene of the Crime*, ed. by Rugoff, pp. 23–36

ZELIZER, BARBIE, ed., *Visual Culture and the Holocaust* (London: Athlone Press, 2001)

INDEX

Abraham, Nicholas, and Maria Torok 9–11, 12, 18, 26, 29 nn. 39 & 42–43, 30 nn. 47 & 49–54, 31 nn. 88–91, 57, 78 n. 2, 146, 157, 164 nn. 12 & 19
after-image 20, 24, 35, 42, 56, 162, 163, 171
alienation 20, 34, 37–38, 42, 43–44, 46–48, 51, 52, 58–62, 73, 75–76, 78, 79 n. 21, 82, 105, 120, 132–34, 137, 141 n. 54, 148, 149
alterity 12–14, 20, 26, 40–41, 44–45, 47–49, 52, 56, 60–61, 73, 76, 77, 93, 115, 117–20, 129, 134–38, 146, 148–49, 157–60, 162, 169, 171
alternate history, *see uchronie*
American Psychiatric Association 19, 31 n. 95
Anisfeld, Leon, and Arnold Richards 165 n. 27,
apparatus 7, 14–16, 25, 31 n. 81, 40, 42, 45, 47, 48, 56–57, 63, 73, 75–78, 82, 114, 123, 125, 129, 132, 134, 171–72
architecture 84–87, 90, 92–93, 96, 98–101, 105–06, 107, 109 n. 11, 116, 118, 121–22, 126–27, 129, 139, 143, 158–60, 161, 163
Assmann, Aleida 139 n. 10
Atget, Eugène 96–97, 110 n. 30
autobiography 28 n. 14, 77–78, 79 n. 17, 112, 138 n. 1, 139 n. 20

Bachmann, Ingeborg 78, 81 n. 51
Bacon, Frances 99
Balfour, Alan 109 n. 11
Barthes, Roland 25, 83–84, 86, 88, 90, 104, 106, 108 n. 4, 109 nn. 6–7, 12, 14 & 20–22, 110 nn. 44, 46–49 & 51–54, 116, 117, 132, 139 n. 11, 141 n. 55, 172 n. 4
Baßler, Moritz, Bettina Gruber, and Martina Wagner-Egelhaaf 30 nn. 74 & 76, 31 n. 79
Becker, Jurek 4, 28 nn. 19–21, 29 n. 23
Benjamin, Walter 25, 42, 54 n. 25, 55 n. 38, 68, 78 n. 8, 82, 83–84, 87, 90–91, 95, 97, 98, 102, 105, 107, 109 n. 23, 110 n. 35, 111 n. 58
Bennett, Tony 110 n. 38
Bergmann, Christian 75, 81 nn. 44–46
Berlin 12, 26, 35, 39, 40, 41, 43, 63, 67, 84–87, 89, 90, 94, 98, 101, 106, 112–15, 123, 125, 126–27, 130–31, 133, 143–45, 153, 155, 157–61, 163, 166 n. 59, 167, 169, 171
Auguststraße 107, 108
Berlin Wall 63, 64, 98; *see also* boundaries
Bernauer Straße 98
Brunnenstraße 92, 94
Friedhof der Sophiengemeinde 105, 106
Friedrichstraße 35, 47, 63, 65
Große Hamburger Straße 84, 89, 92, 93, 94, 102, 103, 105, 107, 117, 119, 121, 125, 139 n. 10, 144, 167 n. 10
Hackescher Markt 96
Hofsynagoge 92–93, 94
Jewish cemetery 144
jüdisches Altersheim 102, 103, 121, 122, 125
Königliche Pfandleihe 100
Krausnickstraße 105, 107
Mitte 35, 87, 109 n. 13, 115, 143, 158, 159, 160
Neue Synagoge 86–87, 109 nn. 11 & 26
Oranienburger Straße 35, 84, 85, 87, 89, 99, 100, 109 n. 10, 121
Pankow 124, 135–36
Postfuhramt 84–87, 92, 99, 109 nn. 10 & 16
Rosenthaler Straße 96, 100, 101
S-Bahn 92, 123, 158
S-Bahnhof Marx-Engels-Platz 92
Tränenpalast 65
Tucholskystraße 85, 99, 100
Unter den Linden 39–41, 126
Wilhelm-Pieck-Straße 100
Berlin Republic 3, 28 n. 17, 79 n. 10
Beyer, Marcel 1

Index

Bickenbach, Matthias 132, 141 n. 56
Biermann, Wolf 35, 37
Bloch, Ernst 51, 78 n. 6, 110 n. 34
Boltanski, Christian 139 n. 10
boundaries 1, 2, 6, 7, 8, 13, 16, 20, 24–25, 27, 31 n. 77, 35, 37, 49–52, 56, 62, 64–65, 68, 69, 75–76, 83, 98, 100–01, 105, 113, 115, 124, 126–28, 130, 137–38, 139 n. 9, 142 n. 69, 152, 156, 157–60, 161, 169–70, 172
  see also thresholds
Braun, Volker 5, 29 n. 24
Brecht, Bertolt 22, 38
Brockmann, Stephen 28 n. 18, 55 n. 33
Buse, Peter, and Andrew Stott 29 n. 31

camera 15, 16, 25, 26, 82–83, 88, 90, 100, 105, 108, 112, 118, 121–22, 125, 127, 131–33, 157, 172
camera obscura 125
Cartesian dualism 70, 80 n. 23, 129
Castle, Terry 29 n. 32
Castricano, Jodey 30 n. 62
censorship:
  of literature 4
  self-censorship 42, 48, 76
Chamisso, Adelbert von 21, 163, 170
Communism 2, 19, 31 n. 94, 161
  see also German Democratic Republic, Socialism
Cooke, Paul 28 n. 17, 51, 55 nn. 44 & 45, 79 n. 10
Costabile-Heming, Carol 80 n. 41
counterfactual history, *see uchronie*
crime 42, 54 n. 27, 97–98, 100–02, 104
  crime scene 96–102, 110 nn. 31–33, 37, 41 & 42
  criminal 36, 42, 48, 50, 51
  guilt 24, 36–37, 42–43, 46, 53 n. 6, 57, 59, 76, 97, 102
  see also detective; forensics

darkness 67–68, 107, 133, 137
Davis, Colin 11, 30 nn. 52, 60, 62 & 66
Dean, Carolyn 137–38, 142 nn. 70–73
death:
  of the body 68, 126, 150, 151–52, 153
  and film 124, 140 n. 31
  of GDR literature 4–5, 29 nn. 24–30

inner mortification 26, 121, 126–28, 134, 137, 150, 152, 141 n. 54
living death 18, 43, 105, 108, 112, 121, 132, 134, 152, 153, 171
and photography 25–26, 88, 90, 104–05, 108, 112, 131–32, 171
and Romanticism 21, 170
Deleuze, Gilles, and Félix Guattari 114, 138 n. 7
Derrida, Jacques 11–14, 18, 30 nn. 61, 63–65, 68, 69, 71 & 72, 31 n. 92, 44, 45, 47, 50, 55 nn. 31–32, 35–37, 42 & 43
detective 97–99, 102, 110 n. 35, 145, 164 n. 20
Doppelgänger 21, 48, 134–38, 142 n. 67
dreams 21, 37–40, 42, 43, 49–50, 54 n. 28, 61–62, 64, 78, 130, 162
Dueck, Cheryl 79 n. 22
dystopia 8, 23, 34, 40–43

Ehrenburg, Ilja 113, 138 n. 4
Eichenberg, Ariane 163 n. 5
ekphrasis 15, 24, 116–18, 121, 139 nn. 12–19 & 22–25
electricity 25, 76–77
empathy 26, 61, 135, 137–38, 142 nn. 70–74, 153
ethics 1, 3, 8, 11–13, 18, 26, 28 n. 16, 46, 62, 103, 135, 138, 139 n. 21, 152, 171, 172
exorcism 11, 12, 57, 152, 165 n. 36
eyes 7, 16, 24–26, 35–36, 39, 44, 47, 50, 56, 67, 72, 74, 76–78, 83, 105–06, 110 n. 29, 114–15, 124, 125–29, 130–32, 134, 138, 141, 147, 150, 152, 154, 162, 165 n. 23, 167 n. 62, 171
  see also vision, faculty of

family narrative 2, 9–11, 26–27, 115, 133, 144–45, 146–49, 150–51, 152, 154, 155–56, 157, 160, 161–62, 167 n. 61
fantastic 7, 22–23, 26, 32 n. 111, 37–39, 127, 156, 162, 170
fantasy 2, 7–8, 15, 18, 20, 21, 23, 36, 39, 155, 157, 160, 162, 172
Farrell, John 31 n. 97
Federal Republic of Germany 1, 2, 4, 5, 8, 22, 28 n. 11, 41, 42, 57–58, 63, 95, 98, 113, 123–25, 130, 135–37, 143, 145, 161, 169, 170
femininity, *see* gender

fiction 8, 15, 21, 23, 26, 27, 53 n. 7, 77, 112–13, 116, 118, 138 n. 1, 143–44, 155–57, 160, 164 n. 22, 171–72
film 14–16, 32 n. 113, 68, 79 nn. 16 & 21, 122–24, 140 nn. 29 & 31, 155
flâneur 39, 98, 129
forensics 96–98, 102
Foucault, Michel 158–59, 160, 166 nn. 53–57
Freud, Sigmund 6–8, 9, 17–18, 19–20, 54 n. 25, 57, 70, 90, 99, 105, 107, 142 n. 68
Fries, Marilyn Sibley 54 nn. 17–27, 55 n. 46
Fuchs, Anne 29 nn. 35 & 40
Fühmann, Franz 22, 32 n. 113, 79–80 n. 22
Fulbrook, Mary 16–17, 29 n. 24, 31 nn. 82–85

Gaderer, Rupert 140 n.42
Gardner, Alexander 88
Gaus, Günter 59, 69, 73
Gebauer, Yvonne 166 n. 52
gender 3, 34
genealogy 3, 34, 99, 144–45, 146, 160, 161–62, 164 nn. 11 & 18, 167 n. 61
German Democratic Republic 1–2, 3, 8, 16–17, 24, 27 n. 10, 36, 41, 63–64, 65, 72, 80 n. 41, 84, 85–87, 89, 92, 95–96, 125, 133, 135, 141 n. 60, 144, 169–70
  legacy of 2, 3–5, 9, 18, 29 nn. 24 & 30, 56–58, 59, 64, 72, 87, 100, 143, 158–59, 169–70
  cultural policies of 4–5, 21–23, 54 n. 17, 170, 172
  Sozialistische Einheitspartei Deutschlands (SED) 17, 27 n. 9, 53 n. 9, 141 n. 60, 144
Goethe, Johann Wolfgang von 21, 32 n. 105, 68, 79 n. 15
golem 23
Gothic 37, 43, 69, 169
  Gothic bodies 69–72, 80 nn. 26–40
Göttler, Fritz 172 n. 3
Graves, Peter 27 n. 7, 78 n. 3
Greiner, Ulrich 53 n. 9
Guerin, Frances 79 n. 16

Hagstrum, Jean 139 n. 19
hands 26, 44, 114–15, 127, 129–34, 141 nn. 54, 56–58 & 61
Hardy, Beverley 54 n. 22

Harvey, John 108 nn. 2 & 3
hauntology 11–13
Heffernan, James 139 nn. 13 & 19
Heimat 8, 29 nn. 37 & 38
  see also home
Hellekson, Karen 166 nn. 41–43
Hermann, Judith 1
Herrnstadt, Rudolf 27 n. 9, 141 n. 60, 145, 156–57, 164 n. 22
heterotopia 157–60, 161, 162, 166 nn. 53–57
Hilzinger, Sonja 28 n. 13, 54 n. 20
Hirsch, Marianne 2, 27 n. 4, 108 n. 5, 110 nn. 50–56
historiography 7, 8, 27, 57, 84, 118, 143, 154–56, 172
Hoffmann, E. T. A. 7, 16, 21, 22, 26, 31 n. 81, 32 nn. 111 & 113, 76, 77, 112, 125, 128, 138 n. 2, 140 nn. 36, 38 & 39–42, 170, 172
  'Die Bergwerke zu Falun' 69–70
  Das öde Haus 32 n. 113, 35, 39, 40–41, 126–27, 129, 130, 140 nn. 39 & 40, 141 n. 50
  Der Sandmann 126, 128
Hölderlin, Friedrich 21, 54 n. 16
Holocaust 1–2, 9, 27 nn. 2 & 7, 102–03, 108 n. 5, 110 n. 50, 110–11 n. 56, 121–22, 125, 139 n. 21, 142 nn. 70–73, 144, 154, 160, 167 n. 61, 172
home 8, 9, 17, 29 nn. 37 & 38, 35, 49–50, 51–52, 60, 74, 105, 113–14, 116, 142 n. 67, 169
  see also houses
homelessness 50, 66, 113, 114, 136, 149
homesickness 8
homunculus 68
houses 35, 48, 49–50, 52, 74, 86, 87, 89, 92, 93, 98, 99, 100, 105, 107, 116, 117–18, 123, 126–27, 129, 130, 136, 139 n. 10, 158
Hurley, Kelly 70–71, 80 nn. 26–40
Huyssen, Andreas 106, 111 n. 57

illness 63, 64, 66, 67, 71–72, 73, 75, 77, 79–80 n. 22, 80 nn. 24, 41 & 42, 130
inheritance 2, 9–11, 13, 22, 58, 145, 146, 148, 152, 163 n. 5, 164 nn. 11 & 18
intertextuality 5, 20, 24, 35, 37, 39, 41, 46, 48, 52, 54 n. 19, 55 n. 38, 60, 62, 65, 73–77, 112, 115, 119, 122, 125–28, 149, 157, 160, 163 n. 3, 164 n. 20, 165 n. 25, 166 n. 44, 167 nn. 60 & 61

Index

189

Jennings, Michael 91, 109 n. 24
Jones, Susanne Lenné 95, 109 nn. 8 & 13, 110 nn. 27-28 & 43

Kafka, Franz 54 n. 27, 70
Kaufmann, Hans 22, 32 n. 114, 38
Kittler, Friedrich 79 n. 21, 132-33, 141 nn. 58 & 59
Köhler, Astrid 28 n. 14, 53 n. 15, 54 nn. 16 & 18, 80 n. 42, 109 n. 15, 122, 138 n. 5, 140 n. 28, 143, 163 nn. 1 & 3, 164 nn. 6, 11 & 21
Konzett, Matthias 53 n. 6
Koskinas, Nikolaos-Ioannis 55 n. 47, 79 n. 15
Kratochvil, Jiři 156-57, 166 nn. 48 & 49
Krieger, Murray 121, 139 nn. 22-24
Kuhn, Anna 37, 53 nn. 7 & 12, 78 n. 7

Ladd, Brian 87, 109 nn. 17 & 18, 169, 172 n. 1
Lammert, Will 122
Langner, Beatrix 79 n. 14
late style 29 n. 30
Leclaire, Serge 165 n. 36
Leeder, Karen 4-5, 29 nn. 24-30
legacy 1-2, 4, 9, 11, 13, 24, 25, 34, 40, 56, 57, 59, 64, 77, 79 n. 10, 84, 109 n. 13, 143, 145, 146, 148, 152, 154, 160, 161, 169-71
Lessing, Gotthold Ephraim 121
Lieb, Claudia 140 n. 39, 141 n. 53
Liebmann, Irina:
  interviews:
    with Susanne Lenné Jones 109 n. 8, 110 n. 43
    with Eva Pfister 135, 142 n. 65, 163 n. 4, 164 n. 20
    with Hans Joachim Schröder 140 n. 30
    with Catherine Smale 30 n. 55, 110 n. 29, 138 n. 46, 140 n. 36, 163 n. 2, 166 n. 49
  works:
    Die freien Frauen 1, 20, 26-27, 33 n. 118, 140 n. 27, 142 n. 65, 143-67
    In Berlin 1, 3, 26, 112-42, 143, 144, 149, 150, 165 n. 25, 170
    Mitten im Krieg 138 n. 9
    Stille Mitte von Berlin 1, 15, 24, 25, 33 n. 117, 82-111, 115-18, 119, 120, 121-22, 124, 125, 127-28, 135, 138 n. 9, 140 n. 26, 145, 156, 159, 160, 164 n. 20, 166 n. 44, 171
    Wäre es schön? Es wäre schön! Mein Vater Rudolf Herrnstadt 141 n. 60, 156, 164 n. 22, 165 n. 23, 166 n. 51
light 21, 42, 79 n. 16, 107, 122, 134, 150
  process of enlightenment 6-7, 12, 38-39, 40-41, 66, 68, 70-72, 84, 90-91, 95, 124, 133, 154, 156, 158-59, 162, 163, 170
  tricks of 66-69, 128
Literaturstreit 3, 24, 36, 53 n. 8, 79 n. 10
Lukács, Georg 21, 32 n. 107

machine 16, 25, 73-77, 133, 172
  see also apparatus
Magenau, Jörg 27 n. 8, 28 n. 13
magic lantern 125, 140 n. 38
Marks, Laura 114, 138 nn. 7 & 8
Marven, Lyn 28 n. 14, 109 n. 15, 138 nn. 1 & 5, 139 n. 20, 142 n. 69, 156, 163 n. 3, 164 n. 21, 166 n. 47
Marx, Karl 95, 161, 170
Mattson, Michelle 3, 28 n. 16, 30 nn. 67 & 70, 62, 79 n. 9
McFarland, Robert 126, 129, 140 nn. 40 & 41, 141 n. 51
McGrath, John 55 n. 30
mediation 1, 14-16, 26, 30 n. 75, 41, 47, 48, 62-63, 64, 82, 84, 87, 112, 126-27, 132, 145, 163 n. 5, 172
medium 14-16, 18, 24-25, 30 n. 76, 31 nn. 77 & 78, 62, 63-66, 68, 73, 77, 82-84, 86-87, 90-91, 105, 108, 120, 127, 132, 171-72
  see also apparatus
melancholia 16-19, 31 nn. 88-91, 83, 104-05, 107-08, 113, 125, 144, 146, 162, 167 n. 60, 169
  incorporation 18, 31 nn. 88-91, 146, 150, 152, 165 n. 35
memory:
  collective 1-3, 14, 30 n. 75, 40, 58, 84, 85, 99, 112, 114, 135, 143, 144
  corporeal 26, 63, 70, 72, 80 n. 25, 147-48, 159
  false 11, 58-59, 117-18
  individual 1-3, 14, 18, 30 n. 75, 54, 64, 84, 117, 124, 127, 133, 143, 144, 146-47, 159, 167

'medallions' of 62, 78 n. 8
memorialization 14, 58, 87, 102, 122, 144, 167 n. 61
and photography 68–69, 108 n. 5, 116–17
concept of postmemory 2, 27 n. 4
and repression 6–7, 10, 14, 25, 42, 65, 66, 70, 82, 85, 97, 114, 135, 144, 146–47, 163
and trauma 9, 10, 14, 163, 163 n. 5, 164 n. 10
Michaelis, Rolf 80 n. 43
mimesis 8, 41, 71, 116–17, 118, 128, 139 n. 25, 171
mirror 40–42, 46, 50–52, 55 n. 46, 87–88, 89–90, 127, 130, 134–37, 142 n. 66
Mitchell, W. J. T. 117, 139 nn. 12–19
mourning 8, 17, 31 nn. 87 & 88–91, 59, 65, 82, 83, 104, 105, 110 n. 50, 113, 145, 146, 151–52, 159
Müller, Heiner 1
Mulvey, Laura 124, 140 nn. 31 & 33–35

Nachträglichkeit 42, 65, 142, 171
National Socialism, *see* Third Reich

objectification 25, 45, 69, 74–75, 119–20
optical instruments 16, 31, 127, 128
optical unconscious 68, 83, 127, 164 n. 18

palimpsest 35, 99, 110 n. 39
paranoia 16–17, 19–20, 31 nn. 86 & 96–97, 32 nn. 98–101, 43, 44, 51, 52
Paul, Georgina 52 n. 4, 55 n. 39
Paul, Jean 141 n. 62
Paul, William 79 n. 16
Payne, Lewis 88
Peucker, Brigitte 54 n. 17
Pfister, Eva 135, 142 n. 65, 163 n. 4, 164 n. 20
phantom 9–11, 12, 15, 18, 21, 23, 24, 26, 30 n. 52, 34, 35, 37, 49, 52, 56–58, 59, 61–63, 66–67, 69, 70, 77–78, 78 nn. 1 & 2, 115, 123, 145, 146–47, 152, 157, 163, 169, 171
Phantombild 20, 24, 35, 36, 42, 43, 45, 47, 50, 52, 56, 57, 123, 171, 172
Philipsen, Bart 27 nn. 2, 3 & 5
photography 14–16, 24, 25–26, 41, 68–69, 82–111, 112, 114, 116–17, 118, 120, 121–25, 127, 131–32, 138–39 n. 9, 150, 157, 159–60, 171

Plowman, Andrew 51, 55 nn. 44 & 45
Poland 157–60, 161
  Gliwice (Gleiwitz) 157–59, 166 n. 52
  Kattowice (Kattowitz) 155, 157–59, 160, 161–62, 166 n. 52
  Opole (Oppeln) 158
  Wrocław (Breslau) 158
poltergeist 50
prison 72, 73, 88, 122, 125, 135–36, 159
psychotopography 131, 139 n. 20, 160, 169

Radisch, Iris 167 n. 60
Rand, Nicholas 10
Rank, Otto 142 n. 68
Rashkin, Esther 10, 30 n. 45
Recht, Camille 97, 110 n. 30
Rechtien, Renate 55 n. 29
redemption 21, 22, 91, 110 n. 50, 171–72
reincarnation 151
Renouvier, Charles 153, 165 n. 37
repetition compulsion 6, 26, 113, 147, 169
Replacement Child Syndrome 151–52, 165 nn. 26, 27, 35 & 36
repression 8, 19, 57, 58, 59, 98, 135, 152, 154, 163
  return of the repressed 6–7, 10, 22, 24, 40, 50, 57, 66, 77, 90, 114, 133, 170
Resina, Joan Ramon 53 n. 5, 54 n. 26
reunification, *see* Wende
Rodiek, Christoph 165 n. 37, 166 nn. 40 & 46
Romanticism 20–23, 24, 32 nn. 104, 105, 106 & 108, 33 n. 116, 34, 37–38, 54 nn. 17, 18 & 22, 139 n. 25, 163, 170
  see also Hoffmann, E. T. A.
Rowe, Katherine 141 nn. 54 & 57
Royle, Nicholas 29 n. 33
rubble 42, 87, 89, 90, 101
Rugg, Linda 69, 79 nn. 17–20
Rugoff, Ralph 98, 110 nn. 31–33, 36 & 42
ruination 40, 41, 42, 43, 70–72, 87, 90
Ruprecht, Lucia 134, 141 n. 61

Salzani, Carlo 99, 110 n. 37
Santner, Eric 164 n. 7
Schreber, Daniel 19
Schubert, Franz 52
Schwab, Gabriele 30 n. 48, 152, 164 nn. 7, 10 & 18, 165 nn. 28–35

Index

Schwenger, Peter 55 n. 41
Sconce, Jeffrey 16, 31 n. 80
Scribner, Charity 19, 31 n. 94
Seghers, Anna 22
shadows 31 n. 87, 43, 68, 79 n. 16, 82, 107–08, 169–70
Socialism 2, 18, 21, 22, 23, 24, 31 n. 94, 37, 55 n. 46, 161, 169
Socialist Realism 21, 22, 57, 172
spectrality 1–2, 4, 5, 12, 14, 16, 17, 21, 26, 29 n. 30, 43–44, 46, 47, 50, 56, 69, 82, 96, 100, 102, 104, 107–08, 115, 120, 122–23, 124, 128, 134, 137, 139 n. 21, 152–53, 169, 172
spectre 2, 5, 11–14, 44, 90, 95, 97, 161, 169–70
Stasi 17, 20, 24–25, 31 n. 86, 35–36, 43–52, 53 nn. 9 & 10, 55 nn. 33 & 44, 59–60, 62, 69, 73–75, 77, 78 n. 3, 81 nn. 44–46, 171
stasis 16, 18, 25–26, 69, 82, 86, 90–91, 104, 108, 112, 118, 120–25, 126, 128, 135, 140 n. 31, 144, 159, 162, 171
Steiner, Wendy 139 n. 22
Stöbe, Ilse 164 n. 22, 165 n. 23
surveillance 17, 34–36, 43–46, 47, 49, 53 n. 9, 55 n. 30, 56, 60, 73–74, 76, 119, 137, 171

Tanner, Laura E. 110 n. 45
Tate, Dennis 3, 28 n. 17, 32 n. 113, 77, 79–80 n. 22, 81 n. 50
telegraphy 15
Third Reich 1–2, 9, 21, 26, 57, 65, 86, 98, 99, 109 n.13, 119, 133, 150, 169
Thompson, Peter 8, 29 nn. 37 & 38
thresholds 1, 8, 50, 106, 113, 116, 129, 137, 160, 169
Tiedemann, Rolf 109 n. 23
time:
　chronography 113–15
　chronology 6, 13–14, 27, 38, 113, 151, 154–55, 158, 162
　chronotope 161
　temporality 8, 26, 38, 61, 62–63, 64–66, 83, 88, 90, 112, 120–22, 124, 137, 138 n. 5, 138–39 n. 9, 154, 158, 160–62, 170
　topography 63–64, 85, 113, 126, 143, 146, 158, 160, 161–62, 169
touch, sense of 44, 104, 109 n. 7, 115, 118, 130–32, 133

haptic perception 114–15, 131
　see also hands
trauma 2, 9–11, 14, 40, 97, 113, 141 n. 60, 142, 144–48, 152, 163, 163 n. 5, 164 n. 10, 172
Trotter, David 19–20, 32 nn. 98–101
typewriter 132–34, 172

uchronie 27, 88, 135, 153–57, 158, 163, 165 n. 37, 166 n. 38, 172
Ulbricht, Walter 144
uncanny 6–8, 9, 16, 21–26, 34, 37, 40, 42–43, 46, 49, 50, 52, 55, 65, 67, 69, 72, 77, 79 n. 16, 83–84, 87, 90, 112, 126, 131, 133–34, 145, 158, 162, 169–71
unconscious 9, 11, 18, 20, 59, 60, 65, 68, 70, 78 n. 2, 127, 133, 146, 151–52, 164 n. 18
utopia 2, 5, 8, 22–23, 24, 34, 41, 78, 80 n. 42, 87, 117, 139 n. 19, 154, 158, 166 nn. 38, 39 & 45, 169–70

vampires 5
Vidler, Anthony 31 n. 81, 55 n. 40, 102, 109 n. 19, 110 nn. 41 & 55, 128, 140 nn. 43–47
Vieira, Fatima 166 n. 39
vision, faculty of 7, 23, 26, 39–40, 41, 43–44, 45, 57, 61, 67, 73, 76–77, 86, 96, 110 n. 29, 114–15, 119, 126–29, 130–31, 134, 138, 163
　blindness 7, 43, 44, 67, 115, 129, 132
　blind spot 6, 7, 58
　second sight 7, 39–40, 43, 57, 67, 128, 129
　see also eyes
visitation 44, 46, 49–52
voice 20, 61, 62, 75, 118–20, 124, 139 nn. 19 & 21

Wackwitz, Stephan 1
Walther, Joachim 53 n. 10
Warner, Maria 31 n. 78, 79 n. 11, 142 n. 66
Webber, Andrew J. 30 n. 73, 32 n. 104, 33 n. 116, 54 nn. 23–34 & 28, 77, 81 nn. 47–49, 138 n. 3, 139 n. 10, 140 nn. 29 & 37, 141 n. 63, 142 n. 67, 172 nn. 1 & 2
Weigel, Sigrid 29 n. 41, 54 n. 25, 109 n. 25
Wende 1–2, 3–5, 8, 9, 21, 23, 27 nn. 7 & 8, 34, 36, 56, 58–59, 61, 65, 87, 112–13, 122, 169
Werner, Hans-Georg 22, 32 nn. 109 & 110, 54 n. 27

Wesseling, Elizabeth 155, 166 n. 45
Wilpert, Gero von 1, 27 n. 1
windows 40–41, 42, 43, 46, 47, 74, 75, 84, 85, 87, 92, 98, 99, 105, 106, 117, 121–22, 123, 125, 126–27, 130, 137, 160
Wolf, Christa:
  biography:
    role as *informelle Mitarbeiterin* 24, 36, 53 n. 10, 59, 69
    see also Literaturstreit; Stasi
  concepts:
    self-actualization 58, 60, 62
    subjective authenticity 5, 9, 15, 55 n. 46, 58
  fictional works:
    Der geteilte Himmel 38, 80 n. 42
    Kein Ort. Nirgends 37, 53 n. 7
    Kindheitsmuster 25, 28 n. 15, 61, 62, 65, 68, 78 n. 2, 79 n. 13, 80 n. 25
    Leibhaftig 1, 24–25, 28 n. 15, 56–81
    Moskauer Novelle 57
    Nachdenken über Christa T. 62, 78 n. 7, 167 n. 60
    Sommerstück 37, 53 n. 7, 54 nn. 16 & 19
    Unter den Linden: Drei unwahrscheinliche Geschichten 22, 24, 37–40, 41–43, 45–46, 48, 54 nn. 17, 18 & 21–23, 58, 64, 65
    Was bleibt 1, 3, 20, 24, 33 n. 117, 34–55, 57, 60, 65, 73–76, 79 n. 12
  interviews and correspondence:
    with Günter Gaus 59, 69, 73
    with Catherine Smale 34, 53 nn. 1 & 13
  non-fictional works:
    'Abschied von Phantomen: Zur Sache Deutschland!' 56–58
    Auf dem Weg nach Tabou 56
    Ein Tag im Jahr 28 n. 13, 35, 52 nn. 2 & 3
    'Krankheit und Liebesentzug: Fragen an die psychosomatische Medizin' 80 n. 24
    'Krebs und Gesellschaft' 80 n. 24
    'Lesen und Schreiben' 39, 62, 77
    'Rede für Hans Mayer' 58
Wolff, Theodor 164 n. 22
Wolfreys, Julian 20, 32 n. 102

zombies 5

www.ingramcontent.com/pod-product-compliance
Lightning Source LLC
Chambersburg PA
CBHW071444150426
43191CB00008B/1236